D1131621

PAY AND ORGANIZATIONAL EFFECTIVENESS: A PSYCHOLOGICAL VIEW

McGraw-Hill Series in Psychology

Consulting Editors

NORMAN GARMEZY

LYLE V. JONES

RICHARD L. SOLOMON

HAROLD W. STEVENSON

Hirsh   *The Measurement of Hearing*
Hurlock   *Adolescent Development*
Hurlock   *Child Development*
Hurlock   *Developmental Psychology*
Jackson and Messick   *Problems in Human Assessment*
Karn and Gilmer   *Readings in Industrial and Business Psychology*
Krech, Crutchfield, and Ballachey   *Individual in Society*
Lawler   *Pay and Organizational Effectiveness: A Psychological View*
Lazarus, A.   *Behavior Therapy and Beyond*
Lazarus, R.   *Adjustment and Personality*
Lazarus, R.   *Psychological Stress and the Coping Process*
Lewin   *A Dynamic Theory of Personality*
Lewin   *Principles of Topological Psychology*
Maher   *Principles of Psychopathology*
Marx and Hillix   *Systems and Theories in Psychology*
Messick and Brayfield   *Decision and Choice: Contributions of Sidney Siegel*
Miller   *Language and Communication*
Morgan   *Physiological Psychology*
Nunnally   *Psychometric Theory*
Rethlingshafer   *Motivation as Related to Personality*
Robinson and Robinson   *The Mentally Retarded Child*
Rosenthal   *Genetic Theory and Abnormal Behavior*
Scherer and Wertheimer   *A Psycholinguistic Experiment on Foreign Language Teaching*
Shaw   *Group Dynamics: The Psychology of Small Group Behavior*
Shaw and Wright   *Scales for the Measurement of Attitudes*
Sidowski   *Experimental Methods and Instrumentation in Psychology*
Siegel   *Nonparametric Statistics for the Behavioral Sciences*
Spencer and Kass   *Perspectives in Child Psychology*
Stagner   *Psychology of Personality*
Townsend   *Introduction to Experimental Methods for Psychology and the Social Sciences*
Vinacke   *The Psychology of Thinking*
Wallen   *Clinical Psychology: The Study of Persons*
Warren and Akert   *The Frontal Granular Cortex and Behavior*
Waters, Rethlingshafer, and Caldwell   *Principles of Comparative Psychology*
Winer   *Statistical Principles in Experimental Design*
Zubek and Solberg   *Human Development*

John F. Dashiell was Consulting Editor of this series from its inception in 1931 until January 1, 1950. Clifford T. Morgan was Consulting Editor of this series from January 1, 1950 until January 1, 1959. Harry F. Harlow assumed the duties of Consulting Editor from 1959 to 1965. In 1965 a Board of Consulting Editors was established according to areas of interest. The current board members are Richard L. Solomon (physiological, experimental), Norman Garmezy (abnormal, clinical), Harold W. Stevenson (child, adolescent, human development), and Lyle V. Jones (statistical, quantitative).

EDWARD E. LAWLER III
*Associate Professor of Administrative
Sciences and Psychology
Yale University*

PAY AND ORGANIZATIONAL EFFECTIVENESS: A PSYCHOLOGICAL VIEW

HD
4909
.L27

McGraw-Hill Book Company
New York
St. Louis
San Francisco
Düsseldorf
Johannesburg
Kuala Lumpur
London
Mexico
Montreal
New Delhi
Panama
Rio de Janeiro
Singapore
Sydney
Toronto

Pay and Organizational Effectiveness: A Psychological View

Copyright © 1971 by McGraw-Hill, Inc. All rights reserved. Printed in the United States of America. No part of this publication may be reproduced, stored in a retrieval system, or transmitted in any form or by any means, electronic, mechanical, photocopying, recording, or otherwise, without the prior written permission of the publisher.

Library of Congress Catalog Card Number 73-139558

07-036700-0

1 2 3 4 5 6 7 8 9 0   MAMM   7 9 8 7 6 5 4 3 2 1

This book was set in Modern Number 21 by Monotype Composition Company, Inc., and printed on permanent paper and bound by The Maple Press Company. The designer was Marsha Cohen; the drawings were done by John Cordes, J. & R. Technical Services, Inc. The editors were Walter Maytham and Helen Greenberg. Stuart Levine supervised production.

To my parents
whose generosity and support
have greatly enriched my life

CONTENTS

PREFACE

This is a book about money and the role it plays in organizations. It focuses on the psychological problems that arise when money is used to pay people for their work. In this sense it is problem-centered. But the book was not written simply as an exercise in using psychology to solve the problems of pay administration. It does attempt to do this, but it also addresses some fundamental questions that deal with human behavior in organizations.

It is my conviction that by studying the impact of pay administration practices on individual and organizational effectiveness it is possible to contribute to the understanding of human behavior, and to test psychological theory in the areas of motivation, need satisfaction, learning, communication, and group effectiveness. From this point of view, pay serves as a convenient object to study in order to answer basic questions about human behavior. Just as problem solving without contributing to basic theory is sterile, however, so is basic theory that is not used to solve significant problems. Thus, five chapters of this book use the theory and research that are presented to solve problems that arise in pay administration. These chapters do not go into detailed descriptions of how to carry out job evaluations or how to set up stock option plans, but they do consider such issues as when pay will operate to motivate job performance and what the effects of pay secrecy are. The implications of the psychological research on pay for organizational effectiveness are emphasized in Chapters 4, 9, 11, 14, and 16.

Perhaps the most concise way to describe this book is to say that it deals with the psychological issues that arise when pay is administered in organizations and that in dealing with each issue it emphasizes theory, research, and practice. These emphases suggest that the book has something to say to both the academic researcher who is concerned with human behavior in organizations and the thoughtful practitioner.

For me this book represents the culmination of seven years of research. It is impossible to thank all those who have assisted me in my work. Thousands of people have completed questionnaires and allowed me to interview them, and numerous colleagues have spent hours discussing my research with me. In 1962, Mason Haire was instrumental in leading me to think about the psychological issues in pay administration. During the entire seven years of my work, Lyman Porter has been a friend and fellow researcher and has contributed immeasurably to my thinking. More recently Chris Argyris has been of great assistance. He has helped me locate research sites, has read this book several times, and has been an invaluable colleague. I could go on thanking people, but if I do I surely will run the risk of slighting someone, so let me stop here and make the obvious point that no work of this nature is ever solely the work of one person.

Edward E. Lawler III

Chapter 1
PAY: PSYCHOLOGICAL AND PRACTICAL SIGNIFICANCE

In most societies money represents and symbolizes wealth and property. For this reason, it is one major vehicle for conducting transactions in which goods and services are involved. This book focuses on one of the situations in which money is used to compensate people for services rendered: specifically, to pay employees for work or services rendered to an organization. The major focus is upon the payment of full-time permanent employees, although some attention is given to paying temporary and part-time employees as well. It deals with the nonfinancial rewards that people receive for working only as they relate to issues involving financial payment. In line with this the term "pay" will be used to refer to the money, fringe benefits, and other commodities that have financial value which organizations give to employees in return for their services.

Pay is typically thought of as performing a number of functions that contribute to organizational effectiveness. Primarily it is considered a reward that can be used to make employees feel satisfied with their job, motivate them, gain their commitment to the organization, and keep them in the organization. Questions about the impact of pay upon job satisfaction, motivation and commitment are basically psychological. Thus, by using a psychological frame of reference we can learn a great deal about how pay affects attitudes and behavior, and how it can contribute to organizational effectiveness. This certainly is reason enough to study the psychological aspects of pay. But it may be too modest a reason. Potentially, the psychological study of pay can reveal more than simply how pay operates. Analysis of the impact of pay on attitudes and behavior can be a means of developing and testing general principles of how atttiude and behavior patterns in organizations are influenced. The pivotal role of pay should make it possible to learn a great deal about the determinants of human behavior by studying its role in organizations.

Just as it is unrealistic to state a theory of human motivation without taking into account people's reactions to such objects as pay, it is impossible to state a valid theory of how people react to pay without contributing to the understanding of many basic psychological influences on behavior. Because of this, work on the psychological issues involved in pay can make important contributions to fundamental research and thinking in such areas as motivation, attitudes, and social comparison theory. Most of the research done so far has been directly concerned with motivation, and it is in this area that work on pay probably has the most to contribute to the field of psychology. As we shall see, pay has been used as a variable in testing the validity of hypotheses extrapolated from many of the current theories of motivation. This variable has been useful in proving some currently popular theories of motivation to be better predictors of behavior than others. The research on pay has also stimulated and encouraged further research and theory building. Thus, it meets perhaps the most important criterion of relevancy to the literature of psychology: opening new fields of inquiry and ultimately extending the boundaries of knowledge.

The main reason for focusing on the psychological issues concerned with pay, therefore, is that any knowledge gained from this study is likely to contribute to our basic understanding of human behavior at work. There are, however, a number of other reasons. Unlike other organization variables that are difficult to change and influence (e.g., leadership style), pay can be easily controlled and changed. This is important to the researcher; he can use pay as an experimental variable that is altered either by him or by an organization. But, it is also important to the practitioner, who potentially can use and implement research evidence on the effects of pay. As we shall see, the research on pay has a number of clear practical implications.

Pay is, in other ways, a desirable variable to explore. It is easy to quantify, and it has a meaning that is shared across many cultural and ethnic groups. Because of this, pay can be used as a variable in projects designed to study a number of different issues. It is also important to remember that most people spend at least half their waking hours working under a pay system. Thus, in looking at pay, we are considering a major influence in most people's lives. This fact increases the likelihood that any findings concerning pay will relate to general views of what influences human behavior.

In short, the way people react to their pay is just one of many aspects of human behavior that can be studied. It is a significant one, however, because it is one research area where it is possible to do work that has important practical and theoretical implications.

PLAN OF THE BOOK

Most psychological research on pay is divided into three areas. The first deals with the importance of pay. The studies in this area essentially treat the importance of pay as a dependent variable or as the variable which is to be predicted. Originally these studies were concerned only with how important pay was, but lately more attention has been given to determining why pay is important and what factors influence its importance.

The second area of research deals with the ability of pay to motivate employees to work. These studies have sometimes been concerned with the importance of pay as an independent variable or a variable to be considered because of its ability to modify behavior.

The third concerns satisfaction with pay. It has been treated as both an independent and a dependent variable. One set of studies has tried to measure employee satisfaction with pay and to determine the causes of different levels of satisfaction. Another set of studies has tried to determine the consequences of high and low pay satisfaction. Here, satisfaction has essentially been treated as an independent variable; turnover, absenteeism and performance have been treated as dependent variables.

Since this book deals extensively with the psychological research on pay, it is organized around the focuses and emphases of this research. The book is, therefore, divided into four parts: (1) the importance of pay, (2) pay as a source of motivation, (3) satisfaction with pay and (4) an overview. These parts obviously relate to the problem areas just described. But they are more than just a convenient grouping. Different psychological theories are relevant to each of the first three parts. At the moment, no one existing theory can explain all of the data on pay. But it is possible to state three related models that can explain the data in each of the three parts. Thus, this organization is designed to facilitate the development of theoretical explanations of the pay research.

The order in which the topics will be discussed is also closely related to the kinds of theoretical models that are needed to explain the relevant data. Importance is treated first because it is an input variable relevant for both motivation and pay satisfaction. Discussion and understanding of why pay is important are basic to an understanding of the data on motivation and satisfaction. Satisfaction is treated last because the outcomes of the motivation model, performance, and in some cases pay, are major inputs into the satisfaction model. Thus, in moving from importance to motivation and then to satisfaction, the discussion will follow the logical progression of the models that have been developed in each area. To the extent that the models can be interconnected, they fit precisely in the order in which they are being discussed.

Many theories and models can be drawn from the basic psychological literature to help us understand the issues surrounding why pay is important, how it motivates people, and what pay satisfaction means. Admittedly, none of these theories perfectly fits the issues that are to be discussed, since they are not designed to deal with the research on pay. But they offer important clues on what theories must contain if they are to account adequately for the data on importance, motivation and satisfaction. So in developing a set of models or theories to explain these data, we must first assess the relevant existing theories and models to determine what they can contribute to understanding of the psychological aspects of pay. Thus, at the beginning of each of the first three parts, we shall briefly discuss the relevant theoretical work. We shall then develop models to deal with these three psychological issues. Finally, in the fourth part, we shall look at how the three models fit together.

In addition to the presentation and development of theory, we shall in each part review the research that is related to the model or theory that has been developed. Finally, the implications of the research and theory will be considered with an eye to designing more effective pay administration practices. This final step is crucial: As is so often pointed out, one of the best ways to find out if you really understand something is to change it. One of the best ways of determining how adequately the psychological aspects of pay are understood is to try to design a pay system that is more effective than the ones commonly used.

When these three topics have been covered, most of the research and theory on pay will also have been covered, but not all. A pay system exists within the context of a total organization, and one very important facet of any organization is the style of management that is practiced. A pay system that motivates very effectively in an organization with one kind of management philosophy may fail completely in an organization with a different management philosophy. This suggests that pay plans and styles of management may interact. Thus, no discussion of pay is complete unless we consider the consequences of implementing certain pay policies in organizations with different styles of management. This issue will be considered in the final part.

Many research findings on pay have come from industrial studies. Fortunately, most of these findings are relevant to all types of organizations where people are paid for their services. Still, we must not limit our discussion of pay to only those issues that arise in industry. We must also consider issues that occur in nonindustrial organizations. Different issues are sometimes involved in paying employees of profit-making and non-profit-making organizations. Most profit-oriented organizations can develop plans for paying employees on the basis of profitability or some other economic indicator of the organization's success. In many other organizations, however, such measures are often difficult or impossible to obtain and generally are not seen to be a valid basis for determining pay. There is a great deal of evidence to suggest that people often work for profit-making and nonprofit organizations for different reasons; as a result, the two kinds of organizations are made up of people who perceive pay quite differently. For example, employees are often willing to work for a nonprofit organization for less money than they would accept from a profit-making organization. To reiterate, in many instances different pay issues arise in different types of organizations. This point, however, should not obscure the fact that the vast majority of research findings probably are applicable to most types of organizations.

HISTORY OF RESEARCH ON PAY

Despite the obvious advantages, psychologists have until recently done relatively little research on pay. As has been pointed out, "It is a strange thing that there is so little psychological research on pay. The basic assumption—that it motivates people to work—is a psychological one. The details of wage and salary systems—e.g., decisions about the size of increments—demand further assumptions about the way people see pay and its structure" (Haire, Ghiselli, & Porter, 1963, p. 3). The fact that little such research has been done, however, has not kept people interested in personnel and organizational administration from writing about it. Figure 1-1 shows the percentage of articles in two journals that mention some aspects of pay in their title. Data are shown for 1956 and 1957 and for 1966 and 1967. For each of these periods, about 10 percent of the articles appearing in *Personnel* dealt with pay. *Personnel* is a practice-oriented journal; these articles tended to be prescriptive rather than research reports. The large number of articles on pay clearly illustrates its importance to practitioners. Figure 1-1 also presents data for the *Journal of Applied Psychology,* which is the logical place for psychologists to publish their empirical studies concerned with pay. It shows that in 1956–1957 no studies on the subject appeared in the journal, but that in 1966–1967 a few did appear. These data reflect the fact that for a long period very little basic research on pay was done, but that recently the amount has increased.

The lack of psychological research on pay means that many of the articles on organizational practice are not based upon empirical evidence, although they often deal with topics for which empirical data can be collected. For example, Rodney (1967), writing in *Personnel Administration,*

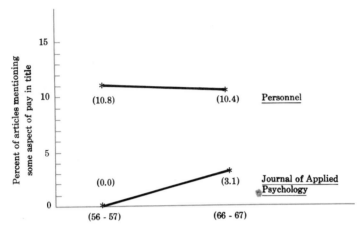

FIGURE 1-1. Percent of articles in Journal of Applied Psychology and Personnel concerned with pay.

asks whether pay can motivate better job performance. The question is important both for practice and for understanding human motivation, yet Rodney cities only two empirical studies directly related to it. His article is symptomatic of the great gap between research findings and practice in the field of pay administration. The result is that most pay administration practices are not research-based. Nor could they be in many instances even if administrators so wished, because until recently the research knowledge simply was not available.

Because most pay administration practices are not research-based, they tend to be faddish and assumptive (Dunnette & Bass, 1963). Practices have developed as a result of the personal experience of a few people and have been heavily influenced by chance and circumstance as well as by the policies of other organizations. Often, practice seems to be characterized by a desire to do whatever the more "successful" big-name companies are doing. Thus, the policies of many companies have a "me too" look. As Haire, Ghiselli, and Porter (1963, p. 8) have noted, "Few other areas of industrial practice have the layers upon layers of traditional thinking that characterize wage and salary administration. We are in danger of being trapped in a kind of institutionalized way of dealing with the problem simply because we have done so for so long. We have made the same assumptions and not tested or questioned them."

Why have practitioners had so little psychological knowledge upon which to build sound pay administration practices? Two reasons. First, relatively few attempts have been made to translate the basic laboratory research findings about motivation, satisfaction, etc., into organizational practice. Missing is what Haire (1964) refers to as developmental research. He points out that such work is needed in many areas of the behavioral sciences. For example, we have learned a great deal about the motivational effects of different reinforcement schedules from the work of Skinner and others interested in operant conditioning, yet this work has had little impact on practice. The second reason is that applied research on pay simply has been out of style; only recently has there been a revival of interest in it. Stating this fact, however, does not explain it. To understand it, we must consider the historical context within which research on pay has been done. This is particularly important because, as we shall see, this context has strongly shaped the kind of research that has been done. Different eras have produced their own unique type of research on pay.

Pay first became a prominent research subject during the "scientific management" era (1900–1930). Little of the research, however, considered the relevant psychological problems. F. W. Taylor emphasized that employees must be given an economic incentive if they are to work to their full capacity. This view was, of course, congruent with the concept of "economic man" which was popularly accepted during the early 1900s. Economic man is, according to J. A. C. Brown,

a rational creature who uses his reason primarily to calculate how much satisfaction he may obtain from the smallest amount of effort, or when necessary, how much discomfort he can avoid. "Satisfaction" does not mean pride in one's job, the feeling of having accomplished something or even the regard of others; it refers only to money. Similarly "discomfort" refers, not to failing in one's task, or losing the respect of one's comrades, but solely to the fear of starvation. [Brown, 1954, p. 16]

During the scientific management era, most research on pay was concerned with measuring the effectiveness of the many piece rate incentive plans that were introduced. Good estimates indicate that during the early 1930s, 75 percent of the firms in the United States used some form of incentive plan (NICB, 1946). From 1900 to the early 1930s, time study and incentive plans became a way of life in most companies. As a result, research on pay became associated with scientific management. This was not entirely unjustified, since much of the research on pay done during this period accepted the scientific management philosophy. It examined such things as the cost savings attributable to the incentive plan and wages before and after the plan was installed. The research shows that even crude piece rate plans often led to increased productivity. This fact is often forgotten. Still, this research is easily criticized on two psychological grounds: (1) It did not consider the psychological basis for expecting pay to be an incentive. (2) It did not consider all the ramifications of using pay as an incentive. Thus, this research—and, in fact, the whole scientific management movement—was ripe for criticism when the "human relations" movement took over in the 1930s and 1940s.

The human relations movement stressed the importance of non-economic factors and their influence on performance. In place of the psychological effects of pay, researchers focused on the impact of the informal organization, group pressure, and social relations. In this milieu there seemed to be little room for pay research. What research there was on pay during the early part of the human relations movement was directed toward proving that pay is not important to employees. A number of studies asked workers to rank or rate job factors in order of importance. These studies have been consistently interpreted as showing that pay ranks about sixth in importance behind such factors as security, job interest, advancement, appreciation (from supervision), and management. The findings seemed to confirm the "fact" that pay was relatively unimportant to employees and that researchers were justified in not studying it in any detail. It seemed more fruitful to study such factors as job interest and appreciation, which were believed to be more important.

At the beginning of the human relations movement there existed no theory to explain why pay was not important to most employees. An explanation did appear later with Maslow's statement (1943) of his theory of motivation. According to this view, needs are arranged in a hierarchy, with security and physiological needs at the bottom, social and esteem needs in the middle, and self-realization needs at the top. Once the lower needs are satisfied, they cease to be important and the higher-order needs are activated. Since many people saw pay as satisfying only the lower-order needs, they argued that it is important only when these needs are not satisfied. Carrying this line of reasoning further, they argued that since most lower-order needs are satisfied in our society, it is hardly surprising that pay is not important to employees. This argument seemed to be the *coup de grace* for research on pay; suddenly, the package was complete. Pay, and to some extent research on pay, became associated with lower-order needs and with scientific management, neither of which was the most exciting topic to study. Thus, it is hardly surprising that during the human relations movement, little research on pay was done.

The tendency of researchers to ignore pay during the human relations era provides an interesting example of the power of the *Zeitgeist* of the period. A great deal of evidence existed to suggest that pay was important to employees and that it could motivate them, yet it was systematically ignored or distorted. Most of the studies of piece rate plans, for example, showed that pay could increase output. Many studies found that pay was ranked as the most important job factor by employees. But perhaps most ironic was the fact that the Western Electric studies, which are credited with having started the human relations movement, showed that pay *can* be an important motivator of performance (Roethlisberger & Dickson, 1939). Later Western Electric experiments established that about half of the productivity increase in the relay assembly test room was due to the change in the pay plan that took place when this room was created. The other half of the increase in productivity apparently was due to a *combination* of *all* the other factors that were changed. This was shown by the 15 percent increase in productivity in the second relay assembly test room, where only the system of pay was changed, as compared with the increase in the mica-splitting test room of about 15 percent, when all other factors were changed (Roethlisberger & Dickson, 1939). It is indeed strange that this study, which clearly seems to show the importance of pay as a motivator of performance, is so often cited as conclusive proof that other factors are more important than pay. Some recent commentators (e.g., Carey, 1967) have even argued that this study shows that pay is the key factor in motivating employees. But again, given the philosophy of the period, the study was not interpreted that way.

The interpretation of pay as satisfying only lower-order needs is another example of the peculiar way in which pay was viewed by people interested in organization theory. There would seem to be no reason for arguing that pay satisfies only lower-order needs, since as will be shown in later chapters, it can satisfy such higher-order needs as esteem and recognition. Yet Maslow's theory is used by some (e.g., McKersie, 1963) as a basis for arguing that pay may be unimportant once lower-order needs have been satisfied.

During the last 10 to 15 years, increased attention has been given to higher-order development and growth needs and to concepts of human nature that stress these needs. This tendency can undoubtedly be attributed to such events as the statement of Theory Y by McGregor (1960), to Maslow's discussion of the importance of self-actualization, and to White's incisive argument (1959) for the existence of a competence motive. These have caused many people to abandon the old human relations concept of social man as their model of man. The recent trend toward the theory of "self-actualizing man" has not, of course, directly stimulated psychological research on pay. As in the social man era, pay research has been out of fashion during much of the self-actualizing-man era. After all, if man is now thought to be primarily motivated by higher-order growth needs, then pay is not likely to be a significant variable.

Fortunately, a number of researchers have tired of simplified views of human nature that stress only one need and build theories of organization based upon the assumption that man is primarily motivated by that need. Schein (1965), for example, has called for a model of what he calls "complex man." Basically, this model argues that man is motivated by a number of different needs and that all of them must be studied. For this view the theories of social man, self-actualizing man, and economic man were important because each served to emphasize one of man's chief needs. But Schein argues that we now need a more sophisticated concept which stresses all these needs and attempts to determine how and when they infleunce behavior.

Clearly, this view of man is more supportive of doing research on pay. In fact, a growing amount of pay research—significant research—has been done in the last few years. Pay research seems to have become more respectable. The climate for this kind of research is getting better, and it is very likely that much more will be done. Recent studies have contributed a great deal to our understanding in a number of areas of psychology, and it has become possible for the first time to write a research-based, psychologically oriented book on pay in organizations.

It is difficult to identify any one study or theory as central in stimulating the recent research on pay. Rather, a number of events have combined to stimulate this work. On the one hand, several theories have been formulated in the nonapplied areas of psychology which have lent themselves to verification in pay situations. For example, Adams' theory of equity (1961, 1963a) is a general theory of social exchange, yet Adams quite rightly felt that a suitable place to test it would be in the area of wage inequity. An interest in testing expectancy theories of motivation has led several researchers (e.g., Porter & Lawler, 1968a) to look at the effects of wage systems on motivation. Patchen (1961) has tested some of the predictions of dissonance theory by considering people's reference groups in evaluating their pay. Research has also been stimulated greatly by the appearance of some interesting theories on pay in the work of Jaques (1961) and Herzberg and his associates (1957, 1959) In addition, several symposiums and many recent conferences have dealt with the psychological research on pay (Andrews [ed.], 1965; Dunnette [ed.], 1967).

In 1966, in reviewing a short monograph on pay (Andrews [ed.], 1965), I stated:

At our present state of knowledge, it would be premature to expect a book that would provide a comprehensive treatment of the psychological issues involved in management compensation. However, it does not seem improbable that as the kind of research described in this monograph is carried out, the area will spawn a more comprehensive volume. [Lawler, 1966d, pp. 238–239]

As this book testifies, the research has been done. It is now possible to write that "more comprehensive volume."

PRACTICAL SIGNIFICANCE OF PSYCHOLOGICAL RESEARCH ON PAY

The money spent on pay represents one of the largest costs any organization incurs. In many organizations it presently exceeds 50 percent of the total budget. Payroll expenses account for a particularly high percentage of the budget in most service-related organizations, because they are essentially selling labor. Service organizations are becoming more and more common throughout the world. Thus, despite automation and other technological changes, most organizations will continue to spend a significant percentage—perhaps an increasing percentage—of their gross income on pay. Recent history has shown that employment costs are rising at the rate of 10 percent per year in many organizations. Two comments by Blough (1958, p. 7) perhaps best summarize the situation:

If you took all of the products that are made in America, put then in one huge pile, and added up the price tags on the lot, upwards of three quarters of this total value would represent the employment costs that were incurred all along the line of production. The remaining quarter or less would cover not only the basic cost of all the raw materials, but would also pay for the rental of property, the interest on debt, and the dividends that pay for use of all of the tools of production that were employed in the manufacturer of these products.

. . . the undisputed evidence in the record of the [United States Senate Antitrust and Monopoly] committee shows that during the past 17 years, United States Steel's employment costs, per man-hour, have gone up at an average rate of more than 8 percent per year.

The significance of salaries as an expense factor to most companies can be determined by considering what the effect of a 5 percent reduction in their wage bill would mean in terms of company earnings. In 1967 AT&T had earnings of $3.79 a share. If the company had been able to reduce its payroll expenses by 5 percent, it would have had earnings of $4.45. Similar increases could be shown for almost any company. In the case of a relatively small manufacturer, Rogers Corporation, the increase in 1966 would have been from $1.66 to $2.10. Rogers spends about 36 percent of its income on wages.

It is hardly necessary to belabor the point that pay is a large and important cost for organizations. Management certainly realizes this, as do unions and other employee groups. Less obvious is the point that management has often done a poor job of assessing the return that it gets from the money it spends on wages and fringe benefits It fails to approach payroll expenses as it approaches raw materials costs. As in the case of raw materials, it does analyze carefully the costs relative to quantity, market value, and what competitors are doing. It does this by making salary surveys, cost analyses of fringe benefits, etc. In other words, it looks at pay extensively from the point of view of economic outlay. But it never really seems to look at what is gotten in return. Instead, it is primarily concerned with keeping the outlay in line with that of competitors. When much smaller amounts of money are spent on raw materials, organizations typically spend considerable effort analyzing the quality and value of the materials they purchase. By measuring only costs and not the returns on money spent for pay, organizations are falling into the trap of measuring those things which are easily measured and ignoring important factors which are more difficult to measure. Without accurate assessment of what a pay system buys, it is impossible to talk intelligently about which system is best. In fact, the lack of good measures is undoubtedly one of the main reasons organizations are so willing to switch their pay programs when a new fad comes along. They simply do not have any evidence on the effectiveness of their present program.

The money spent on salaries should be thought of not as a cost which buys a certain number of people but as an investment in human beings. It is an investment that may or may not yield returns in terms of employee job satisfaction, motivation, and commitment to the organization. These are difficult dimensions to measure and ones that most organizations do not adequately measure, but still, the returns from a salary program must be assessed in these areas. To conclude the raw materials analogy, it is as if the quality of the materials was never assessed, only their quantity and cost. A pay system can look fine in terms of economic feasibility and straight economic accounting, but if we conceive of pay as an investment in people and their behavior, the system may not seem so impressive. Chapters 4, 9, 11, 14, and 16 will deal directly with the practical implications of the research and theory for organizational effectiveness. These chapters will emphasize pay as an investment in the human resources of the organization and what this means in terms of pay practices.

Part 1
THE IMPORTANCE OF PAY

Wine maketh merry; but money
answereth all things.

(Ecclesiastes)

To some people money seems to
represent social respectability; to others
it may mean recognition for achievement; to still others it stands for
worldliness, materialism, and the "root
of all evil."

(Gellerman, 1968)

Chapter 2
THEORETICAL
EXPLANATIONS

Observational evidence abounds that pay is important to people. As Opshal and Dunnette (1966) note, people everywhere seem to behave as if money were a prime goal. "Executives strive mightily to advance to high-paying jobs, entertainers work toward more and more lucrative arrangements; bankers embezzle; robbers rob; university professors publish to win increased salary and to enjoy royalty checks" (p. 108). What is less clear is why and how an intrinsically neutral object like money becomes valuable to people. It is also not entirely clear how important pay is to employees or what factors influence its importance.

A number of theories have been stated to explain why money takes on value. Most of them have not dealt with pay, but since money is an important part of the pay package, they can contribute to our understanding of the importance of pay. We will review some of these theories before developing our own model to explain (1) the importance of pay and (2) why certain factors affect its importance. It is vital that many of the explanations for the importance of money be considered, because different theories have quite different implications for action and for the interpretation of the research on pay. Any model or theory of the importance of pay must meet three criteria. First, it must be able to explain research data on the relative importance of pay and on the factors that influence its importance. Second, it should stimulate further research. Third, it should produce valid implications for practice. Four of the many theoretical explanations for why money can become important are especially well developed and will be considered in this chapter. Then the major differences among them will be discussed in terms of our three criteria. Finally, a model to explain the importance of pay will be presented. This model draws upon some of the key points in the earlier work, but it is distinctly different from any previously offered theory.

THEORETICAL EXPLANATIONS

Money as an Acquired Drive

Few people have seriously argued that man has an innate biological drive for money. A number of theorists, however, have stated that people can develop learned or acquired drives for various objects. According to this view, people can develop a drive for money that is independent of any other drive, so that even if all their other drives are satiated they will still seek money. Dashiell (1928), Anderson (1941a), and others have argued that external stimuli can acquire drive properties when the stimuli occur often enough in contiguity with primary drives. Anderson has called this idea the "externalization of drive." In order to test his thinking, Anderson (1941b) trained rats under conditions of hunger and food reward. He conducted a substantial number of trials in one maze and then transferred the rats to another maze. Although the animals were hunger-satiated at the time of transfer, they still learned the new maze. Anderson explains the rats' learning by arguing that the rats developed an acquired drive for learning the maze and entering the goal box that was independent of their hunger drive. Hull (1951) cities Anderson's work as an example of how a learned drive can be acquired. Calvin, Bicknell, and Sperling (1953) have also provided evidence that is frequently cited as proof that drives can be acquired. They placed two groups of rats in distinctly colored boxes for 30 minutes each day for 24 days. One group was very hungry when placed in its box, the other was not. Both groups were then made equally food deprived and were placed in the boxes. The group that had previously been in the boxes when very hungry ate more than the other group. This was interpreted as indicating that the box had the power to arouse an acquired drive to eat.

To apply this line of reasoning to money, it is argued that because money is often associated with the presence and reduction of such basic drives as hunger and thirst, over an extended period of time it takes on drive properties. That is, people seek it even though they are not hungry or thirsty. This theory is somewhat similar to Allport's (1937) concept of functional autonomy. Allport argues that types of behavior like earning money can somehow acquire their own motive powers. Such behaviors persist despite the absence of primary motives. Thus, these types of behavior must have become independent of the motives upon which they were based, developing, in effect, a motive of their own.

So far, the suggestion has been made that money can become an acquired motive or drive because of its pairing with the reduction of positive drives, such as hunger and thirst. We can also argue that money can become an acquired drive because of its pairing with the reduction of avoidance drives. Brown (1953, 1961) illustrates how money can be paired with the reduction of anxiety. He suggests that very young children, in the course of painful experiences such as illness, falls and accidents, come to associate these experiences with worried and anxious behavior on the part of their parents. If parents then act in a similarly worried and anxious manner when they deal with financial problems, the children's anxiety may be transferred to the topic of money. Getting money will, of course, reduce this anxiety, and the behavior which accompanies obtaining money will be strongly reinforced so that acquiring money or earning it will be a strong motivating force for the individual. Brown himself does not argue that the motivation to obtain money will persist even if the anxiety is removed. Thus, he says it s wrong to speak of a motive or drive for money. It is, however, possible to argue that the desire to acquire money can become functionally independent of avoidance or anxiety drives just as it can become functionally independent of positive drives. Certainly Horney (1937, 1939, 1945, 1950) seems to suggest that, because of its original ability to reduce anxiety, acquiring pay might later become an institutionalized (i.e., functionally autonomous) "neurotic need." Rapaport (1959, 1960) has suggested that the ego may be capable of nontension-reducing functions even when not directly gratifying specific basic drives. He does not identify the ego's source of energy, but he points out that an act like acquiring money can be motivated by what is essentially its own drive.

Money as a Secondary Reinforcer

It has been widely suggested that money can best be thought of as an object that can become a secondary reinforcer because of its frequent pairing with a primary reward. A secondary reinforcer has the power to maintain behavior when primary reinforcement no longer occurs. It also may serve as a "reward" for learning acts which are never followed by primary reinforcement. The concept of secondary reinforcement has an important role in the Hullian theory of motivation (Hull, 1943, 1951, 1952) and in the theories of Spence (1956) and other stimulus response (S-R) drive theorists. A typical example of secondary reinforcement in the experimental psychology literature is the persistence of a turning behavior in a simple T maze when the empty goal box on the side to which the animal is supposed to turn is a box in which he has frequently been fed. The analogy to money is rather direct, and since the presence of money is often associated with receiving primary rewards, it could become a secondary reinforcer and have reward value, just as the goal box has in the T maze.

Most proponents of the concept of secondary reinforcement point out that secondary reinforcers usually work only when the subject is in a state of deprivation. When a secondary reinforcer has been associated with the reduction of only one kind of deprivation, presumably that particular deprivation must be present for it to act as a reinforcer. This is a crucial point for distinguishing between the acquired-drive argument and the secondary reinforcement argument. The acquired-drive argument essentially maintains that the acquired drive is independent of the deprivation or drive upon which it was originally based.

Skinner has stated that generalized secondary reinforcers can be developed. In contrast to specific secondary reinforcers, generalized ones have been paired with more than one primary reinforcer. As Opshal and Dunnette have pointed out, one widely held hypothesis is that money acts as a generalized secondary reinforcer because of its repeated pairing with a number of primary reinforcers (Holland & Skinner, 1961; Kelleher & Gollub, 1962; Skinner, 1953). The argument is that a generalized secondary reinforcer should be extremely effective because some deprivation will usually exist for which the conditioned reinforcer is appropriate. In the case of pay this might mean that deprivation of food, water, or even social relations and esteem could lead to money being a reinforcer if it had been associated with the appropriate primary reinforcers earlier.

The distinction between money as a specific secondary reinforcer and as a generalized secondary reinforcer is not a trivial one. If pay is a generalized reinforcer, it is likely to be a very effective reinforcer since it should take on reinforcer properties when almost any kind of deprivation exists. However, if it is a specific secondary reinforcer, then it will function as a reinforcer only when a certain kind of deprivation exists.

Money as a Conditioned Incentive

Incentives are objects that have the power to stimulate behavior. In the classic experiments of Wolfe (1936) and Cowles (1937) chimpanzees learned to associate tokens with the acquisition of food rewards. Initially, the chimps learned to operate an apparatus that required lifting a weight to obtain grapes, but they continued to operate it when the only visible reward was a token. The token could later be exchanged for food (Wolfe, 1936). An explanation for this behavior is that the token became a conditioned incentive; once it became associated with food, it then had the power to stimulate the behavior associated with obtaining it.

Presumably, money can become either a generalized conditioned incentive or a specific conditioned incentive. That is, it can become an incentive because of its pairing with only one reward or because of its pairing with a number of different rewards. This is an important distinction, since most of the proponents of the conditioned incentive view maintain that conditioned incentives are effective only when the need or drive to which they are conditioned is operating. Thus, if pay is a specific incentive it will have much less motivational power than if it is a generalized conditioned incentive.

J. S. Brown (1953, 1961) essentially argues that money gains value because of its conditioned association with anxiety. Brown speaks of money as a goal which has its basis in anxiety. Presumably he would argue that money will be sought only when anxiety is present. Brown thus sees money as a specific conditioned incentive that can activate money-seeking behavior.

Money as an Instrument

Vroom (1964) has set forth a cognitive model of motivation that is based on the expectancy theories of Peak (1955), Lewin (1938), and others, which will be discussed in Chapter 5. According to one part of this model, money acquires valence or importance as a function of its perceived instrumentality for obtaining other desired outcomes. Thus, the valence of money to an individual is determined by the valence of all the outcomes that he perceives to depend upon money and the subjective probability that money will lead to them. Therefore, the valence of each outcome (where valence varies from +1 to −1) that is perceived to depend upon money should be multiplied by the subjective probability (where this probability varies from +1 to −1) that it is obtainable from money. The sum of the products of all these multiplications determines the value of money to the individual. The greater the sum, the greater the valence. For example, if an individual desires security and esteem and perceives that he can obtain them directly from money, then money will have a high valence for him. If he does not desire esteem or security or if he does not see money as leading to them, money will not have a high valence for him.

This view argues that pay is important when valued outcomes or objects are felt to be obtainable as a result of having it. Thus, pay is seen as a means to an end. Vroom does not specify how the valence of outcomes originates. He states no theory of needs or drives that might determine the valence of the outcomes to which pay leads. According to him, the outcomes to which pay leads have value only if they are seen to lead to other valued outcomes, and so on. Thus, whether deprivation must exist for pay to be important is not considered by Vroom. He does agree, however, that money is not likely to become an end in itself and that people will not seek money unless it leads to something else that is valued.

Gellerman's view (1968) of how money works in industry is somewhat similar to the view stated by Vroom. Gellerman points out that money has no intrinsic meaning but that it can acquire significance when it comes to symbolize intangible goals. For example, he comments that money can represent a sort of shield against disaster; it can come to symbolize love and security. "Money is the paper doll that other fellows cannot steal." Thus, money is of value only because of its ability to satisfy needs for love, security, esteem, etc., and presumably it is important only when these needs are important.

MAJOR ISSUES IN THE THEORIES

The theories that have been discussed so far make a number of similar points about the importance of money. All of them view money as essentially a neutral stimulus that in time takes on value because of its association with other stimuli. The theories differ in a number of respects, however, and in order to develop a model of the importance of pay, we must examine the differences and, where possible, determine the validity of the various views. The following sections attempt to do this by considering the major questions that are raised by the differences among the theories.

Can Acquired Drives Develop?

The acquired-drive theory maintains that money gains its importance through its association with other stimuli, but this view differs from the others in that it argues for functional autonomy or for the idea that seeking money can eventually become an end in itself. There is a considerable amount of experimental evidence relevant to this point. The research clearly suggests that acquired drives simply cannot be established on the basis of positive drives (Cravens & Renner, 1970). The chimpanzees in the studies by Cowles and by Wolfe, for example, would not work for the tokens unless they were in fact hungry. Presumably, if they had developed an acquired drive for the tokens, they would have continued to work for them even though they were not hungry. Anderson's findings (1941b), mentioned above as suggesting that drives could be acquired in this manner, were not replicated in a study by Siegel (1943). Calvin, Bicknell, and Sperling (1953) presented a study which they claimed proved that such drives can be established. A number of attempts to replicate their study, however, have consistently gotten negative results (Parkes, 1958; Scarborough & Goodson, 1957; Siegel & MacDonnel, 1954).

When considered together, therefore, the evidence does not make a convincing case for the view that money should be thought of as an acquired drive based on positive primary drives. It should be pointed out, however, that much of the evidence is not directly relevant to the issue of pay. All the studies were done on animals, and typically the frequencies of the pairing of the acquired-drive stimulus and the primary stimulus were much lower than would be expected where money is concerned, since money is so often paired with positive drives and reinforcers. Still, the only reasonable conclusion is that an acquired drive for money cannot develop based upon associations with positive drives. This does not rule out the possibility that a drive for money could develop because of its pairing with the reduction of a negative drive, such as fear or anxiety.

There is a considerable amount of evidence that objects can acquire avoidance drive characteristics as a result of being associated with anxiety or fear. N. E. Miller (1948, 1951) has shown that once animals are shocked in a box they will develop an acquired-fear drive when placed in that box. This drive will motivate them to escape from the box, and they will work and learn to execute responses in order to escape. For this study to be relevant to pay, however, it would have to show that the box *to which* the animals escape takes on reward characteristics. It would in effect have to show that the animals not only are running away from something but are also running toward something, as people do when they seek money. There is some evidence that animals will seek previous escape boxes when they are placed under fear motivation. Lawler (1965b) has shown that when rats are placed in a fear situation, they will escape to boxes that have previously been associated with shock reduction rather than to neutral boxes. Hence, it seems that escape objects can, like money, be secondary reinforcers and conditioned incentives when fear is present. There is no evidence, however, that animals will seek out escape objects or locations when they are not afraid. Thus, it has not been established that acquired approach drives can be created on the basis of associations with reduction of primary avoidance drives (Lolordo, 1969). Overall, then, the evidence is not strong enough to support the view that a learned or acquired drive can be established for money or another previously neutral stimulus. In fact, as Cofer and Appley (1964) have stated, it probably is not very useful to employ the term "drive" at all. As they point out, it cannot explain a great deal of the human behavior observed and has not been successfully related to physiological functions in a way that would allow it to explain animal behavior either.

Incentive or Reinforcer?

According to both the secondary reinforcement view and the conditioned-incentive view money is a stimulus which gains value by being paired with primary rewards. The theories differ, however, in the function they

see money performing. One stresses its role as a reinforcer of past behavior; another stresses its role as a stimulator of future behavior. This is
an important difference, since these are two distinct—but not mutually
exclusive—functions. In fact, some evidence indicates that pay probably
serves as both an incentive and a reinforcer (Cofer & Appley, 1964). The
important point for our discussion is that these two theories suggest that
an object can take on value through its associaton with other objects or
stimuli and that its continued value depends upon the maintenance of the
value of the other rewards. The tokens and the behavior of the chimps in
the Cowles study show this. Thus, it is reasonable to assume that money
acquires its value as a result of its association with other valued objects.

Generalized or Specific?

Once it has been decided that it is not possible to establish an acquired
drive for money and that money gains value only through its connections
with other stimuli, then the issue of how broadly generalized these connections can be becomes important. Can money become associated with a
number of rewards or only with a few? Evidence from experimental animal studies is not very supportive of the view that stimuli can become
generalized conditioned reinforcers and conditioned incentives. Wike and
Barrientos (1958) did show that a goal box previously paired with both
food and water deprivations was a more effective reinforcer for rats than
goal boxes which had been previously paired with only one of these deprivations. As Opshal and Dunnette (1966) point out, the difference between the effectiveness of the goal boxes was small, but statistically significant. Ferster and DeMyer (1962) have done a study in which coins
were paired with rewards of games and candy. They report that autistic
children could be effectively trained when the coins were used as reinforcers Ayllon's work (1967) with mental patients shows that coins can
be successfully used as rewards when they are paired with multiple rewards. Unfortunately, neither of the studies which used human subjects
tested to determine if the coins were more effective when paired with
multiple rewards than they were when paired with a single reward.
Clearly, there is a need for studies with human subjects in which a stimulus
is paired with multiple outcomes and the strength of the subjects' desires
for the various outcomes can be manipulated. With this kind of design it
should be possible to determine the value of a stimulus, such as money,
when it leads to more than one outcome and what happens when some of
the outcomes it leads to are more desirable than others.

Despite the lack of evidence that stimuli can be effectively generalized secondary reinforcers and incentives, Cofer (1967) has argued

that pay can best be thought of as a stimulus that becomes a generalized reinforcer or incentive. As he points out, "Somewhere in the histories of each of us money has been associated with many reinforcers—it has bought us food and drink, clothing, shelter, entertainment, social relations, security, and many more." It is hard to find fault with Cofer's argument. In fact, it is easy to add to his list of reinforcers. As J. S. Brown (1961) has stressed, money can also be an anxiety reducer, and as we have seen, this view probably has validity. In addition, money can buy prestige and status. Much of the negative evidence with respect to the ability of stimuli to become generalized incentives or reinforcers is from animal studies. Given the more complex cognitive structures of human beings, it is possible that stimuli could be effective as generalized incentives or reinforcers for man but not for animals. Certainly, a great deal of casual evidence suggests that money can be paired with a large number of positively valued outcomes. Thus, it is logical to conclude that money probably is important because of its association with a number of desired outcomes and that as long as these outcomes are valued, money will be valued.

Instrumentality Theory or Drive Theory?

Little has been said so far about the nature of the connections between money and the other stimuli that give money its value. Reinforcement theory speaks of these connections as being conditioned through frequent pairing in the learning history of organisms. Instrumentality theory speaks of people having subjective probabilities of the likelihood that money will lead to other outcomes, but it says very little about how these connections are built up. Part of this difference in the two theories may be attributable to the fact that reinforcement theory has dealt mainly with animals, while instrumentality theory has typically been concerned with human behavior.

Perhaps it makes sense, when dealing with animals, to think of stamping in associations and habit strength, but when talking about humans, it seems best to think of behavior as based on subjective probabilities. Indeed, there is evidence to indicate that people do operate on the basis of subjective probabilities. Thus, it seems logical to think of people as future-oriented, concerned about the expected results of their behavior. This view of human behavior naturally implies that money attains its value as a function of its perceived ability to lead to valued rewards. This does not mean that conditioned associations are not important; certainly, they are one of the foundations upon which people build their subjective probabilities about what money can lead to. Still, they are only one influence, and because of this it is important to identify a person's actual subjective probabilities in order to get the best understanding of why money has value for a particular person at a particular time. By accepting the influence of conditioning, we are going further than most instrumentality theorists; typically, they say very little about how subjective probabilities are established. Perhaps the most reasonable conclusion is that subjective probabilities about money are based partly upon the associations people have experienced between money and other stimuli and partly upon the information available to them about particular situations in which they find themselves.

An individual may never have personally experienced the fact that money leads to a particular outcome, and yet have a high subjective probability that it will lead to that outcome. For example, a person may believe that if he enters a certain section of town, money will buy him the attention of young ladies, yet he may never have actually experienced the association between money and female attention. What we mean to convey, of course, is that our subjective probabilities are founded not only on associations we have personally experienced, but also on those which are verbally communicated to us by others and those which we see operating in a situation. To view the associatons we make with respect to money as based solely upon our previous conditioned associations is too limiting; as human beings we learn from other people's experiences and often develop means-end hypotheses even when we encounter a unique situation.

Drives, Needs, or Just Outcomes?

Many theorists who have advanced secondary reinforcement or conditioned-incentive views of how neutral objects gain value have spoken of the association between the objects and primary rewards, or rewards that reduce primary drives. Vroom (1964), on the other hand, does not use drives or needs at all in his theory. He simply says that money has value when it is associated with other valued outcomes. He does not say what it is about people that causes them to value those other outcomes, nor does he say what other outcomes are likely to be valued. Certainly it would be unreasonable to argue that objects gain value for human beings only by association with primary drives. It might be possible to argue this for animals, but not for human beings. There is ample evidence that people seek objects and do things that are in no way related to the satisfaction of primary needs (Harlow, 1953; White, 1959). Cofer and Appley (1964) state that this is probably also true for animals. Animals will, for example, learn mazes just for the opportunity to explore new goal boxes. One solution to the problem of trying to understand why individuals place valence on certain outcomes is simply to do as Vroom and others have done, and say that this is not amenable to explicit statement at this time. But a theory which deals with the problem in this way sacrifices predictive power, in contrast to a theory of needs which states in advance what outcomes are likely to be valued and what affects their value.

A theory which states that certain needs are important to individuals and that certain factors influence the importance of these needs can make some valid predictions about when pay will be important and about the effects of certain pay practices that cannot be made by an instrumentality view like that presented by Vroom. For example, if it is known that pay is important to an individual because it leads to prestige, instrumentality theory can only predict that as prestige outcomes become less important, so will pay. On the other hand, a theory that combines instrumentality theory with a theory of needs can make predictions about what conditions will affect the importance of prestige outcomes (e.g., satisfaction of esteem needs or lower-level needs), and can then make predictions about what the effect of a number of factors (e.g., a promotion) will be on the importance of pay.

For our purposes, a theory of needs does not have to specify why people have needs (e.g., whether they are learned or innate), since it can say something about the needs people have and conditions under which certain needs operate without doing this. All it has to say is that certain stimuli (or outcomes) can be grouped together because when one is sought the others are sought and when one is obtained the others are no longer sought. People often have several groups of such stimuli. The groups can be called "needs," and if the same ones are sought by most people, then it is reasonable to speak of a "human need" for whatever group of outcomes is sought. Perhaps it should be added that, before a group of outcomes is called a need, they should be sought as ends in themselves rather than as instruments to obtain other outcomes. For example, food outcomes are sought as an end in themselves, and thus we can speak of a need for food, but a big office is not an end in itself and thus cannot be called a need.

Perhaps the most widely accepted theory of needs is that of Maslow (1954). It is a hierarchical theory and somewhat similar to one stated earlier by Langer (1937). With some modification it would seem to suit quite well the requirements for a model of the importance of pay. Basically, it states that man's needs are arranged in a hierarchy and that higher-level needs operate only when lower-level needs are satisfied. Maslow's hierarchy of needs (slightly modified) is as follows:

Self-actualization (competence)
Autonomy
Esteem
Social
Security
Physiological

The bottom level of the hierarchy includes a number of physiological needs (e.g., hunger, thirst, sex, oxygen). For our purpose, needs can be viewed as names given to groups of desired outcomes. For example, "social needs" refers to the desire for such outcomes as friendship and relationships with others. Once the lower-level needs are satisfied, according to the theory, individuals should desire the next higher set of outcomes, and so on, until they reach those of the highest order—self-actualization. Here outcomes like self-development, learning new skills, and developing new competences become important.

As has already been suggested, pay is an outcome that can be used to obtain a number of other outcomes. Money, typically, can be used to obtain outcomes relevant to the satisfaction of most of the needs listed by Maslow. Money can buy food, security, social relations, and esteem, and to some extent, it can satisfy self-actualization needs. But unlike food or water or respect, money will never be sought unless it leads to other outcomes. Thus, we do not speak of a need for money.

A MODEL OF THE IMPORTANCE OF PAY

Figure 2-1 presents a model of the way pay gains its importance and summarizes what has been said so far. It shows that a given amount of pay derives its importance from its perceived associations with the six types of needs mentioned by Maslow. Future research may suggest that more than six needs are needed to explain human motivation. If this should happen, more needs could be added to this model without changing its basic structure. Current research suggests that these six exist and are important influences on behavior. Basically, the model contends that a given amount of pay will be important to the extent that it is perceived to be instrumental in obtaining satisfaction of a person's needs and to the extent that these needs are themselves important. The instrumentality of pay for each need should be multiplied by the importance of that need. Multiplication is suggested because, when either the instrumentality or the importance of a need is zero, then pay will derive no importance from that need. The model also indicates that the result of the six instrumentality-by-importance multiplications should be summed. The instrumentalities themselves are shown to be influenced by past conditioned associations involving pay as well as by general means-end learnings and by situational factors.

Finally, the importance of each need is shown to be influenced by how satisfied needs lower on the hierarchy are and by the degree to which the need itself is satisfied. The more the lower-level needs are satisfied, the more important the higher-level needs should be; and at least for the lower-level needs, the more satisfied they are, the less important they are.

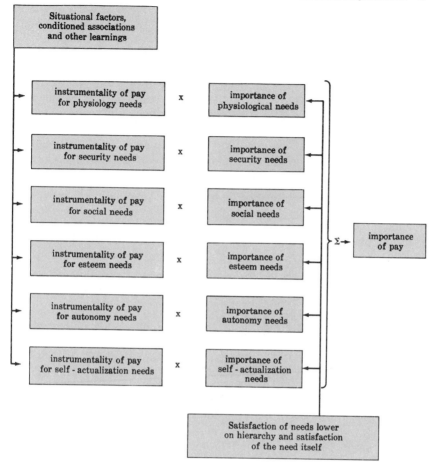

FIGURE 2-1. Model of the Importance of Pay.

As far as the higher-order needs are concerned, there is some evidence (e.g., see Alderfer, 1966, 1969) that they can become more important as they are better satisfied, particularly those related to self-actualization. Porter's work (1964) shows that as one moves up the management hierarchy, self-actualization needs become both more important and better satisfied. This phenomenon does not occur for other needs. Rather, the reverse seems to hold; that is, greater satisfaction is associated with lowered importance. The one study that does not support this view was done by Hall and Nougaim (1968), who found that as lower-order needs became satisfied they did not decrease in importance.

The general point made by Maslow—that lower-order needs have to be satisfied before higher-order ones become important—is supported by a great deal of anecdotal evidence and some empirical research. As Cofer and Appley (1964) note, there is considerable evidence that unless lower-level needs are satisfied, they can be a person's sole concern. Keys, Brozek, Henschel, Mickelsen, and Taylor (1950) found that starving subjects thought of little else than food. Their normal interests and activities were completely forgotten. Wolf (1958) has shown that thirst can have similar effects. There is also evidence that extreme hunger and thirst can reduce exploration behavior in rats and that hunger can interfere with the performance of tasks by monkeys (Harlow, 1953) and chimpanzees (Birch, 1945). Alderfer (1966) found that employees' satisfaction with fringe benefits is associated with increasing desire for satisfactory peer group relations. Hall and Nougaim (1968) also have reported some findings that are congruent with a hierarchical theory. Still, the evidence is not as conclusive as it might be, particularly when different levels of higher-order needs are concerned. It does seem clear that the physiological needs must be satisfied before other needs begin to operate. But it is not entirely clear that social needs, for example, have to be satisfied before self-actualization needs become important. At this time, it is perhaps wise to think in terms of a two- or three-step hierarchy of needs. Alderfer (1969) has argued for a three-step hierarchy in which peoples' basic existence needs must be satisfied first, then their relatedness or social needs, and finally their self-actualization needs. According to the two-step hierarchy view, lower-level physiological and safety needs must be satisfied before social, autonomy, esteem, and self-actualization needs come into play. It makes no predictions about which of these second-level needs will come into play once the lower-level needs are satisfied. Nor does it order them in any particular way. There is abundant evidence that needs do exist on at least two levels. The question that cannot be answered empirically at this time is whether they exist on more than two levels. Thus, at the present time it is probably prudent to accept the two-step view.

Although it is not shown explicitly by our Model of the Importance of Pay in Figure 2-1, larger amounts of pay are probably more attractive than smaller amounts. Larger amounts are more likely to be seen as leading to need satisfaction, particularly satisfaction of higher-order needs. For example, a pay rate of $10,000 per year is more likely to be seen as leading to esteem and security than is a pay rate of $5,000. A similar situation is expected to hold when pay raises are considered: the larger the raise, the more it should be valued because of its greater perceived ability to satisfy important needs. Still, very high pay may reduce the importance of pay. If the needs upon which pay depends for its importance are satiable then a person's desire for pay may decrease once he has attained a high income. This suggests that the value a person places on a given amount of pay is influenced by the amount considered, by the amount of pay he has received in the past, and by the amount of money he presently has. The larger the amount, the more highly it will probably be valued, but if the person has earned an even larger sum in the past, he is likely to place a lower value on it. Also, the more money he has, the less likely he is to value a given amount of pay. The research on equity theory, which will be considered in Chapter 8, also suggests that large amounts of money may not be desired when they are not felt to be earned.

INSTRUMENTALITY OF PAY FOR SPECIFIC NEEDS

The model and the discussion so far suggest that pay can be seen as instrumental for satisfying most needs. The model does not specify, however, what the perceived relative instrumentality of pay is for different needs. This is a very important issue: If pay is not typically seen as instrumental for satisfying some higher-order needs and if a modified version of Maslow's theory is accepted, as we have tended to do, then pay will not be valued beyond a minimum amount. Specifying the perceived instrumentality of pay can also give pay administrators some clues about how pay practices can affect the instrumentality of pay and thus its importance. Note that we are talking about the instrumentality of pay, not the instrumentality of money in general. As the model indicates, money, whether it is pay or not, acquires its value in the same way. But pay very likely has different instrumentalities associated with it than money that is inherited or won at the race track. Regardless of the way money is obtained, it undoubtedly does have the same ability to satisfy lower-order needs. It may not, however, have the same instrumentality for satisfying esteem and recognition needs. For example, pay that is a reward for good performance may be perceived as much more instrumental for satisfying esteem needs than money that is simply a windfall.

Unfortunately, there are no studies that have directly asked people about the instrumentality of money for them. It might, in fact, be very difficult for people to respond validly to direct questions about the instrumentality of their pay, since, as we shall see later, so many social desirability problems arise when pay is discussed. Studies that provide indirect evidence on the subject are of four types: (1) those which have examined the effect of actual pay rates on the satisfaction of a variety of needs, (2) those which have dealt with the degree to which the importance of various needs correlates with the importance of pay, (3) those which have looked at the degree to which the satisfaction of other needs correlates with pay satisfaction, and (4) the large number of studies that have attempted to test Herzberg's two-factor theory.

Pay Rates and Satisfaction

Lawler and Porter (1963) found that in comparison with low-paid managers, those who are high-paid report greater satisfaction in the security, esteem, and autonomy need areas, but not in the self-actualization and social need areas. No data were collected on physiological needs. Lawler and Porter argue that those need areas which are satisfied by pay should appear as more satisfied in high-paid people than in low-paid people; thus, they conclude that pay is instrumental for satisfying security, esteem, and autonomy needs. A number of other studies have shown similar relationships between pay levels and satisfaction in these need areas (e.g., D. C. Miller, 1941; Hall & Nougaim, 1968; Porter, 1961; Thompson, 1939). The problem with most of these studies is that job level and organization level are confounded with increments in salary so that higher-paid people also have higher-level jobs. Lawler and Porter did control for organizational level, however, and still found that greater satisfaction in these need areas did exist among the more highly paid. Thus, there is fairly good evidence that pay is instrumental for the satisfaction of security, esteem, and autonomy needs.

Correlates of Pay Importance

A second way of trying to discover the instrumentality of pay for the satisfaction of needs is to measure the correlation between the strength of needs and the importance the individual attaches to pay. Presumably, the strength of those needs for which pay is most instrumental will be most highly correlated with the importance of pay. This is expected since pay gains its value from the importance of needs, and its value should vary as a function of the importance of the needs it satisfies. It should not, of course, vary as a function of the importance of the needs it does not satisfy. Thus, the correlations between the importance people attach to pay and the importance they attach to needs should tell us something about the instrumentality of pay for satisfying different needs. The higher the correlations the more instrumental pay should be.

Alderfer (1966, 1969) has reported a low but significant correlation between workers' desires for more respect and their desire for pay, but an insignificant relationship between the importance of pay and the strength of self-actualization needs. Two studies have factor-analyzed employees' statements about the relative importance of a variety of objects to them. Bendig and Stillman (1958) factor-analyzed eight incentive statements given to college students. They found three factors. Salary loaded highest on the "fear of failure" and "job autonomy" factors. Wilkins (1949, 1950) has factor-analyzed eight statements that were rated by 300 men in terms of importance. Pay loaded on one of the two factors he obtained. Other items loading on this factor were workmates, hours, and leave. These, of course, are not the kinds of items that other studies have found to be correlated with pay. Wilkins' unusual finding can be explained by the fact that esteem and autonomy need items were not rated. Security tended to load on the other factor, but this should not be generalized too much since the data were collected from eighteen- and nineteen-year-olds at army induction centers in Great Britain. Schaffer (1953) has also established clusters of needs according to the correlations among the reported importance of needs. His data are very much in line with what has been presented so far. One of his clusters consists of items related to recognition, dominance, socioeconomic status, and independence. It reflects the fact that the ranked importance of socioeconomic status correlated most highly with the importance of recognition, dominance, and independence, while it correlated least with the importance of social welfare items. Although Schaffer did not include pay explicitly, it is, of course, interesting that economic status was grouped with esteem and autonomy items.

Correlates of Pay Satisfaction

A third way of trying to determine the instrumentality of pay for satisfying needs is to examine the correlations between pay satisfaction and satisfaction with other factors. Presumably, pay satisfaction should be most highly correlated with the satisfaction of needs for which it is instrumental. This reasoning is based upon the proposition that if pay is instrumental for the satisfaction of a need, an individual cannot be satisfied with his pay unless the need itself is satisfied; he will always be seeking more pay in order to satisfy the need. Similarly, the need itself will not be satisfied if pay is felt to be too low—unless it is satisfied in other ways. Thus, satisfaction with pay should be most closely, but not perfectly, related to the satisfaction of those needs for which it is instrumental.

Several studies have simply correlated pay satisfaction with satisfaction in other areas. Another set of studies have factor-analyzed employees' satisfaction reports in an attempt to determine the basic components that influence satisfaction. We shall look first at the studies that have correlated pay satisfaction with satisfaction in other areas. Morse (1953) reported a financial and status satisfaction cluster in her study of white-collar workers. It contained items concerned with status and advancement as well as a salary item. Locke, Smith, Kendall, Hulin, and Miller (1964) found that pay satisfaction correlates most highly with promotion satisfaction. They did not include a status-satisfaction item in their study.

Table 2-1 presents a brief summary of the relevant parts of the factor-analytic studies that have been concerned with satisfaction. These studies generally tend to support the view that pay is most instrumental for the satisfaction of esteem and recognition needs. Six of the studies found factors on which both pay and status items loaded. Where pay did not load along with status and security, it was usually due to the way the analysis was done or the way the questionnaire was designed. In some studies, for example, no items were included to measure satisfaction with status and security; and, of course, you get out of a factor analysis only what you put into it. In other studies, only a general satisfaction factor was extracted, so it was impossible to tell where pay satisfaction fell with respect to other kinds of satisfaction.

Overall, pay loaded on the same factor as did status in most studies where it was possible. In a smaller number of studies, security, growth, and autonomy satisfaction had loadings on the same factor as pay. Perhaps the best way to illustrate what the factor-analytic studies reveal is to look at the correlations between pay and the other kinds of satisfaction that Baehr (1954) found in her study. Pay satisfaction correlated .50 with status satisfaction, .40 with security satisfaction, .14 with growth satisfaction, and .12 with social need satisfaction.

Herzberg Research

The research on Herzberg's theory of work motivation has yielded data of a fourth type that reflect on the instrumentality of pay. In Herzberg's original study (Herzberg, Mausner, & Snyderman, 1959) the data demonstrated that pay was mentioned in two quite different contexts: (1) as a source of dissatisfaction when it was unfairly low and (2) as a source of satisfaction when it was seen as a form of recognition or a reward. Employees interviewed in this study made comments to the effect that raises can mean progress in work or a reward for good performance and that pay is often a form of recognition for a job well done. The implication of these comments and of the results of this study is that pay is often seen to be instrumental in the satisfaction of the need for recognition and esteem. Herzberg's theory has been subjected to heavy criticism during the last few years (Dunnette, Campbell, & Hakel, 1967; House & Wigdor, 1967). None of this criticism, however, has been directed at the finding that pay can often be seen as a form of recognition or reward and thus can contribute to job satisfaction. In fact, it has been said that Herzberg did not emphasize this point strongly enough (see, e.g., Lawler, 1964; Opshal & Dunnette, 1966). The tendency for pay to be mentioned as a contributor to satisfaction as often as it is mentioned as being unfairly low or dissatisfying has appeared in most of the studies that have

TABLE 2-1. Factor-analytic studies of reported satisfaction with different job factors

Study	Results
Wilkins (1949)	Pay, hours, workmates, and leave load on one of two factors (no status or recognition items).
Katz (1951) also Kahn (1960)	No data presented, but indicates satisfaction with wages is empirically grouped with status satisfaction. Some indication that chance to learn new things also loads on this factor.
Schreiber, Smith, & Harrell (1952)	Extracted only general satisfaction factor; pay item loaded on general factor.
Ash (1954)	Job reward factor that had high loadings on pay, benefits, and status, low loadings on growth and security.
Baehr (1954)	Pay factor that had high loadings on recognition.
Wherry (1954)	A pay, benefits, and status factor.
Dabas (1958)	Pure pay factor. Loadings for security and status not mentioned.
Roach (1958)	Pure pay factor. No item to measure security and status satisfaction used.
Wherry (1958)	A financial rewards factor showing no loading for status or security.
Kahn (1960)	Rewards and mobility factor that includes pay.
Clarke & Grant (1961)	Do not report data on pay.
Harrison (1961)	Found pay cluster. Cannot tell what items load on cluster.
Hinrichs (1968)	Pure pay factor does not report loadings of other items on it.
Ronan (1970)	Pay and prestige items tend to load on same factor.

attempted to replicate or test Herzberg's theory. Thus, the data from the research on Herzberg's two-factor theory clearly suggest that pay can be instrumental for the satisfaction of esteem and recognition needs.

SUMMARY AND CONCLUSIONS: INSTRUMENTALITY OF PAY

The literature reviewed so far suggests some well-founded conclusions can be drawn about the instrumental value of pay for the satisfaction of needs, even though no studies have approached the subject directly. The evidence rather clearly suggests that pay can be instrumental for the satisfaction of a variety of needs and that it is likely to be seen as more instrumental with respect to some needs than to others. The evidence is perhaps clearest with respect to the ability of pay to satisfy esteem and recognition needs as well as basic physiological needs. In the case of esteem, for example, the factor-analytic studies (Table 2-1) show that pay and esteem tend to load on the same factor, and other data show that highly paid people are more satisfied in the esteem need areas. The evidence also suggests that pay can be an anxiety reducer in the sense that it leads to feelings of security: Higher-paid people feel more secure. Still, according to the evidence, pay is less instrumental for the satisfaction of security needs than for the satisfaction of esteem and physiological needs.

A surprising amount of evidence suggests that pay is instrumental for satisfying autonomy and independence needs. Several of the factor-analytic studies show that independence and pay load on the same factor, and higher-paid people report greater autonomy need satisfaction.

Finally, the evidence suggests that pay is not particularly instrumental for satisfying social and self-actualization needs. These needs did not load on the same factors as pay in the factor analytic studies, and there appear to be only slight correlations between their importance and the importance of pay.

In summary, the data suggest that pay can be instrumental for the satisfaction of most needs but that it is most likely to be seen as instrumental for satisfying esteem and physiological needs, secondarily to be seen as instrumental for satisfying autonomy and security needs, and least likely to be seen as instrumental for satisfying social and self-actualization needs.

The fact that pay is differentially instrumental for the satisfaction of various needs has some interesting implications. Stated in the strongest terms, it suggests that unless esteem, security, and physiological needs are strong in an individual, he is not likely to value pay. In other words, people who are primarily concerned with satisfying social needs or self-actualization needs are not likely to value pay very highly, because it is not seen as instrumental for satisfying these needs. Further, pay will be important to people for different reasons, depending upon how much they receive. Presumably, it will be very important to low-paid workers, because it can satisfy security and physiological needs. It should be important to higher-paid people because of its ability to lead to recognition and provide independence. If conditions are such that pay cannot lead to recognition and independence, then pay may not be very important to higher-paid employees.

It also seems that the desire for pay may be satiable both as a function of the amount of pay people receive and as a function of the ability of other rewards to satisfy needs. If autonomy and esteem needs are satiable, as seems likely, then pay should become less important the more these needs are satisfied, since pay is not particularly instrumental for the satisfaction of the next higher order of needs—self-actualization needs. Presumably, very high pay and many other factors can lead to the satisfaction of esteem and autonomy needs, thereby reducing the importance of pay. As we shall see, this is a key point when an employer is trying to determine how large a raise must be to motivate his employees.

It is possible that other rewards to some extent can substitute for higher pay. Once pay is above a certain minimum, it will probably be important only if it is seen as a satisfier of esteem and recognition needs and these needs can be satisfied by other rewards. If they are, pay will not be important. For example, if a manager values high pay for the esteem it brings, presumably other signifiers of esteem, such as a larger office or a new title, would also be valued and could reduce the importance of pay. In effect, satisfying certain needs by rewards other than pay may lead to pay itself becoming less important.

The Model of the Importance of Pay introduced in this chapter and presented graphically in Figure 2-1 attempts to show how pay derives its value from its perceived associations with man's important needs. In the next chapter, the usefulness of the model will be tested by comparing predictions derived from it to the results of a number of empirical studies.

Chapter 3
RESEARCH ON THE IMPORTANCE OF PAY

A substantial amount of research has been done on the relative and absolute importance of pay. Most of the early studies were concerned solely with determining whether pay is more or less important than other job factors. Many seemed to be primarily interested in showing that pay either is or is not a crucially important factor. Some of the recent studies, however, have taken a more sophisticated differential approach. That is, they have been concerned with the degree to which the importance of pay varies as a function of the employee's position in the organization and of certain personal characteristics, such as age, sex, and family background.

Our Model of the Importance of Pay (Chap. 2) leads to no direct predictions about how important pay on the average should be to employees. Only by knowing the strength of all the needs of employees and the perceived instrumentality of pay for satisfying these needs can one predict from an instrumentality model the importance of pay to a particular group of employees. The model does, however, permit some interesting predictions about the effect of certain factors on the importance of pay, as we shall see later in this chapter. The model makes no specific predictions about the overall importance of pay simply because, in the context of the model, it is not particularly useful to make such predictions or to ask whether pay is worthy of concern. The model is a differential one. It argues that pay can be important for many reasons and in varying degrees, depending on who is being considered and what the situation is.

To look at the average importance of pay alone would hide these facts and lead to false conclusions about how important pay can be and the degree to which, under the right conditions, it can motivate job performance. The point is that the importance of pay is not fixed; it must not be thought of as constant or, on the average, as always significant or insignificant. Further, large individual differences both in why pay is important and in how important it is to people should be expected.

Pay might be first in importance for one individual because it satisfies his strong need for security, while for another it might be first because it satisfies his need for esteem. For still another person, it might be last in importance because it cannot satisfy his strong social needs. If we want to determine the average importance of pay, we have to combine the data from the three employees. Such a combination would show that pay is of moderate or average importance. But what have we really learned? In effect, we have added apples and oranges together; we have found out nothing about what factors influence the importance of pay or about when pay will be more or less important.

The average importance of pay to the members of an organization is likely to be strongly influenced by the organization's pay policy since a change in it can affect the instrumentality of pay and thereby either raise or lower its importance. For example, in one organization pay may be administered in a way that makes it highly instrumental for the satisfaction of esteem needs, while in another organization it may not be. Data from these organizations would show that pay is more important in the first than in the second. This is an interesting finding, but combining the data from these two firms in order to determine the average importance of pay is not likely to produce useful data. Unfortunately, the majority of studies have taken such an approach. They have simply asked nonrandom samples of employees how important their pay is to them and then combined the data and made statements about the relative importance of pay. Needless to say, the results of the studies are difficult to interpret.

HOW IMPORTANT IS PAY?

In 1957, Herzberg, Mausner, Peterson, and Capwell reviewed the studies that had attempted to determine the importance of job factors. Their survey of sixteen studies showed that the average worker ranks pay sixth in importance behind security, interest, opportunity for advancement, appreciation, company and management, and intrinsic aspects of the job. They pointed out that in the different studies, "Wages rank consistently in the middle of the list." In other words, pay ranks about the same from situation to situation.

Despite the fact that our Model of the Importance of Pay makes no specific predictions about what the average importance of pay should be, the results of the Herzberg et al. review are somewhat surprising in light of the major thrust of our model and the research on the instrumentality of pay. For example, because of the situational emphasis of the theory, pay should be found to vary in importance fairly widely from one study to another. Further, it would seem that pay should, in most instances, be rated high in importance because of its assumed ability to satisfy a large variety of needs. Thus, even though pay might be important for reasons that vary from situation to situation, it generally should be important if it has the kind of instrumentality that was ascribed to it in Chapter 2.

Table 3-1 summarizes briefly many of the studies in the literature which present data on the relative importance of pay. Note that many studies carried out before 1957 were not included in the sixteen surveyed by Herzberg et al., and that many more have been done in the past fifteen years. The table shows the ranking of pay in forty-nine studies. These studies give pay a much higher rank than the sixth place assigned to it by Herzberg et al. In fact, its average rank is closer to third than sixth, and 27 percent of the studies found that pay ranks first in importance among job factors. The data also show that there is indeed substantial variance in the importance of pay, since it varies in rank from ninth to first. Thus, the results of this literature review lead to conclusions that are the reverse of those reached by Herzberg et al. The conclusions suggested by the present review probably are more in line with the instrumental view stated in Chapter 2. As has been mentioned, from this model, one would expect pay to vary in importance from situation to situation, and, typically, to be ranked relatively high in importance.

It is difficult to determine why the Herzberg et al. review and the present one reached such different conclusions. Unfortunately, Herzberg et al. did not indicate the studies upon which they based their conclusions. Thus, it is impossible to tell if the present review includes the studies they covered. Clearly, the present review covers more studies. It is possible that the conclusions reached by the previous review were justified, based upon the evidence that was available at the time it was done. It might be that the more recent studies have tended to find pay ranked more highly than did the earlier ones. However, Table 3-1 suggests that both the early studies and the later ones tend to show that pay is ranked highly. Thus, there appears to be no simple explanation for the different conclusions reached by the two literature reviews. If we are to reach any conclusion about the average relative importance, of pay, then it is a matter of choosing between these two reviews. This is not too important a decision, since as was pointed out, it is not particularly useful to talk about the average importance of pay. Further, as we shall see, there are many methodological problems involved in making valid conclusions about its relative importance. Still, where it is necessary to say something about the importance of pay, it would seem that the results of the review presented in Table 3-1 probably provide the best basis for making an

TABLE 3-1. Studies of the importance of pay

Study (by year)	Population Sampled	No. of Factors Ranked	Ranking of Pay	Terms Used for Pay	Rating Instruction
Ho (1930)	Employees quitting department store		1	Wages	Important as reason for quitting
Chant (1932)	Young men in variety of occupations	12	6		
Hersey (1936)	Factory workers	14	1	Amount of pay	Important management policy
Wyatt & Langdon (1937)	Factory workers (women)	10	4		
Watson (1939)	National sample	8	3	Pay	Important as morale factor
Blum & Russ (1942)	Males	5	3		
	Females	5	4		
Berdie (1943)	Male high school graduates	12	3		
Foreman Facts (1946)	Employees	10	5	Good wages	Important
Mayo (1946)	Male and female employees	36	1	Pay	Frequency of mention
Jurgensen (1947)	Job applicants, one company	10	6	Pay (large income during year)	Important to you
NICB (1947)	Employees, five factories	71	2	Compensation	Most important
Centers (1948)	Cross section, male working population	10	6	Very highly paid job	Choosing job
Jurgensen (1948)	Job applicants, one company	10	5.5	Pay	Important to you
Lindhal (1949)	Employees	10	5	Good wages	Important
Wilkins (1949, 1950)	Young men entering Army	8	2	Pay	Important about job
Evans & Laseau (1950)	GM employees		1	Wages	Frequency of mention as desirable feature
Fosdick (1950)	Retail employees	8	3	Pay	
Stagner (1950)	Employees, one large company	10	2	Pay rate	Important to you
Stagner (1950)	Workers in large firm	10	2	Pay rate	
Stromsen & Dreese (1950)	Civil servant interns		3	Financial rewards	Career problems in civil service
Worthy (1950)	Retail store employees	14	8	Pay	Important for high morale
Bose (1951)	Workers (India)	10	1	High pay	

TABLE 3-1. Studies of the importance of pay (*Continued*)

Study (by year)	Population Sampled	No. of Factors Ranked	Rank-ing of Pay	Terms Used for Pay	Rating Instruction
Hardin, Reif, & Heneman (1951)	Men	10	4	Pay	Important to you
Schaffer (1953)	A typical sample of males	12	No clear pay items (one on economic security, one on economic status)		
Smith & Kerr (1953)	Employees quitting forty-eight companies	18	1		
C. Dickinson (1954)	College seniors	7	4	Salary	Importance in selecting job
Ganguli (1954)	Factory workers (India)	8	1	Adequate earning	Rate on what wanted from job
Graham & Sluckin (1954)	Workers (England)		1	Pay	Important as job factor
Troxell (1954)	Heterogeneous sample	10	3	Good income	Important for satisfaction
Bendig & Stillman (1958)	College students	8	3.5	Good salary	Selecting job
Kahn (1958)	Workers and foremen	10	1	Steady work and steady wages	Want from job
Rosen & Weaver (1960)	Managers, one plant	24	No clear pay item		How important condition is
Porter (1961)	Middle-level managers	7	4	Pay	Important to me
Rim (1961)	Students (Israel)	12	4	Good salary	Selecting job
Bhatt (1962)		9	3	Wages	
Dill (1962)	Masters students	12	4	Earn enough money	Importance of job characteristics
Gruenfeld (1962)	Supervisors, eleven companies	18	9	Higher wages	How preferred the characteristic is
Stuhr (1962)	Office workers	8	1	Recommendation for pay increase	Desire for rewards
Singh & Wherry (1963)	Factory workers (India)	10	2	Adequate earnings	Important to you
Chalupsky (1964)	Scientists	23	1	Merit salary increases	Important as an incentive
Spitzer (1964)	Supervisors	9	3	Make money in long run	Important
Heller & Porter (1966)	Managers (U.S.)	8	3	Pay	Preference
	Managers (England)	8	2	Pay	Preference
Centers & Bugental (1966)	Cross section, working population	6	1	The pay	Remaining on present job

TABLE 3-1. Studies of the importance of pay (*Continued*)

Study (by year)	Population Sampled	No. of Factors Ranked	Rank-ing of Pay	Terms Used for Pay	Rating Instruction
Lahiri & Choudhuri (1966)	Workers (India)	21	1	Adequate earnings	
Lawler (1966c)	Managers	6	2	Pay	Important to you
Schwartz, Jenusaitis & Stark (1966)	Workers	10	3	High wages	Personal preference
LIAMA (1967)	College students	9	3	Good income	Important
Charnofsky (1968)	Pro baseball players		1	Personal gain	As reason for playing baseball
Poduska (undated)	Retail store executives	14	3	Pay	Importance

estimate. The review is more recent, and thus more complete, than that of Herzberg et al. It also specifies the studies included, so the reader may refer to the research himself and determine whether the author's conclusions about the studies are justified.

METHODOLOGICAL PROBLEMS

Although it probably is safe to assume, based upon the literature reviewed, that pay as a job factor typically ranks about third, it is important to note some of the methodological problems involved in combining data from a number of studies. There are essentially two kinds of problems. One kind has to do with issues of questionnaire design and sampling, and the other has to do with the broader issue of whether preferences can be validly measured by self-report approaches. Some idea of the problems of questionnaire design and sampling can be gained from Table 3-1. It presents data on the sample investigated in each study, the number of factors ranked or rated, the term used for pay, and the rating or ranking instructions given to the subjects. One cannot help being struck by the diversity of the approaches used. For example, the number of factors studied ranged from five to seventy-one. Obviously, pay is more likely to be ranked high when fewer factors are considered. Further, as Bendig and Stillman (1958) have pointed out, many of the factors included are not independent. Thus, pay may rank sixth only because the five items ranked above it are all related to the importance of security or intrinsic job interest. In studies where a number of security-type items are grouped and called "security," for example, pay is ranked high; but when they are listed as separate items, pay tends to be ranked low.

Pay is referred to in a number of different ways in the studies, and this seems to affect the results. Centers and Bugental note, in explaining the results of their most recent study:

Pay was the most important job factor at all occupational levels except "professional-managerial." This contrasts sharply with Centers' early study in which financial profit was shown to be a very weak job motivation. This discrepancy is probably due to the difference between asking respondents the value of a *great deal* of money (earlier study) and asking them the value of the amount of pay they were currently earning. [1966, p. 196]

This is not surprising, since "a great deal of money" and "amount of current pay" are likely to have quite different instrumentalities and valences for the typical employee. Similar inferences can be made about many of the items used in the various studies. In some cases the rank of the pay item is, in effect, determined in advance by its wording. For example, people probably are reluctant to admit that making a great deal of money or having a very high salary is important to them, but they are not hesitant to say that the amount of their present salary and earning a fair rate of pay are very important.

Table 3-1 also shows that studies have varied widely in the kind of importance rating or ranking people have been asked to make. Typically the question has been simply, "How important is pay to you?" But the question has also been stated in terms of the importance of pay for morale, staying on the job, leaving a job, and selecting a new job. Bass (1965) has argued that pay may, in fact, be more important as a determinant of the choice of where to work than as a determinant of the motivation to work. A look at the studies summarized in the table suggests that this may well be true, although the data are not very consistent. Centers (1948), for example, obtained a low rank for pay when people were asked to rank it in terms of their trying to decide what job to choose. The finding is difficult to interpret, however, because Centers used the phrase "very high paid job."

The studies sampled widely different populations, and undoubtedly this accounts for some of the differences in the ranking of pay. We cannot, however, tell how much of the variance is due to this factor, because it is obscured by other differences among the studies. Where studies differ on populations sampled, as well as number and type of items ranked, it is impossible to determine the causes of the differences in the ranking of pay. This is particularly unfortunate, since it is tempting to look at the table and compare the importance of pay for managers (Porter, 1961) with the importance of pay for students (Rim, 1961) and to conclude that, of the two groups, managers rate pay as more important. Such a conclusion is not warranted, however, because the two studies vary widely in the items they include and the kind of ranking procedure they use. As we shall see, it makes sense to talk about pay as being more important to one group than to another only where both are presented with similar stimuli and given identical instructions.

These methodological problems suggest that variations in instrument design and sample characteristics can influence the reported findings. It seems clear, for example, that such factors as the wording of items and the number of items listed can influence the relative ranking of the importance of pay. Because the rated importance of pay is so sensitive to variations in research design, it is very difficult to reach any firm conclusion about whether pay is the second, fifth, or eighth most important job factor. In fact, a strong case can be made from a research design point of view that the only legitimate conclusions and comparisons about the importance of pay are those which involve group differences on the same instrument.

Opshal and Dunnette (1966) and Vroom (1964, 1965) have criticized studies of the importance of job factors on a quite different level. They have pointed out that self-report techniques are not appropriate ways of measuring importance under any conditions. As Opshal and Dunnette state, "The question, 'How do people value money?' will not be answered accurately simply by asking them." They base this conclusion on three points: (1) There may be a social desirability response set that pervades self-reports about pay. People may not feel it is acceptable to admit that they are running after the "almighty dollar" at all costs. A twinge of conscience may, in short, cause people not to rank pay highly. (2) The reinforcement contingencies present in filling out a self-report questionnaire are quite different from those which apply in a real-life situation. A person is clearly reinforced for actually obtaining money and behaving as if it were important, but it is not so clear that he will be reinforced for simply admitting he wants money. (3) People are poor judges of what they really want, particularly when they are making judgments in the abstract. They may not know themselves what job factors are important until they actually have to make some difficult choices.

Opshal and Dunnette, as well as Vroom, conclude that in order to gain a real understanding of people's preferences we must observe them in actual choice situations. Their argument is a very persuasive one, and indeed, it is hoped that such observational data will be collected. But, before labeling the existing studies as too biased to be useful, let us consider what the impact of the three points suggested by Opshal and Dunnette might be. Basically, they should serve to change the relative ranks of different job factors. That is, people might say pay was less important than intrinsic job interest, when, in fact, for them it is not. This suggests that any conclusions about the relative importance of pay compared to other factors, like intrinsic job interest, that are based on self-report data are shaky.

The crucial questions that arise from our Model of the Importance of Pay, however, are concerned with what factors influence the importance of pay, and when pay will be important, not with how important pay is relative to other factors. Most of the studies that have investigated the two issues we are concerned with have compared the importance of pay for one group with the importance of pay for another group by giving both groups the same instruments. The assumption is that if highly paid people, for example, rank pay as more important than do lower-paid people, the amount of pay influences the importance of pay. The question that now arises is, Do the criticisms discussed above show that it is methodologically unsound to try to determine whether pay is more important to one group than to another? The answer would seem to be no— if the studies use the same instruments with both groups. Presumably, what would, for example, be a socially desirable response for one group would also be one for another group, so that, while both might tend to play down the importance of pay, if they do this equally it can still make sense to compare the responses of the two groups. This can be true even though both groups report that pay is less important to them than in fact it is. If the studies are going to provide useful data, it is necessary, of course, that the same biasing tendencies appear equally in all the populations. Clearly, this condition does not always exist, but in many cases it does. Where it does, it is possible to talk about pay being more important to one group than to another, or to talk about the importance of pay being related to a person's education level or some other characteristic.

In summary, this discussion of methodological problems has emphasized the difficulty of basing any conclusions upon the literature reviewed about the importance of pay in comparison with other job factors. These methodological problems include, for example, the nonindependence of factors, the wording used to describe the factors included in the ranking, and the social desirability of saying that pay is important. In light of these problems, it is not wise to place much faith in the statement that, on the average, studies have found that pay ranks about third in importance. The kind of study of the importance of pay that is viable from a methodological point of view is one in which similar data-gathering approaches are used with different groups in order to determine solely if a job factor is more important to one group than to another. There are two points here: (1) The aim is not to compare the importance of various factors, but to determine the importance of one factor to various groups. (2) The same instrument must be used with all the groups studied.

FACTORS RELATED TO THE IMPORTANCE OF PAY

A substantial number of studies have tried to answer the question, What characteristics distinguish people for whom pay is relatively important from those for whom it is relatively unimportant? Many of the factors that have been studied are not ones that our model would suggest should necessarily be related to pay. In some instances, however, when the theory is combined with empirical findings, predictions do become apparent. Many studies have looked at the relationship between the importance of pay and such variables as intelligence and age simply out of curiosity. They clearly were not guided by any theory, nor were they testing any hypothesis; they were merely gathering facts.

According to the model, a factor should be related to the importance of pay only if it influences (1) the perceived instrumentality of pay for certain needs or (2) the valence of needs for which pay is instrumental. There is little reason to believe that intelligence, for example, influences either. Therefore, there is little reason to predict that it will be related to the importance of pay. Nevertheless, we shall review the literature related to it and a number of other variables in order to illustrate the variety of factors that have been studied. By looking at the full range of evidence, we may be able to determine if pay is related to some variables in a way that the model cannot explain. Such a discovery would, of course, raise questions about the validity of the model.

Two groups of factors have been studied. One group includes the following personal background characteristics that people bring with them to the job:

Sex
Intelligence
Age
Personality traits
Family background
Educational level

The second group includes job-related factors, such as:

Pay level
Job level
Type of organization
Union membership
Promotion
How pay is determined

Personal Factors

SEX. A surprisingly large number of studies have asked whether pay is more important to male or to female employees. At first glance the Model of the Importance of Pay would seem to offer no clue to the answer. However, there are some data on the strength of needs in men and women which do lead to a clear prediction. Rosenberg (1957) found that women consistently tend to rate working with people, being helpful to others, and being creative as of greater importance than do men. Similarly, Herzberg et al. (1957) concluded that women are much more concerned with the social aspects of work. My own research has shown that women rate social needs higher than do men, but rate esteem needs lower. If we combine these data on need strength with the fact that pay is typically seen as instrumental for achieving esteem, but not particularly instrumental for satisfying social needs or self-actualization needs, the prediction of the model becomes obvious. Pay should be less important for women because it is not highly instrumental for the satisfaction of needs they rank high (e.g., social), while it is instrumental for the satisfaction of needs men rank high (e.g., esteem).

The studies are quite consistent in showing that pay is more important to men than to women. Out of six studies that could be found which compared the importance of pay for men and women where both had completed a similar research instrument, five show positive results and one shows no significant difference. Blum and Russ (1942), and Hardin, Reif, and Heneman (1951) found that men rank pay as more important than do women. Both Mayo (1946) and Gilmer (1957) reported that men talk more about pay when interviewed, and Centers and Bugental (1966) reported that more men than women choose pay as an important job factor. Only a study by Jurgensen (1947, 1948) failed to find a sex difference in the importance of pay. My own research has shown a tendency for women to rate pay as significantly less important, even when they are heads of households. This would suggest that it is not simply a lack of economic necessity that causes women to rate pay as less important, but rather the relationship of pay to their needs and goals.

INTELLIGENCE. It is not readily apparent from our model that the importance of pay should be expected to vary as a function of a person's intelligence. The model would have to say that, barring evidence that the strength of needs or instrumentalities varies with intelligence, intelligence and the importance of pay should be unrelated. The two studies that have investigated the issue have found relationships. Wilkins (1949, 1950) found that persons with a high IQ attached a low importance to pay. Gruenfeld (1962), however, found just the opposite. These studies differ widely in the populations sampled; Wilkins looked at young males in a British army induction center, and Gruenfeld looked at American supervisors. The studies differ in many other respects as well. It is, therefore, impossible to reach any firm conclusion about why the results were so different. At this point, all that can be concluded is that there is little reason to believe that the importance of pay is related to IQ in any consistent manner.

AGE.   Herzberg et al. (1957) concluded from their review of the literature on the effects of age, "Some evidence indicates that wages decrease in importance with age, at least to the age of forty, at which time they then increase in importance." Herzberg et al. seem to be arguing for a curvilinear relationship between the importance of pay and age, although they offer no reason for this relationship. However, little evidence to support this argument seems to exist. Ganguli (1954) reported no significant relationship between age and the importance of pay. Jurgensen (1947, 1948) and Lahiri and Choudhuri (1966) reported a tendency for pay to become less important as people become older. Gruenfeld (1962) also found a negative relationship. Thus, we have three studies which reported a negative linear relationship between age and the importance of pay and one which found no relationship. Since Ganguli's study, which found no relationship, was done among factory workers in India, it is probably safe to assume that, at least in the United States, a negative relationship does exist. Unfortunately, it is impossible to determine how Herzberg et al. came to their slightly different conclusion, since they do not indicate what evidence their finding was based on. It is important to note, however, that at least they agree that pay decreases in importance up to age forty.

We have said nothing about why pay might decrease in importance as people grow older, and indeed there is no definitive explanation. One possibility is that older employees usually are higher paid and perhaps are at higher levels in the organization, and as a result some of the needs that can be satisfied by pay have been satisfied. This explanation is based on the point made earlier that the needs for which pay is instrumental are satiable; and when they are partially satisfied, they—along with pay itself—become less important. It would be possible to test this explanation by comparing younger and older men who are paid the same to see if they value pay differently. Unfortunately, none of the available studies includes such an analysis.

A second explanation might be found in the tendency of needs to change in strength as a function of age. Porter's data (1963) show that when management level is held constant, older managers put more importance on security and esteem needs than do younger managers. This finding does not fit with the pay importance data, however. This finding should mean that pay becomes more important as people get older. Part of the problem here may be more apparent than real, since management level was held constant in this analysis, and only managers were considered. Thus, it is impossible to determine whether security and esteem do, in fact, generally become more important with age. Still, there is no indication that they become less important, as indeed they would have to in order for the model to explain the decreasing importance of pay with increasing age. At this point, then, there is no definite explanation for the reported relationship between age and the importance of pay.

PERSONALITY TRAITS. Gruenfeld (1962) has found a relationship between the self-assurance scale of Ghiselli's "Self Description Inventory" (1954) and the importance employees attach to pay. Gruenfeld's data must be regarded with some caution, since they are based on a small sample. They do show, however, that people low in self-assurance place more importance on pay than do people high in self-assurance. As was pointed out in Chapter 2, pay is probably seen as instrumental for the satisfaction of esteem and security needs. Therefore, it is not surprising that pay is more important to employees who, presumably, wish to bolster their self-assurance. Rim (1961) has reported that people who score high on the Cattell neuroticism scale tend to place high importance on money. This finding may be due to pay's acting as an anxiety reducer (J. S. Brown, 1961) or as an indication to a person that things are okay. In short, it may be seen as instrumental for reducing anxiety and, as such, be very important to high-anxiety people.

FAMILY BACKGROUND. Some of the most interesting research on pay is that reported by Whyte (1955) in *Money and Motivation*. This book provides a number of valuable insights into how people react to pay systems. On the whole, it takes an anthropological approach and it contains a considerable amount of rich data. Included in this book is Dalton's study of "rate busters." Dalton observed strikingly different attitudes toward the importance of pay on the part of two groups of employees. One group (the restricters) was made up of average and below-average producers who felt that the amount of work needed to earn extra money simply was not worth the trouble. As one worker put it, "Don't misunderstand me. I'd like a little bonus. But they don't give it away, and I won't pay the price." A second group of workers (the rate busters) had a quite different view. One worker said, "I am out here to make money. . . . I keep my bills paid and don't owe anybody a damn cent . . . why the hell should I care what a bunch of damn snoopy bums think of me?" The "snoopy bums" this worker is referring to were the restricters, who were displeased with him because of his high earnings. Clearly, Dalton seems to have identified in this plant one group of employees for whom pay was of prime importance and another group for whom it was of less importance than the satisfaction of needs, such as getting along with fellow workers.

The key question in our individual-differences approach to the importance of pay is, What distinguishes the rate busters from the restricters? Dalton tends to see the two groups as quite different in terms of family background. The restricters were typically sons of unskilled industrial workers; they had grown up in large cities, where they were active in boys' gangs. They tended to be Democrats, and they referred to the rate busters as "Republican hogs." Their religious preference was usually Catholic, and they tended to belong to many social groups (e.g., the Elks or other clubs). In general, the rate busters had grown up on farms or in small towns, where they lived under the close supervision of parental authority. One was the son of a farmer who had migrated to the city and become a huckster, while another was the son of a village barber. They tended to be "lone wolves" and did not typically join in group activities. Most of them were Republicans who owned their own homes. For the rate buster, money seemed to be a "mark of virtue," because it was a sign that he worked hard. Overall, Dalton summarized the two types as "the country born (or middle class born), lone wolf, Republican, money-saving and investing worker without outside interests versus the city born, gregarious, New Deal Democratic, spending worker."

It is not hard to explain why pay is more important to the rate buster than to the restricter in terms of our instrumentality Model of the Importance of Pay. The two groups clearly differ in the strength of their needs. The restricters have strong social needs, while the rate busters are motivated to acquire property, to rise in social status, and to give a fair day's work, presumably because it is vital to their self-esteem. Money is obviously instrumental in obtaining higher social class, property, and perhaps self-esteem, but it is not very instrumental in satisfying social needs. Thus, it follows from the model that pay should be less important to restricters than to rate busters. The model, of course, says nothing about the kind of family background that will lead people to value one need or set of needs higher than other needs. Dalton tends to view the urban-rural distinction as important here, as well as social class and religion of the parents. This is an interesting set of observations, and it is unfortunate that they have never really been followed up with a systematic research effort. Clearly, more data are required before one can conclude that urban workers and rural workers have different needs and values. There are a few studies which show that the urban-rural distinction can be important in determining job satisfaction (Blauner, 1964; Blood & Hulin, 1967; Hulin & Blood, 1968), so it certainly would appear to be an insight worth following up.

EDUCATION LEVEL. Ganguli (1954) has reported finding no difference between groups with different levels of education in terms of the importance they attach to pay. Jurgensen (1947) and Troxell (1954), on the other hand, report data which show that more highly educated people place more importance on pay than do less highly educated people. There is no immediately obvious reason why educational level should have any such effect since it is not obvious that education substantially affects the strength of needs or the perceived instrumentalities of pay for satisfying needs. Thus, in light of the somewhat conflicting evidence, it is probably safe to conclude that the two factors are not related, and that it is not clear how they might be.

As a way of summarizing the research that has attempted to relate individual differences to pay importance, consider for a moment the characteristics of a hypothetical employee who is likely to value pay highly. The employee is a male, young (probably in his twenties) ; he has low self-assurance and high neuroticism; he comes from a small town or farm background; he belongs to few clubs and social groups; he owns his own home or aspires to own one and probably is a Republican and a Protestant.

Job Factors

PAY LEVEL. One of the predictions that is directly suggested by our instrumental view of the importance of pay is that the less pay people receive, the more important it should be to them. Basically, the argument is that high pay should lead to the satisfaction of such needs as esteem and security, and they will thus become less important, as will pay, since its value depends on such needs. A number of studies have found evidence to support the first link in this argument, the contention that high pay leads to greater satisfaction in a number of areas. Lawler and Porter (1963) have shown that high pay is associated with greater satisfaction in the esteem and security need areas, while Andrews and Henry (1963), Troxell (1954), and Lawler and Porter (1966) have shown that the amount of pay is associated with pay satisfaction. Many other studies have shown that high pay is associated with general need satisfaction (e.g., Barnett, Handelsman, Stewart, & Super, 1952; Centers & Cantril, 1946; Marriott & Denerley, 1955; Miller, 1941; Smith & Kendall, 1963; Thompson, 1939). Opshal and Dunnette (1966) point out in their review of the literature that it is not clear whether the increased satisfactions of higher pay are due to the pay itself or to the higher job level, better duties, and privileges that so often accompany higher pay. There is some evidence, however, that high pay alone is enough to produce higher satisfaction. Lawler and Porter (1963, 1966) held management level constant (all managers occupied similar jobs) and found that higher pay was associated with greater satisfaction. Thus, it seems safe to conclude that high pay itself is likely to be associated with high job satisfaction.

There is much less evidence to support the expectation that satisfaction with pay and satisfaction of esteem and security needs cause pay to be less important. Alderfer (1966, 1969) reports that high satisfaction with pay is, in fact, associated with its being less important. Porter (personal communication) has found in his large sample of managers that there is a general tendency for high satisfication of a need to be associated with that need having low importance. A similar relationship has appeared in the data I have collected from managers. Thus, despite the paucity of evidence, it seems reasonable to conclude that high pay satisfaction can lead to a reduction in the importance of pay.

Two studies have reported a direct relationship between the amount of pay an individual receives and the importance of pay to that individual (Ganguli, 1954; Lawler & Porter, 1963). Both studies report that the more pay an individual receives, the less important pay is to him. At this point it is probably wise to comment on the strength of the relationships that have been found between satisfaction with pay and its importance and between amount of pay and its importance. All the relationships reported in the literature tend to be moderate. So it certainly is not true, for example, that when an individual is highly paid, his pay is necessarily unimportant to him. All that can be said is that pay is likely to be less important to him than to someone who is lower paid.

Figure 3-1 summarizes the points made so far and indicates the evidence that supports the connections shown. Admittedly, this is only a start in showing how the amount of pay influences its importance to employees, but the evidence supporting some of the relationships is impressive. Clearly, we need research in which data are collected on all the variables shown and in which the key relationships are looked at while the influences of other factors are held constant. In addition, it would be helpful to know the relative size of the relationship between the different factors. It would seem, for example, that the relationship between the

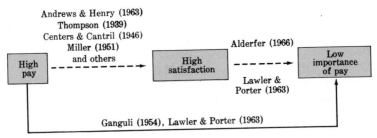

FIGURE 3-1. *Relationship of amount of pay to satisfaction and the importance of pay.*

amount and the importance of pay should always be weaker than the other two relationships shown, since it depends on their strength for its existence.

There is some evidence to indicate that the amount of a person's present pay can strongly influence the importance he attaches to different size raises. In a provocative exploratory study Zedeck and Smith (1968) showed that employee perceptions of what constituted a meaningful raise varied as a function of their present pay. Much larger dollar amounts were needed for a raise to be meaningful to the higher-paid employees. Zedeck and Smith go on to suggest that the importance of a raise to an employee probably can best be understood by considering the percentage increase it represents rather than by considering the absolute amount of money involved.

Hinrichs (1969) has done a large-scale study of employees' reactions to different size pay increases. His results are congruent with those reported by Zedeck and Smith. They show that an employee's evaluation of a raise is a direct function of his present pay. The more he earns, the larger any increase must be if it is to be meaningful. However, his data also suggest that as salary increases, what constitutes a meaningful raise may represent a smaller and smaller percentage of the person's present pay. For example, his data show that employees making under $400 a month regard a 5.1 percent raise as "just noticeable," while employees making over $2,000 a month regard a 2.2 percent increase as noticeable. This suggests that smaller percentage raises may be just as important to high-paid employees as are higher percentage raises to lower-paid people. Of course, this does not negate the fact that raises must be larger in absolute terms for high-paid employees to feel that they are meaningful and important. This point has obvious implications for how large a raise must be if it is to be important enough to motivate job performance.

JOB LEVEL. A good deal of evidence shows that, as one considers higher and higher levels within an organization, pay becomes less important. Skilled blue-collar workers report that pay is less important than do unskilled blue-collar workers (Centers & Bugental, 1966). Blue-collar workers seem to value money more than white-collar workers. For example, 73 percent of blue-collar workers report that pay is the most important job factor, while 62 percent of white-collar workers report that it is the most important factor (Centers, 1948; Jurgensen, 1947). Managers say that pay is less important than do workers (Centers & Bugental, 1966; Kahn, 1958; Ronan, 1970). Lower-level managers place more importance on pay than do middle-level managers. Porter (1961) reports that pay is rated fourth in importance by middle-level managers but second in importance by lower-level managers. Finally, there is evidence that top-level managers rate pay as less important than do middle-level managers (Lawler & Porter, 1963).

Thus, all the available evidence is consistent with the view that the importance of pay to an individual is directly related to the level of his job within the organization. The one study that is sometimes cited as not supporting the conclusion was done by *Fortune* in 1947. It asked employees to choose between jobs offering different degrees of security and pay. Executives tended to weight the amount of salary high, while lower-level employees tended to weight security high. Admittedly, these results could be interpreted as showing that pay is more important to executives than to lower-level employees; and indeed, the study usually has been interpreted this way (see, e.g., Vroom, 1965). It seems plausible, however, that these data actually show that managers are more willing to work under merit-based pay schemes than are lower-level workers. As we shall see later, there is some other evidence that, in fact, managers do prefer greater risks in their compensation system. Thus, the employees in the *Fortune* study who chose the secure, lower-paying job may have been indicating *not* that pay was unimportant to them, but rather that pay was so important that they did not want to risk losing it. This interpretation of the data is, of course, speculative; but it shows that the *Fortune* study does not necessarily provide definitive evidence that pay is more important to executives than to lower-level employees.

There are two possible explanations for the finding that employees at higher organization levels rate pay as less important. According to one explanation, the importance of pay to an individual may determine where he ends up in an organization. Some slight support for this view can be found in Wilkins's study (1949), which showed that people who attached high importance to pay planned on going into blue-collar, unskilled jobs, while men who placed less importance on pay planned to enter higher-level jobs. Unfortunately, Wilkins did not follow up these men to see if they actually took the kind of job they said they would. If it is assumed that they did, it still would be difficult to generalize from Wilkins's data, since he studied only eighteen- and nineteen-year-old Englishmen who were about to join the army. Thus, he clearly did not have a good sample even of the British population.

On logical grounds, it would seem that if the importance of pay determined where an individual ended up in an organization, those people for whom pay is most important would tend to end up at the top. Presumably, if pay is important to an individual, he will be motivated to seek a high-paying job (i.e., high-level job) and will thus be more likely than his less motivated colleague to be promoted to a high-level job. All other things being equal, the people at the top of an organization should, therefore, value pay more. But this does not happen. Higher-level employees seem to value pay less. Thus, we cannot accept the explanation that the degree to which a person values pay will determine his job level.

A second possible explanation for the relationship between job level and the importance of pay rests upon the idea that job experiences or other job factors affect the importance an individual attaches to pay. An obvious possibility, which is in line with our model, is suggested by the fact that people with high pay usually rate pay as low in importance. A strong relationship (see, e.g., Lawler & Porter, 1966) exists between job level and pay level: Higher-level employees almost always receive more pay. The one exception here is that certain blue-collar workers sometimes earn more than white-collar workers. Thus, the relationship between job level and the importance of pay may be explained in terms of the amount of pay received by employees holding the different jobs and the impact of this factor on pay satisfaction and pay importance. Some support for this view comes from a study by Lawler and Porter (1963). Management level was found to be related to the importance managers attached to their pay; but when pay was held constant so that only managers earning the same amount of money were compared, job level was not related to the importance attached to pay. It is probable that actual pay differences cannot explain all of the relationship found between job level and the importance of pay, but they appear to account for much of the relationship.

The fact that higher-level jobs provide a number of nonfinancial rewards and advantages that lead to job satisfaction may also explain part of the relationship between job level and pay importance. Higher-level managers generally report higher levels of need satisfaction, even when they are not higher paid (Porter & Lawler, 1965). Thus, since the importance of pay depends on the degree of satisfaction of such needs as esteem and security, it follows that pay should be less important to higher-level managers; their needs for security and esteem are likely to be better satisfied even when they do not make more money.

Overall, the evidence suggests that differences in the importance of pay at different organizational levels are probably due to such job factors as pay level and the nonfinancial rewards associated with higher-level positions.

TYPE OF ORGANIZATION. There is a great deal of anthropological and survey research evidence that pay is more important to people who work in profit-making business organizations than to those who work in nonprofit organizations. My own research has shown that managers in industrial organizations place the most importance on pay; people who work in government agencies place less emphasis on pay; and people who work in hospitals and social service organizations place the least importance on pay (Lawler, 1964, 1966c). It is very likely that, within each of these groups, high-level employees place less importance on pay than do lower-level employees; but the point is that, on the average, employees in some kinds of organizations place more importance on pay than do employees in other kinds. There is little reason to believe that the difference between the importance of pay to government employees and to business employees can be explained in terms of government employees making more money. To the contrary, the difference seems to exist almost in spite of the fact that business employees earn more.

Although the kind of need satisfaction model we have been using cannot explain this difference merely by considering absolute pay, perhaps another model can at least partially explain it. Rosenberg (1957) measured college students' values before and after they took their first jobs. The data showed that some people changed their values to coincide better with their job choices. Thus, people who chose business careers tended to increase the value they attached to money and status, while those who chose nonbusiness careers tended to decrease it. Such shifts are perhaps predictable from a cognitive dissonance (Festinger, 1957) or a rationalization view of human values and needs. It is important to note, however, that Rosenberg found that, typically, people were more likely to change their jobs to coincide with their values than vice versa.

Probably the best explanation for the variation in the ratings of the importance of pay for employees of different kinds of organizations rests on the fact that people tend to work for organizations that they feel will satisfy their most important needs (Vroom, 1965). There is a great deal of evidence that people who enter business careers value money more than those who pursue careers in other kinds of organizations (see Chap. 10). Thus, the differences are not due to anything the organization does to employees after they join it, but to the kind of people attracted to the organization to begin with. Rosenberg (1957) found that students choosing business careers placed more importance on earning money and gaining social status than did students who chose other kinds of organizations. There is a great deal of evidence that college students preparing for a career in business have significantly higher scores on the economic scale of the Allport-Vernon Study of Values than do other students (Allport, Vernon, & Lindzey, 1951; Cantril & Allport, 1933; Conrad & Jaffe, 1960; Stone, 1933; Vernon & Allport, 1931). Thus, the differences in the importance of pay for employees in different kinds of organizations can be largely explained by the fact that different types of people go to work in business and in nonbusiness organizations.

Note that if the points from this section and the preceding one are considered together, it can be argued that differences in the importance individuals attach to pay are probably very influential in determining the kind of organization for which they work, but may not be so important in determining the level of job they attain. Presumably, this is because an employee has much more choice in deciding the kind of organization he is going to work for than in deciding what job level he is going to be assigned once he joins the organization. Job level is very much a direct function of training and skills, so that most people are limited in the number of job levels open to them. Given their job level, however, most people can work for the government, private industry, or non-government social welfare agencies; and apparently they choose which of these they are going to work for at least partially on the basis of how important pay is to them.

UNION MEMBERSHIP. Two studies have attempted to discover whether union members place more importance on pay than do nonunion members. In terms of our Model of the Importance of Pay, there is no reason to expect that union membership should have any bearing on the issue. Thus, it is not surprising to find that the two studies found no consistent relationship. Ganguli (1954) found that union members tended to rank pay first in importance, while nonunion employees ranked it second. Hersey (1936) found just the opposite result. Thus, barring further evidence, it seems safe to conclude that there is no general tendency for union members and nonunion members to rate pay differently in terms of its importance.

PROMOTION. Festinger (1964) has been engaged in a longitudinal study of a group of managers in order determine how promotion affects the importance they attach to such extrinsic rewards as pay. Our model would predict that promotion should tend to decrease the importance of pay. With promotion would come higher pay, more prestige, recognition, etc., and as a result, individuals would be better satisfied in the esteem need area. Since the importance attached to pay depends partially on the strength of esteem needs, we would thus expect pay to become less important in these circumstances. This view is congruent with the data already presented on the relationship among pay level, job level, and the importance of pay.

Festinger, arguing from a dissonance theory point of view (1957), predicted that pay should become more important to an individual after he is promoted. This is in one sense a typical dissonance theory prediction, since it is the reverse of what might be expected. Festinger maintained that pay should be more important after promotion, because a manager would try to bring his values into line with his changed behavior on the new job. Since getting promoted demands a strong commitment to the organization, Festinger reasoned that people would have to upgrade the rewards that are received from this commitment in order to justify the energy expenditure and the added work load. It is not clear, however, how this argument can explain the fact that higher-paid managers and higher-level managers tend to attach less importance to pay; it would seem to have to predict just the opposite. The data from Festinger's study were only partially analyzed in his initial discussion of the study, but at that time the data showed no tendency for pay to increase or decrease in importance after promotion. Thus, the sketchy evidence available makes it impossible to reach any conclusion about the effect of promotion on the importance of pay. Still, this could be an important research topic, since two theoretical models seem to state different testable hypotheses.

HOW PAY IS DETERMINED.   A substantial body of research (see Lewis, 1965, for a review) shows that the value of outcomes is directly affected by how they are obtained. Objects which have to be worked for and are obtained as the result of effort expenditure are more highly valued than those which are easily obtained. None of the studies reviewed by Lewis were concerned with the effects of effort on the value of money or pay, but there is a fair chance that the findings are generalizable to pay; and in fact, some of the studies did use poker chips and other money substitutes. The finding of increased reward value is congruent with dissonance theory, and indeed, many of the studies that have shown this phenomenon were done to test dissonance theory. This finding can also be seen as congruent with our Model of the Importance of Pay. Presumably, how money is obtained directly influences its instrumentality. Money that is obtained by luck or deception typically will not be instrumental for the satisfaction of esteem needs, whereas money worked for and earned will be. Thus, if it is assumed that the instrumentality of pay is affected by this factor, it follows that money worked for and earned will be more highly valued. The following chapter will show that this point has significant implications for pay policies in organizations.

Relevance of Research to the Model of the Importance of Pay

In general, the research that has related the importance of pay to individual differences and to job factors has produced findings that are both congruent with and predictable from our Model of the Importance of Pay. This would seem to be particularly true with respect to the organizational or job-related factors that have been studied. As expected, because of the relationship between satisfaction and importance, the importance of pay decreased as job level and pay level increased. An instrumentality theory like that of Vroom (1964), which does not include a theory of needs and some statement of what needs pay can satisfy, cannot make these predictions. Thus, as we pointed out in Chapter 2, the predictive power of an instrumentality theory is increased if it includes a theory of needs and their satiability.

Some of the evidence that shows a relationship between individual differences and the importance of pay is not directly predictable from the Model of the Importance of Pay, but neither is this evidence in disagreement with the model. For example, the data which show that females attach less importance to pay than do males in a sense follow from the model once it is known that females attach different levels of importance to certain needs. Without this information, however, there is no reason to predict in advance that females should value pay differently from males. In summary, none of the evidence reviewed tends to disprove our model; some provides support for the model when it is combined with certain other empirical findings, and some offers considerable direct support.

Finally, one last evaluative comment about the research on the importance of pay that has been reviewed in this chapter. It is an excellent example of what often happens when research is not guided by a desire to develop or test some kind of theoretical statement or model. Most of the research is fragmented, noncumulative, and poorly designed. Most of the forty-nine studies that have tried to determine how important pay is represent a great expenditure of effort that contributes virtually nothing to our understanding. By selectively using the data from these studies, one can argue any position—from one which holds that pay is the most important job factor to one which holds that it is one of the least important. Most of this research was done solely because people thought it would be interesting to know how important pay is. It was not guided by any thinking about why pay should be important or what factors should influence its importance; as a result, the research is noncumulative and shows little agreement in either method or result. At this point it would seem to be appropriate to declare a moratorium on all studies that merely want to tell us how important pay is. Only studies that ask why pay is important or seek to test theoretically based hypotheses about the effects of certain variables on the importance of pay should be done.

Chapter 4
IMPLICATIONS FOR PRACTICE

Chapter 3 reviewed the large number of studies that have investigated the importance of pay. In this chapter we will look at the results of these studies, as well as at the research and theory cited in Chapter 2 in terms of their relevance to the practitioner who must make pay decisions in an organization. Unfortunately, little of the research evidence is relevant to some of the most important practical decisions that have to be made. Thus, parts of the discussion must be speculative in the sense that they are not research-based. They are, however, theoretically based, since the discussion draws heavily on our Model of the Importance of Pay.

Originally, much of the research on the importance of pay was motivated by a desire to answer the perennial, very practical question, How important is pay? Practitioners have for a long time been concerned with this question, since its answer is essential in determining whether pay can motivate job performance, be the cause of a strike, a reason for people changing jobs, absenteeism, and so on. Clearly, unless pay is important to employees, it is not likely to motivate any kind of behavior. The practitioner, of course, wants to know more than whether pay is important or not. He must have some idea of its *relative* importance. For example, when trying to hire a new college graduate, the practitioner wants to know whether pay is more or less important to the applicant than other job factors. With this kind of information, he can determine how much stress should be placed on pay as a way of attracting the college graduate to take a job with his organization.

To many, it may seem foolish to even ask whether pay is important enough to motivate job behavior. However, the fact that some social scientists and practitioners interpreted the Western Electric studies (Roethlisberger & Dickson, 1939) and the other earlier research on the importance of nonmonetary factors as showing that pay is relatively unimportant, makes it clear that for some people this is a real question. The conclusions of Herzberg et al. (1957) and others to the effect that pay ranks about sixth in importance have also been taken by some as support for the view that pay may not be important enough to have a great influence on employee behavior. The one conclusion that may safely be drawn from the research reviewed here is that it does *not* make sense to regard pay as relatively unimportant. The forty-nine research studies reviewed presumably provide enough evidence to convince any skeptic that pay can be and usually is important enough to motivate most kinds of job behavior. Admittedly, the evidence does not indicate whether pay is the first, second, or sixth most important factor. What it does indicate is that pay is frequently ranked high in importance, and that as such, it is a potential influence on employee behavior. Thus, when the practitioner asks, How important is pay? perhaps the best answer is that it can be important enough—important enough to influence behavior and to be considered when such problems as motivation, absenteeism, turnover, strikes, and tardiness are discussed.

It is unfortunate that research methodology problems make it impossible to say that when people are choosing a job, pay is, for example, twice as important as working conditions. Or that as an influence on how hard an individual will work, pay is only half as important as peer group attitude. This is, of course, exactly the kind of information a practitioner could use. It could tell him what factors have the most influence in a job situation and thus suggest what changes are likely to have the biggest payoff. To date, the research that has been done is just not the type from which this kind of information can be derived.

SUPERIORS' PERCEPTIONS OF THE IMPORTANCE OF PAY TO THEIR SUBORDINATES

The tendency of some social scientists to underestimate the importance of pay apparently has had little influence on practicing managers. The evidence indicates that managers consistently tend to overestimate the importance of pay to their subordinates. Watson (1939) found that employees ranked pay third in importance on a list of eight morale factors. When the bosses of these employees were asked to rank the factors in terms of how important they were to their employees, however, they ranked pay first. A National Industrial Conference Board study (NICB, 1947) found that executives seriously overrated the importance their employees attached to pay. Similar data are presented in a report in *Forman Facts* (1946) in a study by Schwartz, Jenusaitis and Stark (1966), and in a study by Heller and Porter (1966). Just how important many executives actually think pay is to employees is illustrated by a study mentioned by Viteles (1953). This study showed that, of a sample of executives, 44 percent felt that "money alone is the answer" in gaining worker productivity, and 72 percent felt that either money alone is the answer or that it "is by far the chief thing."

Fosdick (in Viteles, 1953) has reported on a study which shows that employers felt that their employees rated pay number 1, while the employees themselves rated it number 7. The fact that labor union leaders as well as managers tend to misperceive the importance employees attach to pay is illustrated by the NICB study mentioned above. The labor leaders agreed with the executives in saying that pay is the most important job factor for employees. A study by Kahn (1958) nicely illustrates that managers not only tend to overestimate the importance that nonmanagerial employees attach to pay but that they also overestimate the importance other managers attach to it. This study found that foremen overestimated the importance their workers attached to pay and that general foremen tended to overestimate the importance foremen attached to it. Thus, the study suggests that there is a general tendency for superiors to overestimate the importance their subordinates attach to pay almost regardless of the organization level considered. It also seems clear that the one instance where pay is consistently ranked most important is when a superior is asked to estimate how important his subordinates consider pay to be.

There are several possible explanations for the fact that superiors overestimate the importance their subordinates attach to pay. One obvious possibility is that the superiors are fairly accurate, and that subordinates tend to distort their answers (See Chap. 3). We are unable to determine just how much, if at all, a tendency for subordinates to understate the importance of pay to them is actually influencing the data, but even if this tendency is operating to some extent, we find it hard to believe that pay is really as important to employees as managers indicate they think it is. As we have seen, the evidence simply does not support the view that pay is *the* answer in motivating employees or that it is *the* most important job factor. Thus, it is likely that managers do overestimate the importance their subordinates attach to pay, but their estimates may not be as inaccurate as the data seem to indicate because the figures on the importance their subordinates attach to pay may be understated.

It is possible that the superiors' high estimates of the importance their subordinates attach to pay are actually an indication of how important pay is to the superiors. In short, it may be that the superiors are projecting their own desires for pay onto their subordinates. This would suggest that perhaps the best measure of how important pay is to people can be found in their estimates of how important they feel it is to other people. Although this interpretation has a certain appeal, it probably cannot explain completely the degree to which superiors overestimate. The estimates given by the superiors are simply too high to represent either the importance they place on pay or the importance their subordinates place on it. The evidence, in fact, indicates that higher-level managers attach less importance to pay than do lower-level employees. Thus, it is hard to believe that the high estimates of the superiors really can be completely explained by saying they are a projection of their own desire for money. Also, as we shall see, the evidence from motivation theory does not support the view held by managers that pay is the chief or only answer to increased productivity. Further, neither managers nor employees behave as if pay were the number one motivator of their behavior.

There is in the industrial relations literature a considerable amount of evidence that pay is the most frequently mentioned cause of strikes and industrial conflict (Stagner, 1950, Tiffen & Lawshe, 1945). Pay, of course, is an easy grievance to talk about; and it is therefore not too surprising that it is frequently a subject upon which industrial conflict centers. There is also evidence that when workers are asked what will make them work hard, they typically respond by saying that higher pay will (Opinion Research Corporation, 1951). Thus, it seems that pay is likely to be a frequently discussed topic when superiors and subordinates get together, not only because pay is important, but also because it is easy to talk about, socially acceptable to discuss, and subordinates may hope to influence the raises they receive by stressing the importance of money. Other topics that perhaps are as important to employees (such as the opportunity to work on a more challenging job) are more difficult to talk about and as a result may be discussed less. The argument, therefore, is that, because pay is likely to be a frequently discussed topic between superiors and subordinates, superiors may be led to overestimate its importance.

Although no one of these three possibilities seems able to account for the general tendency of superiors to overestimate, taken together they probably offer a pretty good explanation. The combination of (1) subordinates understating the importance of pay to themselves, (2) the tendency of superiors to project their own strong desires for pay onto their subordinates, and (3) the fact that pay is frequently discussed by superiors and subordinates presumably can account for the seemingly high estimates of the superiors. It is quite likely that all these factors operate at the same time, so that cumulatively they may account for most of the overestimation that takes place.

It is interesting to compare the data on managers' estimates of the importance of pay to their subordinates with some other attitude data on the way superiors see their subordinates. Haire, Ghiselli, and Porter (1966) have presented some evidence which indicates that superiors are mistrustful of the skills of their subordinates. Miles (1966) has presented data indicating that superiors, regardless of the organizational level studied, see themselves as very similar to their peers and superiors but quite above their subordinates in the degree to which they possess such positive traits as responsibility, judgment, initiative, and intelligence. If we put all this research together, we get a rather disturbing picture of the attitudes of the typical superior toward his subordinates. He sees them as quite different from himself in a number of ways, all of which are negative. His subordinates are more money-hungry than he, but it does not seem very likely that they will ever earn much money since they are rather low in ability, ambition, and responsibility. He sees himself, however, as very much like his own superior; that is, he is high in ability, responsibility, and ambition, but not too oriented toward money.

Miles (1965) and others have talked about the problems these kinds of perceptions can create in terms of the leadership behavior of superiors. As he points out, superiors may adopt a "human relations" leadership style, that is, a style which uses participation not because it can lead to better decision making but because it leads to better acceptance of decisions and better control. This is congruent with the belief that subordinates really have very little to contribute but that they need a reason for complying with formal authority. Miles maintains that this approach to leadership can be harmful because it ignores the fact that subordinates often have quite a lot to contribute to decisions and because it is likely to lead the subordinates to feel that pseudoparticipation is being practiced.

Although the specific consequences of superiors overestimating the importance their subordinates attach to pay may not be as serious as the consequences which stem from superiors' general tendency to play down their subordinates' abilities, they nevertheless can be serious. All too often, overestimating the importance of pay can lead to superiors relying too heavily on financial incentives and the styles of management which have stressed them (e.g., scientific management) in order to motivate their subordinates. It can also lead to superiors interpreting the symptom of a problem as the problem itself, rather than looking for and trying to solve the real problem. The best examples of this tendency arise in the industrial relations area. As Stagner (1950) has pointed out, "In many cases the workers first get angry and go on strike. Then they look for something to demand. Higher wages and shorter hours are simple and easy to formulate," so they are given as the reason for the problem. If the managers believe that only money counts to workers, they are likely to accept at face value that money is the problem and attempt to solve the problem financially. It may be possible to solve non-pay-caused problems financially, but it can be very expensive.

On the management level, demands for pay raises often represent not so much a desire for more money as a desire to test the system and a desire for feedback (Lawler, 1969). Frequently, all the manager wants to know is how his boss and the company evaluate him. Since he finds it difficult to talk openly with his boss about this, he resorts to asking for a raise as a way to find out. In one sense, the company is forced to pay a higher wage to this person because it has failed to communicate with him adequately. Here, we have a situation in which, again, an economic solution is possible (e.g., giving a large raise), but is expensive and not necessarily optimal.

In the "air hose" case, Whyte (1955) has given an example of what can happen when only economic solutions to seemingly economic problems are sought. For a year a problem concerned with an incentive rate change had defied solution through the normal union-management negotiating channels. Suddenly it was solved in only a few minutes, with the grievance being withdrawn. Why, after such prolonged negotiations, had it suddenly been so easy to solve this problem? Because a new contract had been signed, and a higher level of trust had been established between union and management. As Whyte points out, the economic case put forth by the union must be viewed symbolically.

For the workers and union leaders the case had symbolized the hatred and distrust they bore toward management. It was evident to them that management was unfair and ruthless. So long as they continued to believe that management was unfair and ruthless, the case could have no other meaning to them, no matter what logical arguments were brought against them. But as soon as relations were reorganized so that the hatred and distrust were beginning to be dissipated, there was no longer an emotional need to hold on to that symbol of conflict. [p. 114]

The obvious implication of this discussion is that if union-management relations had not taken a substantial turn for the better, the air hose case could never have been solved on a straight economic accounting basis.

As was mentioned earlier, the tendency of managers to overestimate the importance of pay can lead to the general belief that higher pay for employees is the way to obtain higher productivity and to solve other problems. This is a particularly insidious belief because it often leads managers to spend large amounts of money on giving raises, etc., in the hope that greater productivity will result. When pay raises do not result in greater productivity, the managers may feel betrayed (I was nice to you, why weren't you nice to me?) and then come to the erroneous con-

conclusion that pay cannot motivate or that the workers are lazy. As we shall see in our discussion of motivation, there is absolutely no evidence to indicate that just raising salaries or pay levels leads to higher productivity (Chaps. 6 and 7). A good example of a pay-can-solve-anything philosophy appeared in an interview the author had with a plant manager who stated that because he had poor foremen he had to pay high wages in order to motivate his employees. There is some evidence to indicate that if a company has poor foremen, motivation is difficult no matter how high the wages. Finally, there is the often-heard lament of the college recruiter, "I can't understand why we did not get more graduates from —————— University—we were offering the highest wages of any company that recruited there."

SELECTION

One of the most interesting possibilities suggested by the research on individual differences in the importance attached to pay has to do with employee selection. The research suggests that people do differ in this respect and that certain individual difference factors (e.g., sex, age, background) may be related to this variation. Thus, employers may be able at the time of employment application to identify those people for whom pay will be highly important and those for whom it will not be. This raises the possibility of selecting and placing people in terms of this difference.

Jobs also differ. There are jobs in which it is desirable to have people for whom pay is very important, just as there are jobs where it is desirable to have people for whom pay is less important. In the typical mass-production job, where people work under a piece rate pay system, it may be desirable to have people for whom pay is very important. Whyte's example (1955) of the rate buster's response to this kind of situation shows that people for whom pay is highly important will respond positively to piece rate incentives. On the other hand, on a job in which performance is impossible to measure or in which a restrictive union contract covers the employees, it may be desirable to employ only people for whom pay is not very important. In these situations it is difficult to use pay to motivate performance, so all that is likely to happen if people who value money highly are put on these jobs is that they will be constantly agitating for higher wages or quitting to take higher-paying jobs.

Two kinds of commonly used selection instruments would seem to lend themselves to discriminating among people in terms of the importance they attach to pay. An application blank or a more sophisticated weighted biographical data blank could do this, as could some type of self-report instrument. Whyte's book suggests the kind of biographical items that might be used to identify people for whom pay is very important. Also, in Chapter 3 we gave a brief profile of this type of person. Information about many of the personal characteristics of such a person can be easily obtained by means of a biographical data blank. For example, he is likely to be young, to have a small town or farm background, to belong to few clubs and social groups, and to own or want to buy his own home. All these facts can be obtained from a biographical data blank; and if it turns out that the items can predict the importance attached to pay, then they can be weighted heavily when applicants are considered for certain jobs. For example, for piece rate jobs, individuals might be graded higher if they own their own home and if they come from small towns or farms rather than from urban areas.

Most organizations have some scheme for scoring application blanks or biographical data blanks. They may do this either subjectively or objectively, but they seldom consider the implications of the procedure in terms of how important pay is to the applicant. What is being suggested here is that when selection is made on the basis of age, background, etc., the selection procedure often partially determines how important pay will be to the people who end up in the organization, even though no conscious selection effort is made in this area. The implications of this procedure for the importance of pay need to be considered, since in the case of many jobs the importance of pay to the employee may determine how he will respond in the job situation. Admittedly we are a long way from being able to say exactly which factors are indicators of the importance of pay. Still, the initial data are interesting and, if they can be replicated, potentially quite valuable. What is needed, of course, are studies that relate these individual differences to measures of both the importance of pay to people and the objective performance of people in jobs where we should expect pay importance to have an influence. Presumably, if the data are correct, we should find that because pay is more important to the younger male workers from rural backgrounds, they will be better performers in piece rate incentive situations than will older female workers from urban backgrounds. On the other hand, if we look at a job where salaries are fixed by union contract, we would not expect to find any differences between these groups, because pay is fixed. As we shall see, in this situation, pay cannot be used to motivate job performance.

A number of direct self-report techniques might be used to determine how important pay is to a group of job applicants. Such techniques range from simple rating and ranking procedures to more complicated psychophysical approaches. All, however, suffer from the same problem: the tendency of job applicants to present themselves to the organization as they think the organization expects good applicants to look. In the case of pay, this could mean that applicants, rather than revealing how important pay is to themselves, will actually try to indicate how important they feel the organization thinks it should be to prospective employees. Although there is very little evidence to suggest whether this will lead employees to understate or overstate the actual importance pay has for them, a good guess is that on the average it will lead them to overstate. The point, however, is not that it will lead to their overstating the importance of pay, but that it will lead to inaccurate information; some people will probably overstate, while others will understate. Still, the statements may predict how the applicants will behave on the job. The statements are a sample of behavior in the sense that they tell something about the applicants and how they perceive the environment. Thus, it might be worthwhile to determine whether direct self-reports of this type can indeed predict job performance.

Self-report measures can be designed in such a way as to minimize the degree to which they can be faked. For example, some type of projective test such as the Thematic Apperception Test (TAT) can be used so that the applicant does not know how the test is being scored or what the tester is looking for. Another approach is simply to ask applicants to choose between two job factors on the basis of their importance, but to put items together that are equal in terms of their social desirability in job application situations. The first step in this approach would be to have people rate job factors according to how desirable they think it is to rate them high in importance when applying for a job. Then items that were rated the same in desirability would be paired together. For example, having authority would be paired with high pay if they were rated the same in terms of desirability; and the applicant would be asked to indicate which of the two was the most important to him.

There are several problems with both the projective approach and the approach of equating items for social desirability. Neither of these approaches is a perfect way to prevent faking. Applicants see through projective tests, and the word can get out about what organizations are looking for. But perhaps the biggest problem with using these approaches for selection at this time is that there are no well-developed tests of this type that yield data on the importance of pay. Thus, if an organization wanted to do this kind of testing, it probably would have to develop its own tests, which could be quite expensive. The alternative is to use some of the tests already developed that yield economic importance scores, but which can be faked. The Allport-Vernon Study of Values (Vernon & Allport, 1931), for example, yields a measure of economic values. If an organization regards the importance attached to pay as a good predictor in the selection of people for certain jobs, then probably it should use one of the standard tests of values and also look at the biographical data measures discussed earlier. It should then check the data gathered from these sources against actual job performance to see if either indicator is valid.

LEADERSHIP STYLE AND INDIVIDUAL DIFFERENCES IN THE IMPORTANCE OF PAY

The information that is used to help in selection and placement can also be used by a superior in choosing the style of leadership that will work best with each of his subordinates. It has been stressed for a long time in the management literature that managers should treat subordinates differently, since they are likely to respond to different incentives. Very little evidence, however, has been collected to point out when different styles of leadership are appropriate. The evidence reviewed in Chapter 3 suggests that offering a pay raise will stimulate some people to work hard while it will not stimulate others. This suggests that superiors may have to be very judicious in their use of pay to motivate good performance since in the case of some employees it may not be valued highly enough to be an effective motivator of performance. The key is to be able to determine in advance how much different employees value money so that financial incentives can be used only where they will do the most good.

The evidence presented in Chapter 3 suggests that clues to the importance of money can be obtained by looking at an employee's background information. The superior should use this information in the initial screening of subordinates. By combining this with the information he picks up during his regular supervisory duties, he should be able to make some better-than-chance estimates about which of his subordinates value money the most. These are the subordinates who potentially can be motivated by pay plans, and they should be given jobs where it is possible to use wage-incentive plans. The superior should also accept the fact that those subordinates who do not value money highly are not likely to be motivated by incentive plans, and he should think in terms of motivating them in other ways. In effect, he will have to vary his style of leadership according to the type of employee with whom he is dealing.

INFLUENCING THE IMPORTANCE OF PAY

So far we have focused on issues that arise because of the large individual differences that exist in the importance people attach to pay; we have not talked about the possibility of changing the importance individuals attach to their pay. It has been more or less accepted that the importance attached to pay is a relatively fixed characteristic and that the problem of management is to identify how strong the characteristic is, and then place employees in the appropriate job and influence them with the correct leadership style and pay plan. This way of viewing the importance of pay is typical of the way relatively fixed traits and abilities such as IQ and motor skills are viewed, and indeed unless there is some permanence to the importance people attach to pay, it does not make sense to use it for employment selection purposes. This approach to the importance of pay is viable, since it is relatively hard to alter the importance a person attaches to his pay. Still, the research evidence and our Model of the Importance of Pay suggest that certain factors can have an influence. Thus, it makes sense to talk about how organizations can exert such an influence. The Model clearly suggests two ways this can happen: (1) Organization actions can alter the degree to which employees see pay as instrumental for the satisfaction of certain needs, and (2) they can, by economic and noneconomic means, partially satisfy the needs for which pay is instrumental. Thus, although the importance a person attaches to pay at the time of his job application is probably an indication of how important it will continue to be, the clear suggestion is that what happens to him after he joins the organization will have an influence.

Chapter 3 offered some support for the view that as needs become more satisfied, they become less important. It also showed that the more highly paid people are, the less important pay is to them. One implication of this finding is that as people become more satisfied either with their pay or in the need areas for which pay is instrumental, their pay will be less important. Thus, one way for organizations to be sure that pay will always be important to their employees is to keep the employees underpaid. Obviously, the way to prevent employees from worrying about pay is to keep them highly paid. This point, however, is hardly surprising, and indeed it probably is not very practical to think in terms of keeping people underpaid so that pay will be important to them. Although keeping people underpaid may be desirable in some respects, it clearly can encourage absenteeism, turnover, strikes, and other problems (discussed in Chap. 13). Similarly, although overpaying people may make pay less important to them, economic costs make this impractical, even if an organization wants pay to be unimportant to a certain group of employees. In some instances, however, organizations may be overpaying without being aware of its potential impact on the importance the employees attach to their pay.

Gellerman (1968) has cited a case in which management unintentionally created a pay scheme under which a group of salesmen were so highly paid that their pay became relatively unimportant to them. As a result, the pay-incentive plan stopped working. The men became so well-off that they began looking elsewhere for more satisfying jobs that paid much less money. The company's solution was to cut back on their commissions and to keep them slightly hungry. This case presents a good illustration of one of the binds that arise in wage and salary administration.

On the one hand (see Part 2), if people are to be motivated by money, large amounts must be offered or they will not think it worthwhile to work especially hard; on the other hand, there is the possibility that if pay is high for a period of time, it will lose much of its importance to employees. One way to counter this is to offer larger and larger raises, but this practice can lead to an ever-escalating cycle of pay increases.

By far the most common sin committed by organizations is to offer too small, not too large, a financial reward when pay is used to motivate performance. Organizations seem to overlook the fact that as a person's salary goes up, so must the amount of any raise if it is to be meaningful. Hinrich's (1969) study suggests that they may not have to go up quite as fast, but they do have to go up. All too often organizations try to offer everyone the same dollar increase or incentive. This is, of course, foolish because it will not mean the same thing to everyone. To be meaningful, a raise must represent some appreciable percentage of the individual's present salary.

A second implication of the point that need satisfaction can decrease the importance of pay is suggested by the fact that needs can be satisfied many ways. Because of this, it seems likely that if the needs upon which pay depends for its importance can be satisfied by nonfinancial rewards, then pay itself should become less important. For example, if pay is important to a manager because it satisfies his need for esteem and recognition, it is possible that if he is given a number of noneconomic status-related rewards, his pay may become less important. This would happen because his need for esteem and recognition would be better satisfied and, as a result, less important. Since he values pay partially because it satisfies his esteem need, its importance should decrease as the strength of this need is reduced. There is little hard evidence that this in fact happens, but it is part of the folklore of organizations. In the classic example, the subordinate asks his superior for a raise and ends up with a new title, an executive-type desk, a private office, and the same salary. The supervisor's strategy is clear in this case, although he may not be able to explain it in the terms of our model. The superior is hoping to satisfy his subordinate's needs with nonfinancial rewards, so that the organization will save money and the individual will feel satisfied and stop bothering him about a raise. Observational evidence indicates that, as might be expected, this strategy can be effective on a short-term basis. The problems arise over a longer period, when the subordinate's aspiration level changes, and he wants some more "concrete" reward from the higher-ups to indicate how they feel about him. At this point, money may be the only reward that will satisfy him.

Undoubtedly, the most significant way organizations can influence the importance of pay to their employees is by influencing the ability of pay to satisfy needs. The way pay is administered can directly influence the degree to which it is able to satisfy needs in general and, particularly, the need for esteem and recognition. Organization pay policies influence the degree to which salary will be taken as a mark of accomplishment and status both by the individual and by others. Pay policies influence the degree to which high pay is seen by the employees and others familiar with the company as a mark of accomplishment versus the result of luck, seniority, playing politics, or some other nonmerit factor.

It is important to remember that it is not high pay as such which carries status but what the pay is taken to represent. Pay is simply a shared symbolic way of recognizing accomplishment in our society. Thus, if pay does not represent accomplishment, it loses much of its ability to satisfy such needs as esteem and recognition, and thus loses much of its importance. Although the evidence reviewed in Chapter 3 suggests that pay is generally seen to be instrumental for the satisfaction of esteem and recognition needs, there is no evidence to suggest that it always is or that it automatically is instrumental in satisfying these needs. Quite to the contrary, it is easy to imagine situations where high pay or wealth does not lead to high status. The key, of course, is in how the money is obtained. Almost everyone has at some time asked, "Did that person earn his wealth or inherit it?" The implication of the question (in terms of what his money means to others) is clear. Similarly, in organizations where pay is not based on merit, pay differences are known not to reflect accomplishment; as a result, the amount of a person's salary may not be an important determinant of his status. When this happens, the amount of an employee's pay may become less important to him because he no longer sees it as a way of satisfying his esteem and recognition needs. In short, the first way organizations can guarantee that the absolute amount of salary and the size of pay raises will have the maximum meaning to employees is to let it be known that pay is based upon merit and is an indication of accomplishment. This is not as simple as it sounds, as we shall see in Chapter 9.

The second thing that organizations can do to ensure that pay will satisfy important noneconomic needs is suggested by the statement of a company president who wanted a $200,000 salary rather than $100,000 plus benefits, which would actually yield him more income after taxes. He said he preferred the larger salary because it would look more impressive in the company's annual proxy statement. The fact that his salary was public knowledge made it that much more relevant as a vehicle for satisfying needs such as esteem and recognition, which are inherently public. Similarly, promotion is an important reward because it is public and thus effectively satisfies needs for recognition and esteem. High pay can only satisfy these needs if salaries are in some way known. In most companies, managers' salaries are carefully guarded secrets; as a result it is not immediately obvious who the higher-paid managers are.

Salary levels can, of course, be estimated from the manager's job in the company and from how and where he lives, but these estimates often are not accurate. Undoubtedly, part of the conspicuous consumption behavior that is known as "keeping up with the Joneses" comes about because people want to show that they are as highly paid and successful in their jobs as the next person. The prestige that comes from high pay presumably is derived from the fact that salary size reflects how valuable the organization judges the individual's contribution to be. This is at best an imperfect way of making public how one is regarded by the organization, and as a result, small differences are not apparent. The result of all this is that differences in pay levels and amounts of absolute salary often become less important to managers than they would be if they were public knowledge, since a poor salary can be hidden from others and it is not always obvious who receives the good salary. Salary is a relative matter, and only if other people's salaries are known can one make accurate comparisons for the purposes of deciding what a given salary means in terms of regard by the organization. Thus, making salaries public should sensitize people much more to small differences in salaries and would undoubtedly cause people to be much more concerned about the relative size of their salaries. This, of course, would only happen where pay was seen to be based upon merit and actual salary differences existed for people holding similar jobs.

SUMMARY

This chapter has talked about some of the ways organizations can influence the degree to which their employees value money. It has suggested that organizations can do this by their employee selection process and their pay administration policies. The clear message that should come through from this discussion is that organizations have relatively little direct influence over the degree to which their employees value money. Many of the factors that determine the value people place on money are hardly within the control of the organization. Money is likely to be an important job factor almost regardless of what organizations do, because within the context of the society as a whole it can buy certain goods and tends to carry with it a certain status. The lack of control that organizations have over this factor contrasts sharply, however, to the influence they have over the ability of pay to motivate job performance. As we shall see in succeeding chapters, pay administration practices exert a great deal of influence on whether pay does or does not motivate good job performance.

If we were to pick from this chapter several pieces of advice for a manager who is concerned about how important pay is to his subordinates, they would probably run something like this:

1. Do not assume that pay is necessarily the most important factor to your subordinates.
2. Do not fall prey to the frequently heard cry of social scientists that pay is about sixth in importance.
3. Do assume that pay is about as important to people one level below you as it is to you and other managers at your level.
4. Do look beyond economic complaints and demands on the part of subordinates to see if there are noneconomic causes lurking in the background.
5. Do tie pay to performance and make it a form of recognition if you want pay to be important enough to motivate good job performance.
6. Do look at the backgrounds of people who are going to work on incentive jobs to see if you can identify those for whom pay is likely to be important.

Part II
PAY AS A SOURCE OF MOTIVATION

Money is a big thing in baseball, and
you have your ballplayers who respond
to nothing much except the long green.
You can holler at them until you're
blue in the face and you can pat them
on the back until you've got a callous
on your hand and nothing happens
till you come up with the cash on the
line.

(Bavasi, 1967, p. 45)

Chapter 5
THEORIES
OF
MOTIVATION

Many organization theorists and managers have argued that pay, when properly administered, can motivate good job performance, make employees work harder and induce them to comply with the organization's desires. There has, however, been disagreement on just how much impact pay can have and on what "properly administered" means. Before we consider actual pay administration practices and their impact on motivation, we shall define "motivation" and look at the research and theory on motivation. Psychologists have done a great deal of research on motivation, and although only a small part of it has been concerned with pay, it can contribute to our understanding of pay and the potential of pay to motivate job performance. Psychologists have also developed a number of theories of motivation that can provide leads with respect to what a motivation model must look like if it is to explain the impact of pay on behavior.

The term "motivation" has been used in a variety of ways. Because of this, there has not always been agreement on what kind of behavior should be treated when it is considered. At the present time there seems to be some agreement that the distinguishing characteristic of motivated behavior is that it is goal-directed. Bindra (1959), for example, has said that the core of what is usually called the problem of motivation lies in the "purposive" or goal-directed aspect of behavior. It is generally accepted that in examining goal-directed behavior, one must consider both what energizes the behavior and what directs the behavior toward the goal. Atkinson (1964) maintains that "the study of motivation has to do with the analysis of the various factors which incite and direct an individual's actions." M. R. Jones (1955) has stated that motivation is concerned with "how behavior gets started, is energized, is sustained, is directed, is stopped, and what kind of subjective reaction is present in the organism while all this is going on." Clearly, Jones's definition is broader than Bindra's or Atkinson's. As we shall see, the research on pay has, in fact, touched all the issues raised by Jones's definition; thus, we shall accept his definition, since it will allow the broadest coverage of the literature. We shall, therefore, be concerned with how the ability of pay to serve as a goal object enables it to energize, sustain, direct and stop behavior.

"Commonsense explanations" of motivational phenomena generally consist of verbally linking a given activity with one or another of certain states or events that are culturally recognized as goals or ends. Any given behavior is made intelligible to common sense when the sentence "X does Y in order to . . ." is completed. In Part 2 we shall be concerned mostly with situations in which the goal is money, and the behavior is some aspect of work activity (e.g., working hard, high productivity). Thus, a satisfactory commonsense explanation of why someone works hard can take the form, "X is working hard in order to earn more money." As a scientific explanation of why X is behaving as he is, this is hardly satisfactory. It does not say why X wants to earn more money or why X does Y rather than Z in order to obtain the money. Further, it does not say why X seeks money rather than some other goal or outcome.

An acceptable scientific explanation of X's behavior must specify all these things. It must say why money is the goal; why money is sought, rather than some other goal; and why X pursues it in the manner he does. An acceptable theory of human motives or of the importance of pay has to deal only with why pay and other outcomes are sought (see Chap. 2). This kind of theory should not be confused with a theory of motivation that tries to explain performance. To explain performance, a theory must state not only why goals are sought, but also the factors that influence how they are sought.

Tolman (1925) first stressed the distinction between performance and learning in the following terms: "Previous work . . . has made no distinction between an animal's mere knowledge of the behavior possibilities which will get him to food and his desire for those behavior possibilities" (p. 295). This statement was directed to those learning theorists who assumed that if no performance were present, no learning existed. As Tolman indicated, equating learning and performance is foolhardly, since latent learning may well exist. A different kind of error was made by many early motivation theorists who assumed that, because they had theories of motives (or drives) and could make statements about what objects would be goals, they somehow had a theory of motivation that could explain performance. They were wrong, of course, but for just the opposite reason from that which made the learning theorists susceptible to Tolman's criticism. The motivation theorists failed to consider associative connections and therefore could not explain why a person behaved in a certain way in order to obtain a goal. They were limited to saying why something was a goal and to predicting what might be a goal.

In a very real sense, our discussion of motivation began in Chapter 2, where we talked about why pay is important. That discussion and the

Model of the Importance of Pay provide one of the vital building blocks for the kind of motivation theory that can help us understand the ability of pay to motivate behavior. The model provides a way of thinking about why pay is important which departs from the commonsense explanation that people have an instinct or drive for pay. It helps to explain why pay can become a goal and why people seek pay rather than some other goal. Thus, it provides a basis for answering several of the questions that must be dealt with by a motivation theory. Our Model of the Importance of Pay cannot, however, stand alone as an explanation of behavior. It significantly departs from the commonsense explanation level, since it deals with why pay becomes a goal. But if it is to explain why particular behaviors are tried by employees in order to obtain high pay, some associative or other component must be combined with it.

A number of motivation theories have been stated that suggest scientific explanations for why people choose particular behaviors in order to obtain their goals. Theories have been suggested by social psychologists to explain social behavior, and by learning theorists to explain learning. Similarly, motivation theories with special relevance to clinical psychology, physiological psychology, and child psychology have been developed. In total, the psychology literature contains hundreds of different motivation theories.

Fortunately, for our discussion of pay and motivation, it is not necessary to discuss all these theories. There are two reasons for this: First, many so-called theories of motivation simply are not sufficiently developed to deal with all the phenomena with which an acceptable theory must deal. Many of them, for example, are theories of motives rather than theories of motivation. These, of course, need not be considered, because they do not fit our definition of a theory of motivation. Second, there is a high degree of convergence among the more fully developed theories. The work of Lewin, Tolman, Rotter, and others converges into one stream of thinking that can be called "expectancy × valence" theory. Although these theorists differ somewhat in the way they think about motivation, they are similar in their basic approach. A second clear stream of thinking about motivation is apparent in the work of drive theorists such as Hull and Spence. This approach has been labeled "drive × habit" theory.

Clearly any discussion of pay and motivation theory must consider both drive theory and expectancy theory since these are the two major approaches. But is it sufficient to consider just these two approaches? If we were relating motivation theory to some outcome other than pay, the answer would probably be yes, but the work of Adams (1963a, 1965) makes it vital that we also consider the balance theory approach. Adams took the work from social psychology on dissonance theory and social exchange theory and developed what is called "equity theory." This approach has stimulated a considerable amount of recent research on pay, and it makes a number of predictions that are significantly different from those suggested by the other two approaches.

Brief mention of Herzberg's two-factor theory is also warranted. Although this approach does not qualify as a theory of motivation according to our definition, it has received a great deal of attention from people interested in work motivation, and it makes some specific predictions about pay and motivation.

The remainder of the chapter will be devoted to a discussion of drive theory, expectancy theory, equity theory, and two-factor theory, and to the predictions they make about pay and motivation. In Chapter 6, we shall develop our own Motivation Model. In Chapters 7 and 8, the research evidence on pay as a source of motivation will be considered and related to the model. Chapter 9 will focus on determining what the research and theory mean in terms of specific pay administration practices and their impact on motivation and performance. Finally Chapters 10 and 11 will focus on the role of pay in motivating job attendance. The reader who is familiar with the work of Adams (1965), Atkinson (1964), Cofer and Appley (1964), Herzberg, Mausner, and Snyderman (1959) and Vroom (1964) may wish to skip the remainder of this chapter and begin reading Chapter 6.

DRIVE THEORY

Drive theory is the oldest and probably the best known of the motivation theories. Its origins can be found in the work of the ancient Greek philosophers as well as in the writings of English utilitarians such as Jeremy Bentham and John Stuart Mill (Vroom, 1964; Atkinson, 1964). They first clearly verbalized the principle of hedonism, from which contemporary drive theory has derived. Hedonism assumes that people will always select from possible alternative actions that course of action which they think will maximize their pleasure and minimize their pain. Hedonism, because of its simplicity and commonsense approach to motivation, has at times gained widespread acceptance. Since it contains no clear-cut specification of what type of events will be pleasurable or painful and no explanation of why people behave in a particular way to obtain a pleasurable outcome, however, it is not a testable theory of motivation. It is excellent at "explaining" why people did behave in a certain manner, but it is unable to predict how people will behave in the future.

The first significant conceptual advance beyond hedonism was made by Thorndike (1911) in the law of effect:

Of several responses made to the same situation, those which are accompanied or closely followed by satisfaction to the animal will, other things being equal, be more firmly connected with the situation, so that, when it recurs, they will be more likely to recur; those which are accompanied or closely followed by discomfort to the animal will, other things being equal, have their connections with that situation weakened, so that, when it recurs, they will be less likely to occur. The greater the satisfaction or discomfort, the greater the strengthening or weakening of the bond (p. 244).

The law of effect does not say why certain events are satisfying or dissatisfying, but it does introduce learning and past events into the thinking about motivation. It uses learning and previous stimulus-response connections to explain why present behavior is directed toward satisfying events and away from painful events. If it is hedonism at all, it is a hedonism of the past, since it emphasizes the importance of past events in influencing current behavior. Because it emphasizes the impact of learning, the law of effect has been recognized as an important step toward the development of a testable theory of motivation.

In 1918, R. S. Woodworth introduced the concept of drive as an alternative to the then current emphasis on instinct. The concept of drive is important in the development of motivation theory, because as we shall see, it has been used by Hull, Spence, and others as a basis for explaining why certain events are pleasurable while others are not. It represents an attempt to deal with the criticism of hedonism and the law of effect—that they are untestable because they do not specify in advance what will be pleasurable to the organism. By assuming that drives exist, a theory may state in advance not only what objects will be sought, but also how vigorously they will be sought. Presumably objects which satisfy drives are rewarding and can serve as reinforcers of behavior. This approach has had difficulty in specifying what drives people have and in explaining behavior that does not seem to be related to the satisfaction of biologically based drives.

Modern thinking about drive theory really began with the work of Hull. In a series of theoretical papers published in 1929, he translated the learning experiments of Pavlov and others into stimulus-response terms. Hull recognized that in order to explain behavior it was necessary to consider both the "striving" for goals and the "strengthening of connections" related to goals. It was not until 1943, however, that he published his major work, *Principles of Behavior*. In it he developed the formula $sE_R = f(sH_R) \times f(D)$ to explain what he called the "impetus to respond." This formula suggests that present behavior is influenced by a multiplicative combination of drive strength and habit strength. In Hull's theory, drive essentially has an energizing and a partial directing influence. Hull assumed that when a condition of biological need arose, there would be produced what psychologists at that time (following Woodworth's suggestion) called a "drive," which would activate the animal. Drive was hypothesized to increase as hours of deprivation increased. Hull also assumed that different biological needs produced qualitatively different patterns of internal stimulation (*Sd*). These drive stimuli, he argued, had an important role in determining what kind of behavior the need would elicit, since they provided clues to what the "correct" behavior was: hence, the view that drive has a partial directing influence. Drive was seen as a general exciter of all responses. This was its most important role. Hull argued that drives are cumulative in energizing behavior. Hunger, thirst, and sexual need, when all present at the same time, are expected to produce heightened excitability of whatever habits are evoked by the immediate stimulus circumstance, regardless of whether these habits are functional for the satisfaction of the organism's strongest needs.

After developing the concept of drive, Hull turned his attention to the concept of habit strength ($_sH_R$), which he defined as the connection between a stimulus and a response. Habit strength is for Hull an associative connection that influences the kind of behavior the drive will energize. According to Hull the strength of a habit depends upon four factors:

1. The contiguity of the stimulus and response during training
2. The closeness of the S-R event to a reinforcing state of affairs
3. The number of reinforcements
4. The magnitude of reinforcement during training

It is obvious that Hull's treatment of habit draws heavily on Thorndike's law of effect; both stress the concept of reinforcement in the establishment of S-R connections. Hull made an important contribution, however, because he stressed some of the factors that influence habit strength. For him, habit strength is a gradually built-up association between a stimulus and a response that tends to be stronger the more frequently the S-R connection is reinforced, the larger the reinforcements, the more closely the reinforcements follow the S-R associations, and the closer the contiguity of S and R. In a given situation, therefore, the particular habit that is likely to be energized is the strongest one for that situation, or in terms of the theory, the one that in similar stimulus situations has most frequently led to large amounts of quickly received reinforcements. From this kind of reasoning Hull developed his proposition that the immediate determinants of action are the organism's drive state and habits.

Perhaps the best way to make Hull's thinking clear is to look at the behavior of a rat in a maze and try to understand what determines its behavior at a choice point. First of all, the animal will be stimulated to act only to the extent that some drive is present, since drive is required in order to sensitize habit strengths into action. The particular habit strength that is sensitized into action will depend upon the rat's previous experience in this particular situation. If at the present time he is hungry, and if in the past when hungry he found that, in this situation, turning to the right immediately led to large quantities of food, he is likely to turn to the right. If the only other times he was in this situation he was thirsty and upon turning right he immediately found large amounts of water, he is not particularly likely to turn right now: The drive stimulus (S_d) is now different, so a new S-R connection has to be established. If the previous time the rat found himself in this situation he was hungry and turned right but found little food or found food only later, he will not be particularly likely to turn right this time: His $_sH_R$ for turning right will not be strong, since it has not been properly reinforced. In short, for Hull, the probability of an organism's behaving in a particular way is influenced (1) by the degreee to which its drive state is strong enough to energize behavior and (2) by the degree to which in similar situations this kind of behavior has been closely associated with large appropriate rewards.

Pay can influence behavior in terms of Hull's theory because of its ability to act as a secondary reinforcer. Objects which are frequently associated with stimuli that reduce primary drives can themselves become secondary reinforcers. Hull (1943) cites the work of Wolfe (1936) and Cowles (1937), which was discussed in Chapter 2, to support his point that objects like money can become secondary reinforcers. This means that the ability of pay to motivate good job performance is based on the degree to which it has in the past been a secondary reinforcer of good performance. This emphasis on the establishment of S-R connections has led some to call theories like Hull's "hedonism of the past." The clear suggestion of Hull's work is that it is not the anticipation of a large pay raise that motivates someone, but the previous experiences he has had in similar situations. Thus, offering a large rather than a small raise will not immediately lead to stronger motivation, although in the long run it might, since receiving the raise will result in the gradual establishment of a stronger $_sH_R$. Summarizing briefly, in terms of Hull's theory, it would seem that only under three conditions will pay act to motivate good job performance: A drive must be present; pay must be a secondary reinforcer for that drive; and pay must follow immediately after good job performance.

It is not hard to see why Hull's theory and other reinforcement theories have often been cited as support for a piece rate type of incentive plan. They fit well with the kind of mechanistic S-R bond-building approach that characterizes reinforcement theories. The job is broken down into small, discrete responses, each of which is reinforced when properly performed; that is, workers are paid for each piece they produce (for each correct response). Workers are seldom changed from job to job; in fact, they may give the same response thousands of times a day for years. Presumably, the large number of reinforcements would lead to the establishment of a very strong $_sH_R$. Perhaps the one step in the theory that piece rate plans fail to follow completely is that they do not immediately reinforce the correct response with a pay reward. Normally, the reward does not come until several days after the response has occurred, since workers are usually paid on a weekly basis. Awareness of this missing link has led to the suggestion that workers be reinforced immediately each time they complete the cycle upon which their piece rate is based. Suggestions on how to do this have varied widely: Machines could give workers tokens when they complete a piece of work, or the foreman could give the workers the money on the spot. Tokens given out as rewards could be used in a slot machine which would pay out money. All this may sound a bit unnecessary, but it is in general agreement with the kind of thinking put forth in Hull's 1943 statement of drive theory.

Although Hull's statement of his theory represents a landmark in the development of modern drive theory, he and others have made significant changes in the theory since 1943 in response to certain criticisms about what determines reaction potential $(_sE_R)$. As originally stated, the theory was unable to explain some of the data that were collected on the effects of incentive motivation. Much of the failure of the theory was due to the fact that it was oriented to the past. It did not include any way of accounting for the actual effects of changing the size of reinforcements. According to the theory, changes in size of reinforcement could only gradually influence behavior, because they had to operate by means of changing $_sH_R$; hence, the prediction mentioned earlier that little immediate effect could be expected from giving a large rather than a small pay reward. Studies by Crespi (1942, 1944) and Zeaman (1949) clearly showed that when rats trained to run to a large reward were given a smaller reward they showed abrupt changes in the speed of running. Rats trained to run to small rewards showed equally abrupt increases in running speed when a larger reward was given. These results did not support Hull's prediction of a gradual building of habit strength; they suggested that shifts in size of pay reward might in fact have an immediate effect on behavior.

To accommodate the experimental evidence produced by Crespi and Zeaman, and the evidence on latent learning provided by Tolman and Honzik (1930) and Blodgett (1929), Hull (1952) revised his theory. He introduced amount of incentive as a separate motivational variable (K) in the equation for reaction potential, so that instead of reading $_sE_R = D \times _sH_R$ it read $_sE_R = D \times K \times _sH_R$. Hull used the term K to refer to anticipatory goal reactions that are forward-looking and, therefore (according to Hull), can change quickly in strength as changes take place in reward size. It is a motivational variable like D, because it too can energize habits. This change in the theory allowed it to explain the latent-learning data and the results of the studies on changing the size of rewards.

Perhaps the most striking point about this change in drive theory is that it sharply reduced the areas of disagreement between drive theory and the expectancy theories of Lewin and Tolman. For a considerable time the approaches were easily differentiated by the fact that one was very forward-looking and concerned with anticipated goals, while the other was not. With the change in Hull's theory, the difference greatly decreased. However, drive theory still remains more oriented to the past than does expectancy theory. The work of Spence (1956) breaks down still further the distinction between expectancy theory and drive theory. In his drive theory, Spence also includes an incentive factor (K), but he presents a slightly different formula for combining it with drive and habit: $E = (D + K) \times H$. Spence identified incentive (K) as a goal-response–goal-stimulus mechanism that is in some ways like an expectancy which is also a response-stimulus association factor.

EXPECTANCY THEORY

Expectancy theory, like drive theory, can be traced back to hedonism and the work of the English utilitarians. In the 1930s, however, it began to develop a quite different thrust. It was at this point that Tolman (1932) began to talk about expectations and to argue for an approach that was more cognitively oriented. At this time Kurt Lewin also presented a cognitively oriented theory of behavior that contained terms like "valence" and "force." Out of this early work by Tolman and Lewin a number of very similar motivation theories have developed. All include a concept of valence, or the attractiveness of an object, and a concept of expectancy, or the likelihood that an action will lead to a certain outcome or goal. The theories also converge in that they see valence and expectancy combining multiplicatively to determine behavior; hence, they can be referred to as expectancy × valence theories of motivation.

Notable among the theorists who have picked up the main points of the early work of Tolman and Lewin and built their own motivation theories within the expectancy × valence framework are Atkinson (1958), Edwards (1954), Peak (1955), Rotter (1954, 1955), and Vroom (1964). Table 5-1 lists the terms used by the various theorists. Obviously, there is a high degree of similarity in their approaches. One interesting difference is the use of the terms "motive" and "incentive" by Atkinson, while the other theorists use only one term to refer to the attractiveness or importance factor. This, however, does not represent a disagreement among the theorists; it only means that Atkinson goes further in stating what determines valence. His theory maintains that valence depends on both motive strength and incentive value, while most expectancy theories are notoriously vague about what determines valence. A theory like Atkinson's could alternatively be written: Motivation = (expectancy × valence) where valence = (motive × incentive). The important point about the theories listed in Table 5-1 is not that they use different terminology and reveal minor differences in the way they are stated, but that all agree on certain basic issues. All of them maintain that the strength of a tendency to act in a certain way depends upon the strength of an expectancy that the act will be followed by a given consequence (or outcome) and upon the value of that consequence (or outcome) to the actor.

Vroom's theory (1964) is the only one listed that was specifically stated for the purpose of dealing with motivation in the work environment. Thus, it is the logical theory to examine to see how expectancy theory can be applied to work motivation and pay. For Vroom, "valence" refers to affective orientations toward particular outcomes. Outcomes can be either positive or negative in valence. An outcome is positive if a person prefers attaining it to not attaining it, it is neutral if the person is indifferent to it, and it is negative if a person prefers not attaining it. Vroom emphasizes that valence refers to an outcome's anticipated reward value rather than its actual reward value when obtained.

Vroom argues that outcomes achieve valence because of their perceived relationship to ends. Drawing on the work of Peak (1955), he goes on to state that if an outcome is believed to lead to desired consequences or to prevent undesired consequences, it will be positively valued. If, on the other hand, it is believed to lead to undesired consequences or to prevent desired consequences, it will be negatively valued. This view is, of course, similar to the one presented in Chapter 2, where it was argued that outcomes like pay gain their importance from their ability to satisfy needs. The chief difference is that our instrumentality view of valence or importance is stated in terms of needs and motives, while Vroom's theory is not. Vroom ignores the issue of how outcomes ultimately obtain their

TABLE 5-1. Expectancy theories of motivation

Theorist	Determinants of Impulse to Action
Tolman	Expectancy of goal, demand for goal
Lewin	Potency × valence
Edwards	Subjective probability × utility
Atkinson	Expectancy × (motive × incentive)
Rotter	Expectancy, reinforcement value
Vroom	Expectancy × valence; where valence is (instrumentality × valence)
Peak	Instrumentality × attitude (affect)

valence. That is, he never considers how far back one has to go from an outcome, such as pay, to find the original object upon which its valence is based. In a sense, Vroom's theory continually passes the buck from one object to another and never says what the original source or sources of the valence of all these objects are.

Vroom defines "expectancy" as a momentary belief concerning the likelihood that a particular act will be followed by a particular outcome. Hence, like other expectancy theorists, he sees an expectancy as a response-stimulus, or response-outcome association. Expectancies can be described in terms of their strength. Maximal strength (1) is produced by a subjective certainty that the act will be followed by the outcome, while minimal strength (0) is produced by a subjective certainty that the act will not be followed by this outcome.

Like other expectancy theorists, Vroom argues that expectancy and valence combine multiplicatively to determine motivation or force. The multiplication aspect of the theory is important; it means that unless both valence and expectancy are present in some degree, there will be no force. When either or both are 0 the product will be 0; and motivation will be 0. If, for example, a person wants to perform well but does not feel that his effort will result in good performance, he will have no motivation to perform. Similarly, if a person believes that his effort will lead to good performance but good performance is not attractive to him, he will not be motivated.

Any action may be seen to lead to a number of outcomes; hence, one must consider how the combination of the various outcomes influences behavior. Vroom's theory argues for taking the algebraic sum of the products of the valences of all outcomes and the strength of the expectancies that the act will be followed by the attainment of the outcomes. Thus he writes his theory as follows: Force $= \Sigma(E \times V)$ where the summation is across all outcomes. This is a key point in the theory for understanding the impact of pay on motivation since it means that just tying a valent reward like pay to performance will not be enough to motivate good performance. Pay can be highly valued and can be seen as closely related to performance; but if negative consequences, such as feeling tired or being rejected by a work group, are also perceived as related to good performance, there may be no motivation to perform. The significance of this conclusion will become apparent when we consider the impact of certain types of piece rate incentive plans. Finally, we should note that, according to Vroom, a person will be motivated to perform well in a situation only if performing well has the highest $E \times V$ force in that particular situation. Performing well can have a strong force, but if performing poorly has a stronger force, the person will not be motivated to perform well.

There is one area where Vroom's theory, and indeed all the expectancy theories, get into muddy water. This involves the distinction between acts and outcomes. As Vroom states, "The distinction ... is not, however, an absolute one. Actions are frequently described in terms of particular outcomes which they effect." Vroom goes on to say that he uses the term "action" to refer to behavior that is within the person's repertoire, for example, trying to perform well or seeking a job. He reserves the term "outcome" for distant events that are not under control, such as actually performing well or actually getting the job. Thus, the belief that trying to perform well will lead to performing well is an "expectancy," and the relationship between performing well and a reward (e.g., pay) is an "instrumentality" that affects the valence of performing well.

Others who have stated expectancy theories have taken different approaches. Porter and Lawler (1968a), for example, regard the perceived relationship between putting effort into performing well and receiving outcomes like pay as an expectancy. According to this view, the expectancy that putting forth effort will lead to outcomes is influenced by both the probability that putting effort into performing well will lead to good performance and the perceived probability that performing well will lead to the outcome. Thus, Vroom (1964) and Porter and Lawler (1968a) agree about what factors influence motivation, but they use a different terminology. In a sense, the particular terminology that is used is a function of whether an outcome like pay is seen as the goal or whether the performance itself is the goal. Porter and Lawler's usage emphasizes that pay or other outcomes are the goal, while Vroom's usage emphasizes the role of good performance as a goal.

None of the expectancy theories presented in Table 5-1 really provides a satisfactory way of distinguishing between acts and outcomes when job performance is taken into account. Tolman, for example, says that, for the rat running a maze, the goal is not successfully reaching the goal box, but obtaining the food that is there. He does not say why running into the goal box is the act, rather than trying to reach the goal box. Nor does he say why obtaining the food is the goal, rather than obtaining the goal box. He, like some other theorists, does not clearly state that obtaining the food is a function both of successfully reaching the box and the likelihood that the food actually will be there when the animal arrives. Atkinson (1964) uses the term "expectancy" to refer to both the likelihood that an action will result in successful performance and the likelihood that successful performance will result in such rewards as pay. This is somewhat misleading since it lumps together an action-outcome connection and an outcome-outcome connection and does not recognize that they are different and can vary independently of each other.

Much of the work on expectancy theory has tended to ignore the fact that trying to perform an act does not always lead to performing it. The perceived relationship between performing well and getting high pay often has been considered the only relevant expectancy (e.g., Galbraith & Cummings, 1967, Stagner & Rosen, 1965), and the issue of whether good performance is possible has been largely ignored. In many situations (e.g., in laboratory studies), trying to perform an act is equivalent to performing it; and in these situations motivation is determined by the degree to which performing the act leads to the reward, since expectancies are likely to be 1. In many situations, however, trying to perform an act does not always lead to performing it. For instance, good job performance does not automatically result from trying to perform well; hence, beliefs—the person's subjective probability—about whether or not it will must be taken into account.

Just the opposite mistake is also made. That is, the strength of the connection between pay and performance is ignored, and attention is focused upon the perceived probability that good performance will be possible. In laboratory studies where a subject is told that if he performs at a given level he will receive X amount of money, it is almost always assumed that the subject accepts this condition and, as a result, perceives a perfect relationship between his pay and his performance (see e.g., Adams, 1963b; Atkinson & Reitman, 1956). In some instances, this approach may be warranted, but it certainly is not justified in most field settings; just telling someone that performance and pay are related does not guarantee that he will perceive a perfect relationship between them. Vroom's and Porter and Lawler's discussions of expectancy theory make it clear that, if we are to understand the impact of pay on the motivation to perform effectively, we must consider people's beliefs about the likelihood that they can perform the act and their beliefs about whether performing the act will lead to high pay.

Perhaps the best way to summarize this discussion is to state the conditions that will have to prevail if pay is to motivate good job performance.

1. Employees must attach a high positive valence to pay. Chapter 2 discussed a number of factors that can influence how valent pay will in fact be for employees.
2. Employees must believe that good performance does in fact lead to high pay.
3. Employees must believe that the quality of their job performance reflects to a large extent how hard they are trying. In other words, they must feel that they can control the quality of their job performance. Unless this condition exists, employees will not believe that working hard will eventually lead to high pay.
4. Employees must see the positive outcomes tied to good performance

as greater than the negative ones. According to expectancy theory, when negative consequences are perceived to result from an action, the effect of positive outcomes can be canceled out. Thus, a pay program must create conditions in which a large number of outcomes with a high positive valence and a minimal number of outcomes with a negative valence are seen to be tied to performance.

5. Employees must see good job performance as the most attractive of all possible behaviors. Only then will they be motivated to direct their effort toward performing well. In other words, the force (where force $= E \times V$) toward performing well must be greater than the force toward acting in any other manner.

EQUITY THEORY

Adams (1963a, 1965) has developed a theory of equity that makes a number of interesting predictions about the effects of wage inequity on work output, work quality, and attitudes toward work. Although this theory is a general theory of social inequity, using the exchange model as its basis, it has been largely tested with respect to the effects of wage inequity. As noted earlier, Adams's theory is not a fully developed theory of motivation in the same sense as either drive or expectancy theory. Since it has focused on pay and because it makes some different predictions from those made by the other theories, however, it is important that we discuss it. In addition, some interesting research appears to support the theory. Its predictions seem to be particularly relevant to understanding the effects of offering various sizes of pay increases and to understanding the effects of paying different wage rates. It is in this context that we shall consider it.

Adams (1965) defines inequity as follows:

Inequity exists for Person whenever he perceives that the ratio of his outcomes to inputs and the ratio of Other's outcomes to Other's inputs are unequal. This may happen either (a) when he and Other are in a direct exchange relationship or (b) when both are in an exchange relationship with a third party and Person compares himself to Other. (P. 280)

Outcomes in the job situation include pay, fringe benefits, status, and the intrinsic interest of the job, etc. Inputs include how hard the person works, his educational level, his general qualifications for the job, etc. It must be remembered that what determines the equity of a particular input-outcome balance is the individual's perception of what he is giving and receiving, and this cognition may or may not correspond to an observer's perception or to reality.

Equity theory states that the presence of inequity will motivate an individual to achieve equity or to reduce inequity. Further, the strength of the motivation to reduce inequity will vary directly with the perceived magnitude of the imbalance experienced between inputs and outcomes. Feelings of inequity can be produced in a variety of ways and in a variety of situations. Adams, in his own research, has dealt with inequity produced by overpayment. The present discussion will also be limited to studies concerned with pay inequity, but will consider both over- and underpayment. Feelings of inequity can also be reduced in a variety of ways. Adams has tended to stress changes in productivity and work quality. These two methods of inequity reduction are, of course, ways for the person to alter his inputs. Although Adams has not emphasized the fact, a person can also alter his outcomes. For example, when a subject is paid on a piece rate, he can reduce his output, thereby reducing the amount he is paid. Other ways of reducing inequity include leaving the field, perceptually distorting either inputs or outcomes, and changing the object of comparison.

Not surprisingly, one important issue that equity theory has to deal with concerns what determines the kind of inequity reduction mode a person will choose (Weick, 1964, 1966). Thus, we must pay some attention to this issue. But the most crucial question for our discussion is, what does equity theory predict about the effects of inequity on job inputs—in particular, productivity and work quality?

Equity theory makes predictions concerning four different pay inequity situations. Persons can, of course, be either overpaid or underpaid; but equity theory stresses the point that their reaction to pay inequity will depend upon whether they are on a piece rate or an hourly pay system. According to the theory, overpayment on a piece rate wage will have a different effect on productivity from overpayment on an hourly rate. In the piece rate situation, if the subject increases his productivity he also increases his outcomes (money); in the hourly pay situation, this is not so, because pay and productivity are not directly related. Hence, in discussing the effects of pay inequity on productivity and work quality, we shall consider the four inequity conditions separately.

Overpayment: Piece Rate

Perhaps the most interesting prediction that Adams has made based upon equity theory is that in the piece rate situation, subjects who feel overpaid will produce less but do higher-quality work than subjects who feel equitably paid. Adams states that the overpaid subjects will try to increase their inputs in order to bring them into line with their outcomes, and as he points out, raising quality is one way of increasing inputs.

Lowered productivity is expected because there is usually a negative correlation between quality and quantity; thus high quality will typically lead to a reduction in quantity. It would also seem that subjects should be expected to restrict their productivity even where quantity and quality are unrelated, since in the piece rate situation high productivity leads to higher outcomes. Although this prediction is congruent with his theory, Adams has tended to reject it in his later writings (Adams, 1965), despite the fact that he presents no evidence which shows it to be invalid. At one time Adams (1963a, 1963b) seemed to feel that a desire to reduce outcomes could help explain the low production of overpaid subjects.

Underpayment: Piece Rate

The predictions of equity theory with respect to the effects of underpayment on a piece rate are less surprising perhaps than those made for overpayment. Adams argues that, when faced with a low piece rate, workers will produce large quantities of low-quality work. By doing this they will, of course, keep their inputs low yet raise their outcomes (money). This particular prediction can also be made from other theories of motivation, and thus it has stirred up less discussion than some of the other predictions made by this theory.

Overpayment: Hourly Rate

The hourly rate overpayment situation places the employee in quite a different situation from the piece rate overpayment situation. Since his pay outcomes are fixed, all that he can do to achieve equity is vary his inputs or try to decrease his nonfinancial outcomes. Adams has emphasized that people will strive to increase their inputs by raising both the quality and the quantity of their work. Thus, the prediction is that employees will work harder or be more motivated.

Underpayment: Hourly Rate

In the hourly rate underpayment situation, as in the overpayment situation, financial outcomes are fixed. To reduce inequity, the employee may increase his nonfinancial outcomes and/or decrease his inputs. He can, for example, raise his estimation of the intrinsic interest of the job and thereby increase his outcomes. If a subject chooses to reduce his inputs rather than raise his outcomes, then underpayment on an hourly rate should lead to less effective performance. Presumably, to reduce his inputs, the subject must lower the quantity and quality of his work.

Tables 5-2 and 5-3 present the predicted effects of inequitable payment on productivity and work quality. The predictions are: Overpayment will lead to higher quality in all situations and to higher productivity in the hourly rate situation. It will lead to lower productivity in the piece rate situation. Underpayment will lead to lower quality in all situations and to lower productivity in the hourly rate situation. In the piece rate situation, it will lead to high productivity.

COMPARISON OF EQUITY AND EXPECTANCY THEORY

The predictions derived from equity theory are striking in the degree to which they diverge from those of expectancy theory and drive theory. Much of the divergence arises because equity theory does not include a concept similar to that of either habit strength or expectancy. This difference accounts for the fact that, in the hourly rate situation,

TABLE 5-2. Effects of inequitable payment on productivity

	Hourly Rate Situation	Piece Rate Situation
Overpayment	↑	↓
Underpayment	↓	↑

TABLE 5-3. Effects of inequitable payment on quality

	Hourly Rate Situation	Piece Rate Situation
Overpayment	↑	↑
Underpayment	↓	↓

equity theory predicts that changing the amount of pay will affect motivation; expectancy theory and drive theory do not predict that it will necessarily have any effect. In expectancy theory terms, an increased hourly rate is expected to lead to increased motivation only if the amount of the rate and future rates are seen to depend upon job performance. This comes about because of the multiplicative combination of E and V; increasing the amount of money will increase V, but this will affect motivation only if E is greater and 0. The clear suggestion of equity theory is that changes in pay rate will affect motivation even when E is 0. In fact, statements of the theory make only a passing reference to any need to consider a concept such as expectancy or subjective probability.

The theories also make some sharply differing predictions about the effects of changing reward size when rewards are dependent upon performance (i.e., in the piece rate situation). Both drive theory and expectancy theory have usually been interpreted as predicting that, other things equal, an increase in reward size should lead to increased motivation to act in whatever way leads to the reward. Equity theory suggests that just the opposite may happen in the piece rate situation, where pay depends upon productivity. It suggests that when the piece rate is seen as too large, productivity will decrease. Thus, it argues that increases in reward size can actually lead to decreases in the frequency of the behavior upon which the reward depends. In other words, a large piece rate may lead to lower productivity. Equity theory also makes no specific prediction about whether production should be higher under an hourly rate or a piece rate system, while it would seem to follow from expectancy theory that production typically should be higher under a piece rate system.

As a way of putting the predictions of equity theory into perspective, let us see how the theory would affect the design of pay systems. First of all, with respect to raises, equity theory suggests that it might be unwise to offer a very large raise to employees for performing well. Presumably, if they feel the reward is inequitably large, they might avoid working hard in order to avoid receiving an inequitable amount of money. On the other hand, the theory suggests that people should actually be given very large raises or high salaries to motivate them. Presumably, large raises will lead to feelings of inequity and a tendency to increase productivity in order to reduce the inequity. As far as piece rate situations are concerned, the theory clearly suggests that if rates are too low, a lot of low-quality work will result, while if they are too high, a small amount of very high-quality work will result. Thus, the productivity of piece rate workers can be increased by cutting the rate or setting it low, although this will reduce quality. A company that is having quality problems with its piece rate workers, however, should try increasing its rates, since this should lead to high quality but some loss of productivity.

TWO-FACTOR THEORY

Modern two-factor motivation theory was originally defined in a book by Herzberg, Mausner, Peterson and Capwell (1957), which stated that job factors could be classified according to whether they contribute primarily to satisfaction or dissatisfaction. Two years later, Herzberg, Mausner, and Snyderman (1959) published the results of a research study which they interpreted as supportive of the theory. Prior to the work of Herzberg and his collaborators, Hersey (1936) developed a two-factor theory. Hersey did little research on his version of the theory, however, and it received virtually no attention in the literature. Herzberg's theory, on the other hand, has generated a great deal of research and has attracted a tremendous amount of attention.

According to the theory, satisfiers, or "motivators," as they have been labeled more recently, have the power to motivate outstanding job performance. Dissatisfiers, or maintenance factors, restrict productivity and interfere with it if they are not at an adequate level. Herzberg, Mausner, and Snyderman (1959) further state that satisfiers contribute mainly to job satisfaction, and that they tend to be associated with particularly gratifying and motivating experiences. Examples of these are achievement, recognition, advancement, and responsibility. Dissatisfiers, on the other hand, contribute mainly to job dissatisfaction. For them to occur, conditions must be particularly bad or in some way not "hygienic." Examples of these factors are working conditions, company policies, and supervision. Pay, interestingly, appeared about equally as a satisfier and as a dissatisfier in the data reported both in 1957 and in 1959, but in a somewhat circuitous interpretation of their results Herzberg et al. classified it as a dissatisfier.

Since 1959, a great deal of research has been directed toward testing whether separate factors contribute to satisfaction and dissatisfaction. We will review some of this research in Chapter 13 when we discuss pay satisfaction. Here, it is sufficient to note that the studies have provided only mixed support for the theory. Those by Myers (1964) and Schwartz, Jenusaitis, and Stark (1963) have offered some support, while others (e.g., Wernimont, 1964; Dunnette, Campbell, & Hakel, 1967) have failed to support it. (For a review of this literature see House & Wigdor, 1967; Whitsett & Winslow, 1967; Winslow & Whitsett, 1968). Thus, the validity of this aspect of the Herzberg theory remains in doubt.

Significantly, while considerable research has tried to determine which factors contribute to satisfaction and dissatisfaction, little attention has been directed at testing the motivation and performance implications of the theory. However, most of the implications for practice that have been drawn from the theory (e.g., Herzberg, 1966) concern how the motivation to perform can be increased. The original study of Herzberg et al. (1959) did ask subjects (engineers and accountants) to report how various job factors affected their performance. The subjects reported that the presence of satisfiers boosted performance, while the presence or dissatisfiers reduced it. Overall, satisfiers were reported to have the strongest impact upon performance. At best, this is weak evidence that these job factors influence performance as suggested by the theory. Only self-reports of performance were used; and in many cases the managers were reporting on events that had happened some time prior to the date of the interviews. The evidence, although not at all conclusive, at least suggests the kinds of experiences (with pay, for example) that might lead to a strong motivation to perform effectively. Unfortunately, Herzberg, et al. did not develop any theoretical concepts to explain why the job factors should affect performance. Their theory contains little explanation of why outcomes are attractive, and it fails to consider the importance of associative connections in determining which of a number of behaviors a person will choose to perform in order to obtain a desired outcome. Thus, in the strictest sense of the term, it is not a theory of motivation at all; rather it is a theory primarily concerned with explaining the determinants of job satisfaction and dissatisfaction.

Of special interest for the present discussion are the kinds of experiences with pay that Herzberg et al. (1959) reported were seen by the respondents as leading to high performance. Although salary tended to appear as both a satisfier and a dissatisfier, it was mentioned in a special way when it appeared as a satisfier and motivator of good performance. Specifically, it was mentioned as something that went along with a person's achievement on the job. "It was a form of recognition; it meant that the individual was progressing in his work." Thus in these situations, pay appeared to be seen by the individuals as resulting from good performance and on-the-job accomplishment, and it meant that high pay itself was taken as a sign of accomplishment and recognition. Seeing pay as a satisfier, therefore, apparently means that high pay, recognition and achievement are seen as contingent upon job performance. It is not surprising, therefore, that in the Herzberg et al. study the effective performers were those who saw pay as a satisfier, or in terms of expectancy theory, those who saw pay and other rewards as dependent upon their own efforts to perform well. Interpreted this way, the results of the Herzberg et al. study on performance and on pay as a satisfier appear to be congruent with expectancy theory.

When pay was mentioned as a dissatisfier, it was also mentioned in a somewhat special way. It was "unfairly low" or "unjustifiable." When subjects saw it as unfairly low, they reported that they reduced their work level; thus, Herzberg et al. stress that pay has great power to reduce performance. Perhaps the most striking thing about this prediction is its similarity to the predictions of equity theory about hourly rate underpayment. Equity theory clearly stresses that unfairly low pay will lead the employee to reduce his inputs. On this point, equity theory and two-factor theory seem to converge. As already stated, the two-factor view of pay as a satisfier seems to converge with expectancy theory. Thus, in one sense two-factor theory says nothing that is not said by equity theory and expectancy theory. But this is an unfair way to state the case, since two-factor theory clearly is saying something different. Its attractiveness with respect to pay actually lies in the fact that it combines some of the predictions of equity theory and some of the predictions of expectancy theory into a single theory that is quite different from either of the others.

To be valid, two-factor theory must establish that pay can operate both as a satisfier and as a dissatisfier to influence performance; if it operates as only one of these, then the theory does not make any prediction about the effects of pay on motivation that is distinctly different from predictions made by equity theory or expectancy theory. Note that this discussion concerns pay only; it is clear that with respect to other potential motivators (e.g., security, working conditions, leadership, and autonomy) two-factor theory does make predictions that are quite different from those which would be made by either equity or expectancy theory. This comes about because it classifies objects as either satisfiers or dissatisfiers and because, unlike expectancy theory and drive theory, it does not stress the importance of relating rewards to performance.

Chapter 6
THE
MOTIVATION
MODEL

In Chapter 5 the theoretical work related to understanding how pay can motivate behavior was reviewed as a first step in developing a Motivation Model to explain how pay can be a source of motivation. Perhaps the most striking aspect of the theories reviewed was the similarity between drive theory and expectancy theory. As has often been pointed out, there are few situations in which the two lead to different predictions. These two theories are the best developed, enjoy the widest acceptance, and have survived for the longest time. There is, of course, a good reason: They can handle most of the findings in the literature on motivation. Therefore, a motivation model concerned with pay can profitably use one of them as its starting point. But which one?

The choice between drive theory and expectancy theory is an important and difficult one. Despite the similarities between the predictions of the theories, it is not reasonable to conclude that it makes no difference which theory is used. There are good reasons for choosing one of these theories over the other, although it must be admitted that the reasons involve some rather fine points and that to some extent the choice must rest, at least partially, on one's personal thinking style and preferred way of approaching data. My own inclination is definitely toward expectancy theory. There are some good data-based reasons and some good theoretical reasons for this preference, but it should be stressed that the broad general agreement of the two theories makes the choice difficult.

In this chapter, we shall consider first some of the points that have led to the decision to use expectancy theory as a basis upon which to build our motivation model. Then we shall develop our model.

EXPECTANCY THEORY VERSUS DRIVE THEORY

Expectancy theory and drive theory differ in the way they handle anticipated threats (Atkinson, 1964). This is perhaps the topic on which the two theories agree least. Expectancy theory explains avoidance behavior in terms of perceived negative consequences which suppress or dampen the tendency to perform a given act. Thus, quota restriction and gold-bricking which are so often observed where workers are on a piece rate, are explained as follows: the motivation to produce highly is dampened by such perceived negative consequences of high productivity as social ostracism and rate changes. Drive theory, on the other hand, explains avoidance behavior in terms of anticipatory emotional reactions that have the same functional properties as anticipatory goal reactions. Thus, drive theory emphasizes the nonspecific exciting effects of anticipatory emotional reactions, such as fear, and the specific avoidance habits elicited by the internal stimulus produced by the fear response. The two theories thus differ sharply in the role they assign the emotional response of fear. Drive theory gives it a directing role in terms of selecting specific avoidance behavior and says there must be an anticipatory emotional reaction in order for behavior to be motivated. Expectancy theory does not state that fear must be present in order to be a cause of behavior. It stresses that fear can be a suppressant force and can motivate avoidance behavior when it is perceived to be a consequence of behavior. Expectancy theory sees the emotional reaction itself as a result of behavior or as a symptom rather than as motivating it.

There is some evidence from the research on animals which suggests that the expectancy explanation of avoidance behavior is superior. Basically, the argument rests upon the fact that avoidance behavior occurs so rapidly that it is difficult to imagine that any kind of emotional reaction has taken place. Solomon, Kamin, and Wynne (1953), for example, point out that avoidance behavior in dogs takes place so quickly (nine-tenths of a second in some cases) that it is hard to argue that any emotional reactions have taken place to provide the drive needed to motivate the behavior. Since expectancy theory does not argue that a fear reaction is necessary to motivate behavior, these data pose no problem for it. Finally, there is a great deal of evidence on the persistence of avoidance reactions. An animal that is shocked will continue for hundreds of trials to avoid an area where it was once shocked, even though it is never shocked again. This finding is predictable from expectancy theory, since nothing has been done to change the animal's beliefs about the consequences of behaving certain ways in that situation. Drive theory, on the other hand, has to argue that the emotional response of fear will continue to be present and motivate the animal for all these trials. This seems hard to accept, since after a while the avoidance responses become automatic, and much of the surface evidence of fear disappears.

The expectancy theory approach to explaining avoidance behavior is particularly appealing when the effects of pay-incentive systems are considered. In the piece rate situation, for example, avoidance of high productivity develops and continues, although a real fear or emotional response does not seem to be present. Under many piece rate systems it seems to be generally accepted that high productivity will lead to negative consequences, even though many of the employees have not, in fact, ever experienced the negative consequences that are supposed to stem from high productivity. Merely perceiving the situation this way seems to be enough to prevent employees from producing highly. This is quite predictable and comprehensible from expectancy theory, since the theory stresses the importance of considering the perceived negative consequences of an act. But it is much more difficult for drive theory to handle. Can these employees really be experiencing anticipatory emotional reactions despite the fact that they have never actually experienced the fear-producing situation? It is also not clear how drive theory can explain the avoidance of high productivity by many workers when, in fact, they have never actually experienced a negative consequence as a result of high productivity. Drive theory undoubtedly can explain these phenomena, but they can be explained by expectancy theory much more directly.

Extensive research has been done on the relationship between beliefs about how pay is determined and job performance. This research particularly supports expectancy theory and provides a second reason for preferring it (Lawler & Porter, 1967a). The research shows that verbal statements about the importance of pay and about how high pay is obtained are directly related to performance. It shows that a multiplicative combination of these two kinds of attitudes is the best predictor of performance. These findings are perfectly predictable from expectancy theory, since it emphasizes the importance of knowing a person's response-outcome beliefs and of combining them multiplicatively with the perceived value of the outcomes. Drive theory, on the other hand, stresses the importance of considering $_sH_R$ and how $_sH_R$ combines multiplicatively with drive. It does not stress the importance of the awareness of response-reward connections, and thus it does not lead one to look at these in order to predict behavior. It emphasizes that S-R associations are strengthened by appropriate rewards which do not necessarily have to be related to responses on a conscious level. Working from drive theory, one would be much more likely to look at S-R habit strength than at response-outcome connections in order to predict behavior. There is no evidence to indicate that looking at employees' $_sH_R$ is a particularly fruitful way of studying how pay influences motivation, while there is evidence that looking at response-reward connections is. The research on response-outcome beliefs thus by no means disproves drive theory, but it provides one reason for preferring expectancy theory.

Drive theory and expectancy theory also differ in the degree to which they indicate that the effects of anticipated goals can be generalized. As has been pointed out, drive theory basically states that a drive or an anticipatory goal reaction acts to motivate all responses (habits) that are elicited in a situation. Thus, the strength of the motivation to perform well can be increased by the anticipation of goals that are in no way conditioned to or related to performance. Expectancy theory, on the other hand, does not argue for such a generalization of arousal states. It argues that a person's motivation to perform an act is a function only of the valence of those rewards which are seen to be related to performing that act. The evidence on pay seems, in general, to fit the expectancy theory view better. A study made by Atkinson (1958) is a good example of the research that follows directly from the expectancy theory approach. Atkinson found that, when both achievement motivation and money were brought to bear in an experimental setting, performance was higher than when either one alone was involved. Both money and feelings of achievement were seen to result from good performance, and thus, both contributed to the motivation to perform well.

Similar data have been obtained from many of the expectancy theory research studies (e.g., Galbraith & Cummings, 1967; Lawler & Porter, 1967a). These studies found that motivation is highest when a number of valued rewards are seen to be connected to performance. The findings are more directly in line with the expectancy theory emphasis on the specific motivating effects of the anticipation of rewards than with the drive theory orientation toward generalized drive level. None of the pay studies have shown that the anticipation of rewards that are not related to performance can affect the motivation to perform. Nor have they shown that the general drive level of a person can affect motivation. In short, none of the pay research actually provides support for the concept of a generalized drive level affecting motivation, while a large part of it supports the view that motivation is related to an additive combination of the valence of the rewards that are seen to be tied to performance. This does not prove that drive theory is incorrect; it is merely one more example of the fact that, on the whole, the evidence is more congruent with expectancy theory.

Expectancy theory has been criticized because it fails to specify how people learn what is appropriate behavior in different stimulus situations. Drive theory goes to great lengths to specify just how $_sH_R$ develops and how it can be altered. Atkinson (1964) highlights this problem when he discusses his theory of achievement motivation and its applicability to the ring toss game. His theory of achievement motivation formulates the choice problem as one involving conflict among tendencies to throw a ring from each of several lines that are marked on the floor before the subjects. In other words, it is assumed that the presence of these environmental stimuli will suggest the responses of throwing a ring from each of the several lines. But why does not a person who is strong in need for achievement stand backward on a line up close to the peg and throw the ring over his head? That would be a moderately difficult task, an intermediate risk. The answer is that he does not do this because it never occurs to him to do it. And in giving this answer to the question, we see that habit strength or some concept of learning must be included in motivation theory in order to specify what responses a subject will "consider" in a given situation.

The concept of habit serves this purpose in drive theory, but the problem has been systematically ignored in expectancy × value formulations. Perhaps this point is most clearly made in reference to one of the obvious deficiencies of the early economic theory on decision making. It was assumed that the individual was always completely informed concerning the nature of actions which could be undertaken in a given situation and of all possible consequences of each of the potential actions. This meant, specifically, that an individual would think of all possible actions he might undertake in a given situation and then consider all possible outcomes of all these actions before arriving at a decision. People, of course, do not operate this way. We must now recognize that leaving out habit strength, which defines the set of possible actions elicited (or entertained as possibilities) in a given situation, is a major deficiency of current statements of expectancy × value theories of motivation. This deficiency does not have to exist in our Motivation Model. As will be shown, the problem can be handled by our model even though it is based upon expectancy theory.

Expectancy theory has also been vague and ahistorical in orientation when it comes to specifying how people develop beliefs about the consequences of behaving in a certain manner. That is, expectancy theory has never clearly stated how people develop their response-stimulus subjective probabilities. Why, for example, do some people believe that if they perform well, there is a high probability of a pay raise, while others believe that there is little chance of a pay raise? The vagueness and ahistorical orientation of expectancy theory on this point are both a strength and a weakness. They are a strength because they allow the theory to handle data like those presented by Ayllon and Azrin (1965), which show that a simple verbal statement of what action-outcome connections exist can radically change the motivation level of people toward performing certain behaviors. Similarly, it can handle the fact that inductions like those used in laboratory studies of pay (e.g., Atkinson, 1958) can produce different degrees of motivation, depending upon how the relationship between pay and performance is described. Since expectancy theory focuses on how performance-reward connections influence behavior and not on how they come about, the fact that they often change quickly and can be established by simple verbal instructions presents no problem for the theory. All expectancy theory says is that, once they are established, they will affect behavior in a certain way.

On the other hand, the sudden changes that can take place in response-outcome subjective probabilities and the consequent changes in motivation are not particularly congruent with drive theory. Drive theory has always emphasized the slow building of associatons and the importance of previous experience and temporally close associations. This does not fit well with the ability of verbal statements of reward probabilities to influence performance. Still, many of the points made by drive theory about how associations come about do appear to be generally valid. Clearly, therefore, expectancy theory can profit by specifying some of the more obvious factors that influence response-outcome connections. Perhaps the best way to deal with the issue in building a theory or model of pay as a source of motivation is to take advantage of expectancy theory's lack of specificity and build into the model some points about how response-outcome connections are developed and influenced.

Expectancy theory has also tended to be vague about what factors determine the valence of outcomes. As we said in Chapter 2, it is possible to include in expectancy theory some statements regarding this matter; in fact, we did this in developing our Model of the Importance of Pay. Drive theory, on the other hand, has tended to specify when and how objects become rewards. It has talked in terms of the ability of objects to reduce certain primary and secondary drives. In explaining the behavior of animals, this aspect of drive theory may well be more of an advantage than a disadvantage. When it comes to explaining the role of pay in motivating job performance, however, this facet of drive theory is limiting, because it is difficult to incorporate some needs, such as those for self-actualization or autonomy, into drive theory. On the other hand, because of the vagueness of expectancy theory in explaining how objects obtain valence, it is easy to incorporate them into expectancy theory. This point is particularly relevant when the data from equity theory experiments are considered (Adams, 1965). On the surface these data do not seem to fit into either the drive theory approach or the equity theory approach. However, if expectancy theory is modified to include equity as a factor influencing the valence of pay, these data can be handled (Lawler, 1968c). Drive theory presumably could also be modified in this manner, but a concept of equity does not fit as well with drive theory, since it has nothing in common with any of the drives or needs that are usually assumed by drive theory to give objects reward value.

In summary, the argument has been made that the expectancy theory approach provides the best base upon which to build a model to explain how pay can motivate behavior. Admittedly, the choice of expectancy theory over drive theory is based upon some rather fine points, since the two theories make predictions that are basically similar. Our preference for expectancy theory is based upon the way it handles avoidance motivation, its forward-looking orientation, which has generated the research on expectancy beliefs, and its emphasis on the specificity of arousal states.

THE MOTIVATION MODEL

Figure 6-1 illustrates the proposed Motivation Model that is intended to explain how pay operates to motivate human behavior. The model basically follows an expectancy theory approach as elucidated earlier by Porter and Lawler (1968a), but it goes beyond what is normally included in an expectancy theory. For example, it includes some statements about how objects acquire valence, and it takes past learning into account much more than do other expectancy theories.

Our model shows that the motivation to perform at a given level is primarily determined by two variables. The first of these is the person's belief concerning the probability that if he puts effort into performing at that level, he will be able to perform at that level (Box 1). This subjective probability can vary from 1 (sure that effort will lead to intended performance) to 0 (sure that effort will not lead to intended performance). It is influenced by two factors: (1) the subject's self-esteem (Box 3), that is, his general beliefs about his ability to cope with and control his environment (Argyris, 1964; Rotter, 1966), and (2) his previous personal and observed experience in similar and identical stimulus situations (Box 4). The model also shows that a person's self-esteem is influenced by his job performance (loop *a*). In general, the higher the person rates his self-esteem and the more he has been able to perform effectively in similar stimulus situations, the higher will be his effort→performance (E→P)

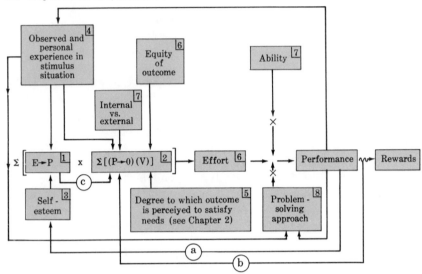

FIGURE 6-1. The Motivation Model.

subjective probability. The one qualification that is necessary here concerns people with very low self-esteem. Some individuals with extremely low self-esteem may distort reality and have high and unrealistic E→P probabilities.

The second factor that influences motivation is really made up of a combination of beliefs about what the outcomes of accomplishing the intended level of performance will be and the valence of these outcomes (Box 2). Figure 6-1 shows that a person's subjective probability that performance will lead to an outcome (P→O) should be multipled by the valence of that outcome (V). Finally, it suggests that the products of all probability times valence combinations should be added together for all outcomes that are seen to be related to the intended level of performance. This is represented in the model by the Σ sign. Valence is considered to vary from +1 (very desirable) to −1 (very undesirable) and the performance→outcomes probabilities to vary from +1 (performance is sure to lead to outcome) to 0 (performance does not lead to outcome). Hence, this second factor will be larger for good job performance, the more positively valued rewards are seen to be obtained as a result of good performance, and the less negatively valued outcomes are seen to result from good performance.

It is important to note when consideration is being given to the outcomes associated with performance that among other things, amount of effort put into the performance can influence the outcomes of the performance. Particularly when performing at a given level is perceived to require a large amount of effort or great sacrifices, this can be a very important influence on motivation. Outcomes like feeling tired can become associated with trying to perform at a given level, and this may decrease the person's motivation to perform at that level or even increase it if the person values the feeling. The point is that the process one must go through to perform at a particular level may lead to certain outcomes being associated with trying to perform at that level, and this may effect the motivation to perform at that level.

In Chapters 2, 3 and 4, some of the factors that can influence the valence of a reward or outcome such as pay were discussed. The points made there are relevant to the present discussion since the same factors must be included in our Motivation Model. The basic argument made in the earlier chapters was that the more an outcome is perceived to be capable of satisfying one or more of a set of needs, the more valued it will be (Box 5). Figure 6-1 also shows that the valence of outcomes can be influenced by the perceived fairness of the input-outcome balance (Box 6). This point is taken from Adams's work on equity theory. As will be shown in Chapter 8, where the specific research on equity theory is discussed in detail, this point is included in order to explain the effect of perceived inequity when piece rate payment is used. The work on hourly pay inequity can be explained by the basic expectancy model without reference to a concept of equity. The assumption here is that perceived overpayment can lead to a decrease in the valence of pay for some people. This suggests a curvilinear relationship between amount of pay and the valence of pay such that small amounts and very large amounts of pay may be less attractive than amounts that are perceived to be fair.

There has been surprisingly little research on the relative value, utility or attractiveness people place on different amounts of money. There has, however, been a long history of theorizing about it. Giles and Barrett (1970) have reviewed some of the theory and research, and they conclude that both the research and the theorizing contain a number of different points of view. For example, in 1928 Cramer postulated that the value of money might be a power function of the amount while Bernoulli hypothesized a logarithmic function.

Giles and Barrett also collected some interesting preliminary data on the utility of different size "merit pay increases" to 64 professional-level employees in one company. Overall, their results gave the most support to the power function model and the least to the logarithmic function model. But they also found some people who seemed to operate in accordance with equity theory. According to Giles and Barrett, "a surprising finding was that seven of the employees did not report satisfaction as a monotonically increasing function of merit increase. For those seven employees more money did not bring more satisfaction, and for some, more money would actually result in a decrease in utility." Thus it seems that for some people very large raises or amounts of money do have less value than small ones, although, based on this preliminary study, it is impossible to determine how many people in the general population react this way to raises. It is also not clear how important an influence the fact that the subjects were asked to react to a "merit" increase had on the results. It is quite possible that the curvilinear relationship would not have appeared if it had not been called a merit increase, since, as has been stressed, the meaning of pay to employees is influenced by the basis on which it is determined.

A person's performance→outcome subjective probability beliefs are shown to be influenced by two factors. One is an individual difference factor that Rotter and others (Lefcourt, 1966) have referred to as a belief in internal versus external control (Box 7). According to this view, some people see the world in terms of internal control (that is, they act on the world), while others see it in terms of external control (the world acts on them). It would seem that the more a person is oriented toward internal control, the more he will feel that performance will lead to outcomes, while the more he is oriented toward external control, the less likely he will be to have high performance→outcome subjective probabilities. Some evidence for this has been found in my studies of managers; managers exhibiting high internal control seem to see stronger performance→outcome associations than those exhibiting high external control. The theory, as presented in Figure 6-1, also shows a feedback loop from the strength of the connection between performance and outcomes to the P→O probability (loop *b*). This is included to illustrate the importance of learning in determining what a person's performance→outcome probabilities will be in a given situation. Clearly, the degree to which performance, in similar situations, has in the past been closely followed by outcomes will influence the person's beliefs about what future outcomes performance will lead to.

The two factors that so far have been said to influence the strength of a person's motivation to perform effectively are briefly: (1) the person's belief that his effort can be converted into performance and (2) the net attractiveness of the events that are felt to come from good performance. These two factors are said to combine multiplicatively, because if the first is 0 or if the second is 0 or negative, there will be no motivation to perform effectively. On the other hand, the greater the product of these two factors, the greater will be the motivation to perform. Thus, if a person does not believe that good performance will follow from his effort, he will not be motivated to perform well, even though he feels that good performance will lead to a number of desirable outcomes. Similarly, unless good performance is seen to lead to positive outcomes, the person will not be motivated to perform well, even if he is sure he can perform well by putting forth effort.

Although on the surface it would seem that motivation will be greatest when the E→P probability is high, there are some situations where this may not, in fact, be true. Atkinson (1964) and McClelland (1961) have suggested that under some conditions the highest motivation may result when effort is seen to have only a 50-50 chance of leading to good performance. Under this condition, a whole set of different rewards get tied to performance that are not involved when there is certainty that effort will lead to good performance. Specifically, feelings of achievement, accomplishment, and growth are seen to result from successful performance when there is a less than perfect relationship between effort and performance. Thus, in some instances, motivation may be highest when the effort→performance probability is not perfect because the perceived consequences of good performance may be greatest when the first term is less than 1. If, as seems likely, once the first term exceeds .5, further increase in it only serves to decrease the value of the second term, then the highest motivation will come where the first term is around .5. This influence of the E→P term on the P→O term is indicated by a line (labeled *C*) joining the two in the model.

When attention is given to the strength of a person's motivation to perform at a given level, it is necessary in some cases to look at more than just the E→P and P→O probabilities that are associated with the person achieving that level of performance. When the E→P probability is less than 1, that is, when a person is not sure he can convert his effort into the level of performance he is considering, then it may be necessary to take into account the subjective probability that trying to perform at a given level will actually lead to performance at a different level. Where a person is trying to perform at a high level, this may mean taking into account the possibility that he will be unsuccessful and will perform at a low level. If other E→P probabilities are considered, they should be combined with the appropriate (P→O) (V) combinations for that level of performance. The results of such additional (E→P) [(P→O) (V)] combinations as are appropriate should be summed with the original one for the probability that trying to perform at a given level will actually lead to performing at that level. This is shown by the Σ sign that precedes the first term of the model.

Figure 6-2 gives an illustration of this point. It shows an example where the person considers the probability of successful performance to be .8 and unsuccessful performance to be .2. In this case, it is important to examine the two E→P probabilities and the outcomes that are seen to be associated with them. Normally, the E→P probabilities should sum to approximately 1 while the P→O probabilities will not.

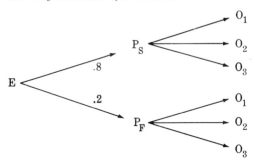

FIGURE 6-2. Example of a situation in which failure is possible.

Taking the E→P probability for failure into account would seem to be particularly important where trying but failing to perform at a given level has strong negative consequences. How motivated a person is to perform well on his job may be strongly influenced by (1) the probability he sees of failing to perform well, even though he tries, and (2) the consequences of trying to perform well and failing. He may feel that if he performs successfully he will obtain a number of positively valued outcomes. But his motivation to perform may be reduced by the fact that if he fails to perform at the high level, significant negative outcomes will come to him, outcomes that might not have come had he been content to try for minimum performance. Consider two hypothetical people, A and B. A feels there is a good chance that he can perform successfully on a task and also feels that if he does he will be rewarded. He feels that even if he fails to perform as well as he would like, he will receive some rewards. B, like A, feels that there is a good chance he can perform successfully on the task and that if he does he will be rewarded. B feels, however, that if he fails to perform successfully, significant negative outcomes will result—outcomes that would not occur if he did not try for the higher level of performance but tried to merely perform at a minimum level. He feels that trying for high performance and failing to achieve it will mean lower self-esteem, lower status among his colleagues and feeling tired because of the effort output. In terms of our model, A should be more motivated to perform the task at a high level than B. B is likely to decide not to try to perform at the high level because of the negative effects he sees associated with trying and failing. This is particularly likely to happen if performing at a minimum level leads to some positive consequences and few negative ones.

The strength of a person's motivation to perform correctly is most directly reflected in his effort, that is, in how hard he works. This effort expenditure may or may not result in good performance (Lawler & Porter,

1967a), since at least two factors determine whether effort is converted into performance. First, the person must possess the necessary ability to perform the job well. A number of authors (e.g., French, 1957; Lawler, 1966a; Locke, 1964; Maier, 1955, & Vroom, 1964) have argued that motivation and ability combine multiplicatively to determine performance. A similar view is presented in Figure 6-1. Ability (Box 7) is shown to combine multiplicatively with effort in order to stress the fact that if ability is 0 so will performance be 0. In other words, unless both ability and effort are high, there cannot be good performance. Great amounts of effort cannot make up for very low ability.

A second factor also is seen to intervene between effort and performance: the person's perception of how his effort can best be converted into performance (Box 8). It is assumed that this perception is learned through previous experience and is somewhat similar to the drive theory $_sH_R$ concept. This how-to-do-it perception can obviously vary widely in accuracy. It is shown to combine multiplicatively with effort in order to stress the point that unless it is accurate, performance will be 0 just as when ability is low. Some evidence to support this position has been provided by Lawler and Porter (1967a) and Porter and Lawler (1968a). Their studies have shown that where erroneous how-to-do-it perceptions exist, the performance of managers is low, even though their effort or motivation may be high. Numerous everyday examples of this phenomenon come to mind: the student who studies the lecture notes assiduously, but finds that the exam is based only upon the assigned reading; or the salesman who pushes the soft sell, but discovers that his boss is interested only in short-term results.

Although not shown explicitly in the model, situational factors often intervene between effort and performance. Such factors block the conversion of effort into performance. A breakdown of machinery, direct interference by other employees, etc., may act in this way.

The final link in the theory is represented by the wavy line that connects performance to rewards. It is drawn as a wavy line to indicate that rewards do not always follow directly from performance. This particular part of the model will be treated in greater detail in Chapter 13, where the relationship between satisfaction and performance is discussed in some detail. It is sufficient to note here that the theory does not see satisfaction as strongly affecting performance or motivation. The motivation to perform is determined by the perceived consequences of good performance and by a person's estimate of the probability that effort can be converted into successful performance.

Finally, a person will actually choose to perform well only if performing well is seen to lead to more positively valued outcomes or fewer negatively valued outcomes than performing at some other level. That is, a person will be expected to perform at the level that has the highest $\Sigma \, [\,(E{\rightarrow}P) \times \Sigma \, [\,(P{\rightarrow}0)\,(V)\,]\,]$ score for him. This means that a person will choose not to try to perform well, even though he feels that a lot of positive outcomes will result, if performing poorly will lead to outcomes with similar or greater valence. The difficulty of motivating someone to perform well is pointed out by the model. Since a person's E→P expectancy is lower for good than for poor performance, it is possible that many more positive rewards must be tied to good performance than to poor performance for a person to be motivated to perform well. In other words, since a person's E→P is usually lower for good performance than for bad, his $\Sigma \, [\,(P{\rightarrow}O)\,(V)\,]$ must be higher if he is to be motivated toward good performance.

Although not explicitly stated as part of the model, the valence of the outcomes that are perceived to come from good performance may influence, and be influenced by, both the perceived probability that they will come from good performance and the probability that E→P. Outcomes which are highly positive may be seen as less closely related to performance than those which are moderately valued. This might be described as a "life is not that simple" phenomenon or "things really are not that easy" view. Also, when very positive outcomes are seen to stem from performance, they may lead to a low perceived connection between effort and the performance needed to obtain the outcomes. This effect is similar to a "you don't get something for nothing" phenomenon or a Protestant ethic belief that you have to work hard for valuable things. It may also be that E→P expectancies can influence the valence of outcomes that are seen to stem from performance. The evidence discussed in Chapter 3 indicates that low E→P expectancies may lead to higher valence, while high E→P expectancies may lead to lower valence. In other words, you really value only what you have to struggle for. Much of this is just speculation and, for that reason, is not included in the model. It does, however, point to an interesting and virtually unexplored area of research. Specifically, research is needed on the degree to which the valence of outcomes and their perceived relationship to performance affect each other and on the degree to which they both influence and are influenced by the expectancy that effort leads to performance.

MAN AS A "SATISFICIER" AND LIMITED IN HIS RATIONALITY

The economic man view of the nature of man pictures man as totally rational. There are no limits to the computations he can go through in order to determine which behavior he should attempt. He is fully aware of all the alternative behaviors and of all the outcomes that will stem from them. He also has clear preferences among these outcomes. Thus any decision he makes is based on full information and is likely to be the optimal one. Further, his decisions will appear rational to an observer who is aware of his preferences. We must distinguish this view from the one presented in our model.

Simon (1957), among others, has pointed out that the economic man view does not present a realistic picture; people simply do not behave in this manner. They do not have full knowledge either of all possible behaviors or of all outcomes. They are not capable of making highly complex computations every time they have to make a difficult decision, and their behavior is not always obviously rational to observers.

Does this mean that man's behavior in organizations is irrational and unpredictable? No, what it seems to mean is that man's behavior is generally predictable but that it does not always appear to be rational or optimal to others. Simon argues that man's behavior is directed more toward "satisficing" than toward "optimizing." By this he means that man generally looks for a course of behavior that is satisfactory or "good enough" and when he finds it he acts. An individual does not continue to search until he has considered all the alternatives and then pick the optimal one. Rather, because of the difficulty of arriving at an optimal strategy, man seems to be oriented toward "satisficing"; at times he has to simplify the world so that he can deal with it. It is beyond his cognitive response capacity to consider all the complexities of the real world in making a decision. In terms of our model this means that man may not consider all performance and effort levels that are possible on his job.

Man's behavior may not always appear to be rational to the observer, but there is reason to believe that it is intended to be rational and is seen as rational by the actor. It may not appear to be rational because the observer may not place the same value on outcomes that the actor does. The observer may see different P→O connections. He may see different E→P connections. He may consider totally different alternative behaviors. Finally he may set a different level at which he is willing to stop his search and act; thus he may be more easily satisfied or harder to satisfy. The actor, however, intends his behavior to be rational and he sees it as rational. It represents his best attempt to deal rationally with the world as he sees it. Because of this, his behavior can be predicted if we know how he perceives the situation and how he values various outcomes. Our Motivation Model stresses the fact that people base their actions on their perception of the situation, and their perception is based both on their own characteristics and on characteristics of the situation. Therefore, behavior is a function of both the person and the situation.

In using our Motivation Model we must remember that people do not consider all alternatives and that they "satisfice" rather than "optimize." When people are considering whether to try a behavior, such as performing effectively, they might not take into account all the outcomes associated with that behavior. Thus, if we used the model and tried to predict a person's behavior by gathering full data on all his perceptions and all the relationships that exist, we might incorrectly predict his behavior because we would have built a more complex model than a person in fact uses. It must be remembered that man bases his behavior on perceptions that are simplified and that he does not consider all factors. Thus, carried to all its permutations and combinations, our model would undoubtedly be much more complicated than the models that people actually use. The model of course does not have to be carried to all the combinations. It can be viewed as considering a limited number of alternatives, just as people do. The important thing the model does is to show the kinds of cognitions people have and how these interact to influence behavior.

The Motivation Model does not purport to explain all the data available on human motivation, but it does purport to be able to do a good job of explaining the evidence with respect to how pay motivates behavior. To the degree that it can explain the data on pay and stimulate future research, it should be judged a useful contribution. It goes further than previous expectancy theories in specifying how subjective probabilities and valences come about: It leads to more specific predictions and to a larger number of predictions. This is an advantage, since it means that more can be said; but it also involves an element of risk, since there is a greater probability that it can be proved wrong. In the next chapter, we shall relate the model to the research that has been done on pay as a source of motivation.

Chapter 7
PAY
AND
JOB
PERFORMANCE:
THE
RESEARCH
EVIDENCE

Research on the ability of pay to motivate job performance has centered on four issues, all of which relate to important parts of the Motivation Model presented in Chapter 6. The first issue and the one which has been most heavily researched concerns the effects of *actually* tying pay more closely to employee performance. The second deals with the effect of changing the size of the pay reward offered for a certain kind of performance. The third concerns the relationship between employee expectancy and valence beliefs about pay, on the one hand, and motivation and performance, on the other. Finally, a number of recent studies have tested the predictions that are derivable from equity theory. These will be reviewed in Chapter 8. The present chapter will be devoted to the research on the first three issues and the way it relates to our Motivation Model.

TYING PAY TO PERFORMANCE

A surprisingly large number of studies have dealt with the effect of tying pay to performance. Typically, they have used productivity as the criterion of effective performance, but some have considered work quality, effort, or other measures. As we shall see, although there is a great deal of research evidence, much of it is not of very high quality, and there are many important questions that remain unanswered. Perhaps the one criticism that applies to most of the studies is that they are nothing more than case studies, lacking any kind of control group that could be used for comparison purposes. Study after study simply reports that a certain kind of incentive plan worked in a given company. In addition to having no control group, many studies report on companies that have changed their pay system as well as a number of other factors at the same time. Thus, it is impossible to determine which factor was responsible for any performance changes.

One of the clear predictions derivable from our model concerns the effect of tying pay to performance. As long as pay is valued and as long as employees accurately perceive the connection between pay and performance, actually tying pay more closely to performance should lead to a stronger motivation to perform effectively. There are innumerable approaches to tying pay closely to job performance, and it appears from the literature that most of them have been tried at one time or another. Many of them are very much alike and, as a result, can be grouped for discussion purposes. It is important, however, to discuss separately those plans which relate individual performance to individual pay and those which relate group performance to some level of group reward. In the group plans, everyone in a given group gets the same pay, regardless of individual contribution, since pay is tied to the performance of the total group. The evidence clearly suggests that the difference between the two plans is significant both in terms of how they are seen by employees and in terms of their effects. It is also worthwhile to distinguish between two kinds of group plans. One type is based upon work group performance, or what Porter and Lawler (1965) have called "subunit performance," while another type, for example, the Scanlon Plan, is based upon the performance of a total organization, usually a whole company or major division or plant. Some pay plans combine these approaches by paying an individual a bonus based upon his performance, but using organization performance to determine how much bonus money will be available. In our discussion, the research evidence on individual, subunit, and organization-wide incentive schemes will be considered separately. The research studies have not typically been concerned with pay programs that involve combinations of these approaches and by separating the studies in this manner, we should be able to get an understanding of the different impact each of the plans has.

Individual Pay Plans

The best-known individual incentive plan is the piece rate approach, in which payment is tied to the number of units produced by the worker. Literally thousands of piece rate plans have been devised and put into practice: differential piece rate plans, multiple piece rate plans, and a variety of task and premium bonus systems, such as the Gantt Task-

Bonus Plan, the Bigelow Plan, the Emerson Efficiency Plan, and the Parkhurst Differential Bonus System. It is beyond the scope of this book to describe each of these plans. The interested reader should look at some of the basic reference material in this area, such as the work of Marriott (1957), Lytle (1942), Balderston (1930), Z. C. Dickinson (1937), and Reitinger (1941). It is safe to say that all piece rate incentive plans are based upon some type of measurement of what constitutes normal or standard production on a given job. Such a measurement is needed for determining how much to pay for each piece in simple piece rate plans and for determining the time savings that result from above-average performance in standard time plans. The difficulty of measuring performance and arriving at time standards and equitable piece rates has been a continuing concern of behavioral scientists interested in pay plans (see, e.g., Viteles, 1953). Certainly, time standards and piece rates are not based solely upon *objective, accurate, reliable,* and *verifiable* data, and because of this they can be a source of unending controversy. Perhaps the one open question with respect to such measures concerns the degree of their susceptibility to error. Industrial engineers often claim an accuracy of plus or minus 5 percent, while Whyte (1955) and other behavioral scientists suggest that the errors are usually much larger.

The piece rate plan is not the only form of individual incentive plan. In fact, it may be the second most commonly used plan. Raises based upon individual job performance, under a merit system, probably constitute the most frequently used type. Under such a system, an employee's salary is adjusted regularly, based upon his performance during a preceding six- to twelve-month period. Performance is typically measured by a superior's evaluation.

As a number of studies have pointed out, both piece rate pay systems and merit raise pay systems are usually subjective and are often ineffective in their attempts to tie pay to performance. Neither can tie individual pay perfectly to performance. Still, compared with straight hourly pay and systems in which raises are not merit-based, they do achieve some success in relating pay to performance. Thus, it is possible to compare situations where employees are working under piece rate or merit raise conditions with situations where employees are paid on fixed-rate systems and find out something about the effect on performance of relating pay to performance. The prediction of our model is clear here. Tying pay more closely to performance should lead to a stronger motivation to perform whatever behavior is being rewarded.

Taylor's early work (1911) provides one of the first examples of how employee motivation can be changed by tying a worker's pay more closely to his performance. Taylor took a "thrifty Dutchman" who was shoveling pig iron and put him on a piece rate plan that offered more money if he shoveled more pig iron. Taylor's subject responded with a several hundred percent increase in productivity, thus providing dramatic evidence that tying pay to performance can affect motivation.

The results of Taylor's work and of other work like it were undoubtedly crucial in encouraging companies to install individual incentive plans. A survey by the National Industrial Conference Board (NICB, 1940) found that 51.7 percent of the 2,700 concerns surveyed used wage-incentive plans. Although these plans have not typically resulted in the kind of performance increase that Taylor obtained from his Dutchman, there is evidence to suggest that they have increased performance. A 1945 government survey of 514 wage-incentive plans in the United States showed that the change to these plans had resulted in average production increases of 39 percent and in average unit labor cost reductions of 11.6 percent (reported in Viteles, 1953). Another survey that was done in the New York area showed that the introduction of wage-incentive programs led to an average productivity increase of 41.5 percent (Despain, 1945). Large productivity increases due to the installation of wage-incentive plans have also been reported in a study of sixty-two companies in the Chicago area (Viteles, 1953).

Viteles (1953) cites the Murray Corporation as an example of what can happen when a company switches from a fixed-wage payment system to an individual incentive plan: Here the change led quickly to average plantwide production gains of 16 percent. Furthermore, accident rates fell, and cooperation with supervision increased. Many such cases have been reported, but all of them suffer from the same methodological flaw that is present in Taylor's original experiment. In addition to changing the Dutchman's pay, Taylor changed a number of other factors (e.g., how he did the work, the shape of his shovel). In the Murray Corporation, the introduction of wage incentives was accompanied by the formation of new standards (which meant new work procedures), by changes in shifts and length of workweek, and by a change in union-management relations. Thus, it is impossible to attribute the changes in productivity solely to the changes in the wage plan. This criticism can be made of most of the studies of companies that have changed from fixed-wage systems to incentive pay systems. As Viteles (1953) has pointed out, "The installation of a wage-incentive plan is generally accompanied by other changes in working conditions, personnel policies, and practices which are frequently major in character" (p. 29).

Undoubtedly, some of the reported productivity increases are due to changes in the wage system that resulted in pay being tied more closely to individual performance. Performance increases of the sizes reported in these studies have not typically been found when only non-pay-related changes are made. Such sizable increases seem to occur only when the nonpay changes are installed in conjunction with a pay incentive plan.

Fortunately, there are a few before-and-after studies that, methodologically, represent an improvement over the type discussed above. These have made an effort to see that only the pay system was changed in the period studied. From a methodological standpoint, however, these studies still leave something to be desired. They include no control group, and although they tried to ensure that nothing was changed except the pay system, it is impossible to control everything that happens.

Undoubtedly, the Western Electric studies are the most famous of the before-and-after studies (Roethlisberger & Dickson, 1939). One of the first experimental manipulations that was tried with the girls working in the relay assembly test room was the installation of a piece rate incentive plan. This was actually a group plan, but it was practically an individual one because of the small size of the group. Following the installation of this plan, production increased about 16 percent.

More important from our point of view, however, are the results from the second relay assembly test room. After the researchers found that in the original relay assembly test room they had obtained a large increase in productivity which could not be attributed to any one change they had instituted, they decided to conduct some additional studies in order to isolate the cause of the increased productivity. To do this, they set up a mica-splitting test room and a second relay assembly test room. The second relay assembly test is of particular interest, because it was designed to test the hypothesis that the results obtained in the first room were due to economic causes. In this room only the method of payment was changed; the workers were put on a piece rate payment plan. This resulted in a 12.2 percent increase in production. Although this increase was not as large as that in the original room, it suggests that a considerable amount of the increased productivity found in the original room might have been due to the change in the pay system. More importantly, however, it provides evidence that tying pay more closely to performance can result in increased productivity.

Wyatt (1934) reported a study in which he switched employees from a fixed weekly pay system to a competitive bonus system designed to relate pay to individual productivity. The immediate effect of introducing the bonus system was a production increase of 46 percent, a rate which was maintained throughout a fifteen-week period. A flat piece rate system was then introduced, and this resulted in a further increase in output of 30 percent. This new high level of production was maintained throughout the remaining twelve weeks of the study. In another well-controlled study, Burnett (1925) had four subjects work on a cross-stitching task for eight weeks, during which time they were paid at an hourly rate. Later the subjects worked for five weeks on a piece rate that was based upon their hourly output. To the best knowledge of the experimenter nothing was changed between the work periods except the method of payment. The immediate effect of adopting the piece rate was an average increase in output of 7.2 percent. This rose to 18 percent for the third week and to 20.2 percent for the fourth week. During the last two weeks, production fell off slightly, but the results clearly suggested that tying pay more closely to performance did bring about a substantial increase in productivity during the five-week experimental period.

In a more recent series of studies among psychotics in a mental hospital, Ayllon and Azrin (1965) tested the effects of tying token rewards to certain kinds of behavior (e.g., serving meals, doing clerical work). The tokens were like money in that they could buy certain privileges and commodities at the hospital commissary. This well-designed series of studies presents strong evidence that, by relating the giving of tokens to certain kinds of work behavior, it is possible to dramatically increase the frequency with which patients will volunteer to do work in a mental hospital. Figure 7-1, which is taken from one of these studies, shows how effective the token rewards were in influencing work behavior. It shows that during days 1 to 20, the receipt of tokens was contingent upon performance, and the forty-four patients worked a total of forty-five hours on an average day. On the first day that tokens were not contingent upon performance, the amount of work fell to about thirty-five hours. On the third day it went down to about twenty hours, and by day 36 of the experiment, it had dropped to one hour per day. When the token rewards were again made contingent upon performance (day 41), the time spent productively immediately increased to forty-five hours and stayed there during the next twenty days.

Finally, we have a few studies that are methodologically more sound than the ones we have covered. These not only restricted their comparisons to situations where changes were made only in the pay system, but they also employed a control group that operated concurrently with the group or groups performing under the incentive system. This type of control rules out the possibility that historical factors account for the changes observed by the researchers. With such a control group, for example, it cannot be argued that a performance difference between the incentive pay group and the control group is due to simply learning the job better or to some event in the outside world beyond the control of the experimenter. Where subjects are simply shifted from hourly to incentive pay systems and no control group is used, these possibilities can never be ruled out.

Atkinson and Reitman (1956) did an experiment with two conditions. In the first condition subjects were given achievement-arousing instructions for performing a task, but were offered no financial reward. In the second condition, subjects were given the same achievement-arousing instructions and were told that a $5 prize would be awarded for the

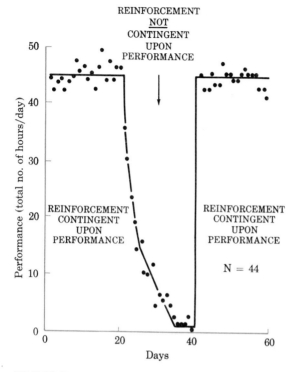

FIGURE 7-1. The total number of hours of the on-ward performance by a group of 44 patients. (Ayllon and Azrin, 1965)

best performance. The results showed that the offer of a financial incentive led to increased performance in general, but particularly among people who were low on achievement motivation. People who were high on achievement motivation worked hard without the offer of a financial reward. In another laboratory study, Kaufman (1962) found higher performance when level of individual performance was related to the amount of a promised economic reward.

A study by Bass, Hurder, and Ellis (1954) showed that offering pay for effective performance can, under some conditions, decrease performance, even though it may increase motivation. This study found that offering an incentive increased performance on a simple task, but cut performance on a more complex one. In discussing this finding, Bass (1965) noted that motivation was already high and that offering the financial incentive simply made motivation too high for the complex task that had to be done. Thus, the study further supports the point that offering financial incentives for performance will lead to increased motivation to perform, but it adds the cautionary note that increased motivation may not always be desirable or productive.

Locke and Bryan (1967) have presented evidence from a number of studies with respect to the effects of financial incentives. Overall, their data seem to suggest that offering financial incentives will increase performance. They interpret this differently from the way it would be interpreted by our model, since they argue that money influences motivation by influencing intentions. The important point for this discussion, however, is not that they present a different interpretation of why money affects motivation, but that they present evidence from a well-controlled series of laboratory studies to show that the offering of individual financial rewards can affect productivity. My own work on equity theory has shown that subjects working on a piece rate system will produce about 20 percent more than subjects working on an hourly system (Lawler, 1968c). This result seems to hold regardless of pay equity. This study, as well as the other experiments discussed, involved comparisons between subjects who had been randomly assigned to different treatment groups and who worked on the same tasks. Thus, they provide good evidence for the view that individual incentive plans can work.

In sum, there is a substantial amount of evidence to support the prediction of the model that tying individual performance to financial rewards results in increased motivation, which under most conditions results in increased performance. The evidence to support this proposition comes in all shapes, sizes, and qualities. Much of it comes from studies of poor quality that used only before-and-after measures, but some of it comes from rather carefully controlled laboratory experiments. Even the most conservative studies seem to suggest that individual incentive plans can increase productivity by 10 percent to 20 percent. Still, a number of studies have asked why larger increases in productivity have typically not been obtained after the installation of individual incentive plans in organizations. These studies have investigated what might be called the "side effects" of individual incentive systems.

The main side effect that has been studied is restriction of output. There is a tremendous amount of evidence that workers on individual incentive systems establish quotas for production that are far below the maximum they could produce. Mathewson (1931), after a large-scale investigation of output restriction, during which he worked as a laborer, machine operator, etc., concluded that output restriction is practiced on an enormous scale by workers at diverse occupational levels and in practically every industry. In one machine shop Mathewson found that men were producing at about 50 per cent of their potential. This low level of production was enforced by the workers, and anyone who produced more was liable for ostracism or even physical punishment. Further observational evidence on the restriction of output is available in the Western Electric studies. The study of the bank wiring room found a rigidly enforced output restriction system. Workers who exceeded the quota could expect to receive a "bing" (punch on the arm) and to be rejected and degraded by the other members of the group. More recent anthropological studies (Collins, Dalton, & Roy, 1946; Dalton, 1948; Dyson, 1956; Roy, 1952; Whyte, 1955) have provided a great deal of additional evidence to support the point that restriction is widespread and that, as a result, incentive plans do not produce the kind of productivity increases of which workers are capable.

On the surface it seems that the widespread existence of restriction indicates that employees are not motivated by money, since they appear to be earning less money than the pay system allows. In fact, many writers have argued that the restriction phenomenon shows that employees are more concerned about social than economic needs; the group seems to be able to force individuals to make less money as the price for acceptance in the group. But is this the only explanation? It seems quite possible that just looking to the group itself for the explanation is not enough. Admittedly, group norms and sanctions are highly visible and clearly serve to keep production low. But group pressure is only the visible enforcement device.

To really understand restrictions, we must ask why the group norms against high productivity develop. This issue has been tackled by Hickson (1961) and by two large-scale attitude studies conducted by the Opinion Research Corporation (Viteles, 1953). The data from these sources suggest that workers feel that more productivity will lead to negative economic consequences. In one of the Opinion Research Corporation studies, 30 percent of the workers felt that high production would lead to higher production quotas, 11 percent felt that it would result in lower piece rates, and a smaller percentage thought that higher productivity would result in no change in wages. Many workers—23 percent—felt that high productivity would be unpopular with other workers. A later study by the Opinion Research Corporation (1949) showed that workers also feared that if they responded to wage incentive plans by producing a great deal they might work themselves out of a job. Overall, 50 percent of one group of workers felt that increased output would be bad for them. Roy's description of his experiences while working on a piece rate job nicely reflects how group pressures operate and suggests that fear of rate changes is an important basis for production restriction:

From my first to my last day at the plant I was subject to warnings and predictions concerning price cuts. Pressure was the heaviest from Joe Mucha, day man on my machine, who shared my job repertoire and kept a close eye on my production. On November 14, the day after my first attained quota, Joe Mucha advised: "Don't let it go over $1.25 an hour, or the time study man will be right down here! And they don't waste time either! They watch the records like a hawk! I got ahead, so I took it easy for a couple of hours."

Joe told me that I had made $10.01 yesterday and warned me not to go over $1.25 an hour. He told me to figure the setups and the time on each operation very carefully so that I would not total over $10.25 in any one day.

Jack Starkey defined the quota carefully but forcefully when I turned in $10.50 for one day, or $1.31 an hour.

Jack Starkey spoke to me after Joe left. "What's the matter? Are you trying to upset the applecart?"

Jack explained in a friendly manner that $10.50 was too much to turn in, even on an old job. "The turret-lathe men can turn in $1.35," said Jack, "but their rate is 90 cents, and ours 85 cents."

Jack warned me that the Methods Department could lower their prices on any job, old or new, by changing the fixture slightly or changing the size of the drill. According to Jack, a couple of operators (first and second shift on the same drill) got to competing with each other to see how much they could turn in. They got up to $1.65 an hour, and the price was cut in half. And from then on they had to run that job themselves, as none of the other operators would accept the job. [Whyte, 1955, p. 23]

The evidence, considered together, leads to the conclusion that, when workers are placed on individual piece rate plans, they often feel that a number of negative social and economic consequences will result if they are highly productive. There is also some evidence to suggest that they do not believe that the company will continue to reward them for higher productivity. Unfortunately, there is relatively little evidence to show how these beliefs develop and what causal sequence they develop in. It is important, for example, to find out why and when the strong social norms against high productivity develop. Group pressures against high production may well develop simply because of the perceived negative economic consequences of high productivity. Thus, they may be present only where such consequences are perceived. Thus, rather than showing that people will forego economic gain for social pleasures, the existence of social pressures may show the ability of economic factors to influence group norms and social interaction—and thus show the great importance of money.

This explanation of why production restriction and goldbricking develop is presented in diagram form in Figure 7-2. The interpretation is consistent with our model, since it explains the low productivity of piece work employees in terms of the perceived negative consequences of performing well. It suggests that when a piece rate incentive is installed in a situation where mistrust exists between management and employees, the employees will develop beliefs to the effect that high productivity will

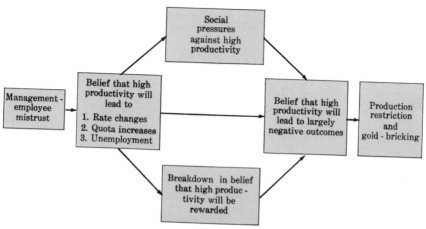

FIGURE 7-2. Model of the determinants of production restriction.

lead to negative economic consequences. These beliefs will in turn lead to the creation of informal pressure groups in which employees seek to protect their economic interests by using social means to control other employees' production. It is also suggested that these beliefs will destroy any perception that high production leads to high pay. The net result is that the individual worker will see more negative than positive outcomes associated with high productivity and consequently will restrict his production.

Note that this argument suggests that group pressures develop because of the economic situation and then combine with economic conditions to produce the restriction. This is not to suggest that social sanctions are not real and important causes of the restriction. It is merely to suggest that they may have an economic basis and that they may be effective only when combined with certain economic realities and beliefs. Unfortunately, there is no experimental research available that adequately tests this view of restriction. We need some well-conducted experimental studies to provide information on the causal basis for production restriction. One implication of our argument that could be tested concerns the cause of group pressures. According to the view stated above, unless certain beliefs about the economic consequences of high productivity exist, group pressure should not develop. This kind of speculation is amenable to experimental test and until it is tested we will not know why restriction takes place. We will only know that it does.

A second negative side effect of individual incentive systems involves the degree of competition they encourage among individual workers. In many cases, competition between employees may not be bad; but where they are working on cooperative tasks (Ghiselli & Brown,

1955), it can be harmful. One study illustrates this point quite well. Babchuk and Goode (1951) studied a group of sales people who were on an individual bonus scheme. They found that this scheme led the salesmen to compete for customers and neglect unrewarded but necessary tasks such as stocking shelves and maintaining accounts. Many other examples could be cited of jobs in which cooperation is necessary between individuals and in which individual incentive systems do not succeed because they do not reward cooperative behavior. The point to remember, however, is that people seem to perform in terms of how their performance is evaluated; and in most individual incentive plans, cooperative behavior is not evaluated. Thus, where cooperative behavior is important in a job, individual plans run into difficulty unless they explicitly measure and reward cooperative behavior.

It is often claimed that individual incentive plans produce high administrative costs (W. Brown, 1962) and lead to higher accident rates. It probably is true that complex piece rate systems are much more expensive to operate than straight hourly or salary pay programs. In addition to clerical help, they demand specialists to study jobs and set rates. Unfortunately, few studies have accurately determined just how expensive it is to install and operate various incentive plans. Thus, it must remain a matter of speculation whether the increased costs of incentive plans cancel out the economic advantages of the higher productivity that they seem to consistently effect. A somewhat similar situation exists when the relationship between accident rates and individual incentive systems is cited. That is, there exists little evidence relevant to the allegation that individual plans tend to lead to higher accident rates.

In summary, it is clear that individual incentive plans can have some negative side effects. There is not enough evidence, however, to establish just how serious the side effects are and whether they can be avoided. Thus, it is impossible to determine whether they are serious enough to preclude the use of individual incentive plans in most situations. It is also difficult to say much about what can be done to prevent the side effects from occurring, although in Chapter 9 we shall discuss this issue. In marked contrast to the small amount of research on the side effects of individual incentive plans is the large amount of research on their effects on productivity. This evidence clearly indicates that, as predicted by the Motivation Model individual plans typically lead to substantial increases in productivity.

Group and Organization Subunit Incentive Plans

Two studies have compared the effectiveness of individual incentive plans and group incentive plans. Marriott (1949) studied the relationship between the size of the work group and the output of male production workers on group incentive plans in two British factories. In both factories, he found a general tendency for production to decrease as the size of the group increased. He also reported that workers paid on an individual incentive basis were higher producers on the average than were workers in even the smallest work group. Babchuk and Goode (1951) have reported on a sales group that developed its own group incentive system. Originally on an individual incentive system and experiencing a number of the side effect problems mentioned earlier, the employees divided the business equally among them so that they were, in fact, on a group bonus system. This change seemed to eliminate many of the negative side effects and it encouraged cooperation.

These two studies nicely illustrate the positive and negative features of group incentive plans. As the Marriott study points out, often they do not lead to as high productivity as individual plans. Campbell (1952) has suggested one explanation for this. Like Marriott, he found lower productivity in larger groups, but he also found that in larger groups employees saw less relationship between their pay and their performance. In large groups pay is clearly not as closely tied to individual performance as it is in small groups or in individual plans. Thus it would be expected from our model that group plans would have less motivational value than individual plans, because they lead to lower performance→pay subjective probabilities. On the other hand, group plans can encourage cooperation and eliminate some of the negative side effects of individual incentive plans. This, of course, represents the real strength of group plans and the reason they are preferred in situations where cooperation among employees is important and needs to be rewarded and where individual performance is very difficult to measure separately from group performance.

Unfortunately, little research has directly compared the productivity of individuals working under group bonus conditions with that of employees working under fixed-payment conditions. Nevertheless, based upon the evidence that does exist (e.g., Campbell, 1952; Marriott, 1949), it seems safe to conclude that production will be higher under the group bonus system since it relates pay and performance at least minimally.

Overall, there are surprisingly few studies of the effects of group bonus systems, despite the frequent suggestion that they are an improvement over individual systems (e.g., Bass, 1965). It is particularly important that we learn more about the kinds of productivity norms that develop where group incentives are used. The Western Electric research on the bank wiring room established that employees working on a group incentive plan could develop restrictive norms just like those on individual incentives. It has been suggested, although not proved, that restrictive norms are less likely to develop when a group incentive plan is used. As we have said, the whole topic is ripe for research. The present discussion suggests that it should be particularly interesting to see if different norms develop under group incentive conditions than develop under individual incentive conditions.

Companywide Incentive Plans

A substantial number of companywide incentive plans have been tried. Typically, they offer everyone in the company a bonus or some form of extra payment, the size of which is based upon some measure of organizational effectiveness. The key characteristic of these plans is that all employees holding similar jobs get the same bonus regardless of individual contribution. The measure of company effectiveness may be profitability, sales, etc. In the best-known plan, the Scanlon Plan, the measure is labor savings, or cost effectiveness. For two reasons, it is virtually impossible to make any strong statements about how effective various companywide incentive systems have been. First, in addition to changing the payment system, most of the plans involve a number of other changes. Thus, we cannot tell what role, if any, the change in the payment system played in any overall increase in organizational effectiveness. When a company adopts the Scanlon or the Lincoln Electric Plan, it is adopting not a method of wage payment but a philosophy of management, only one part of which is concerned with wages. Second, where companies have changed to companywide plans, it has been impossible to establish adequate control groups; thus, it is impossible to prove that any increased effectiveness is due to the changes in the pay system. This criticism is not too serious, however, where large and consistent increases in organizational effectiveness are found, since they are not likely to be mere chance phenomena.

The relationship between organization size and companywide incentive plans is an issue that is frequently raised when these plans are considered because, to an even greater extent than group incentive plans, they separate the individual employee's behavior from his pay. The larger the company, the greater the separation. In one sense, companywide plans exaggerate the advantages and disadvantages that are inherent in group-based plans. That is, they can facilitate cooperation among orgnization members more than group plans, but they break down even further the close connection between performance and pay that is the chief strong point of the individual plans.

The Scanlon Plan is undoubtedly the best researched of the companywide incentive plans. Puckett (1958) has studied the impact of the plan in nine firms and reports that the increases in productivity are extremely impressive. In the first year under the plan, productivity increased an average of 22.5 percent. In the second year, productivity increased an average of 23.7 percent over the base period. Puckett discredits the common criticism that the plan is successful only in firms that are experiencing severe economic problems. He points out that several of the companies he studied were already quite profitable, but that the plan still served to make them more successful. He is less convincing in answering the criticism that the plan works only in small companies. He found no relationship between company size and the success of the plan for the firms he studied, but his sample covered a very limited size range. The largest organization had under 1,200 employees. This is hardly large enough to prove that the Scanlon Plan can work as well in large organizations as in small ones. In fact, the overall record of the Scanlon Plan shows that it has seldom been tried in large firms. The upper end of the size range of firms that have tried it seems to be around 7,200 employees, while most firms that have tried it employ fewer than 1,000 (Schultz, 1958).

The Kaiser Plan has been tried in a large company (NICB, 1963). Its impact is very difficult to evaluate, but it seems clearly much less successful than the Scanlon Plan.

The Lincoln Electric Plan (Lincoln, 1951) represents an interesting attempt to combine the advantages of an individual plan with those of a companywide plan. The amount of bonus money paid out is determined by the profitability of the company, but the amount each individual gets is based upon how his performance is rated. Thus, it is possible for an individual to get no bonus, even though the company had a good year, and to get a big bonus in a mediocre year. The plan tries to relate individual performance more closely to individual pay, while at the same time encouraging employees to work together in a cooperative spirit to increase the amount of bonus money. As with most companywide incentive plans, it is difficult to establish how successful this one has been. Lincoln (1951) presents a great deal of evidence to suggest that it has been very successful. His data show that in 1949, Lincoln Electric Company had sales of over $25,000 per employee, while the industry average was less than $15,000. The data also show that sales per employee have steadily risen since the plan was installed. Based upon this and other evidence, Lincoln argues that the plan has greatly increased productivity. It is impossible to determine whether employees would have been just as productive without the plan, but it seems unlikely.

In summary, there is some evidence that under companywide incentive plans which relate pay to performance, worker productivity is higher than under fixed-pay conditions. The evidence is subject to a number of methodological problems, however. Further, there is no reliable evidence that compares the relative effectiveness of the various types of individual, group, and companywide plans. It is true that the data from the Scanlon Plan companies showed that they experienced larger average increases in productivity than are typically reported by companies who switch from fixed-payment to individual incentive plans. But the evidence can hardly be used to support the conclusion that moving to the Scanlon Plan typically leads to larger increases than does moving to individually based incentive plans. There are, in fact, some theoretical reasons for predicting that it should not, since the Scanlon Plan does not tie pay closely to individual performance. Its real strength is that it can tie other rewards to good performance and does not lead employees to believe that negative consequences will follow effective performance.

The important issue is not which type of pay plan is on the average most effective, but the differential question, Under what conditions will each plan be most effective? It seems very unlikely that one plan will always be more effective than another. Quite to the contrary, under certain conditions an individual incentive plan might be more effective than a companywide plan, while under other conditions just the opposite might be true. A number of the conditions that must be considered have already been mentioned: the size of the company or group, the extent to which performance is quantifiable, the degree to which cooperation among employees is important, and the degree of superior-subordinate trust. Chapter 16 will consider this subject further and discuss the problems associated with choosing a pay plan for a particular organization.

When all the evidence already discussed is considered, it is obvious that there is a tremendous amount of empirical support for the proposition that productivity can be increased by making pay dependent upon performance. Admittedly, much of the evidence is from studies that have methodological problems, but some of the evidence reviewed in the discussion of individual plans is quite good. One fact stands out: Regardless of the methodology and the kind of plan considered, when individual pay is clearly dependent upon individual performance, job performance is higher than when pay and performance are not related.

EFFECTS OF PAYING DIFFERENT AMOUNTS OF MONEY

In discussing the effects on performance of altering the amount of an employee's pay, we must be sure to distinguish between situations where pay is closely related to performance and those where it is not. There is reason to believe, on the basis of our model and expectancy theory, that offering larger amounts of money in return for a certain kind of performance should increase a person's motivation to perform in the rewarded manner. This should be true as long as the reward is not seen to be inequitably large and as long as the person does not accumulate so much money that he satisfies all the needs upon which the importance of pay is based. Thus, in a piece rate situation, increasing the size of the piece rate offered within equitable boundaries presumably should increase the subject's motivation to perform, since it increases the valence of the rewards offered for performing the task. On the other hand, arbitrarily increasing or decreasing an employee's wages where pay is not based on performance should not affect his job performance at all.

The possibilty that increasing wages may increase motivation has been discussed by Vroom, and his summary of the evidence still appears to hold true:

One possibility is that the strength of a worker's motivation to perform effectively is directly related to the amount of his wages. The more wages he receives the higher his motivation to do an effective job. There is little evidence in support of such a relationship. To this writer's knowledge there is no reliable data indicating that increases in wages increase levels of performance, or that decreases in wages decrease levels of performance. [Vroom, 1964, p. 252]

As far as this author knows there is still no evidence to show that simply increasing wage levels will lead to an increase in performance.

The situation is quite different, however, when pay is tied to performance. A number of studies have analyzed the effects of changing the size of pay rewards where the reward is tied to job performance, and they have generally found that there is a relationship between the size of the pay reward offered and the performance obtained. Unfortunately, the results from the studies are not entirely consistent, and thus, it is not clear what the effects of paying different amounts of money will be in some situations.

Atkinson (1958) has reported a study in which he examined the effect of offering women college students different amounts of money in return for the successful performance of a task. Subjects were told that they were competing with other subjects and that the best performer would receive the money. The results of this study were very much what might be expected from our model. Subjects who were offered $2.50 for successful performance performed better than those who were offered $1.25. This finding is also consistent with the results of a number of animal learning studies which have shown that size of reward is positively related to learning and to motivation (Cofer & Appley, 1964). Studies by Crespi (1942), (1944) and Zeaman (1949), for example, have shown that, with hunger held constant, rats given a larger food reward during training run faster than those given a small reward. They have also shown that if the amount of reward is varied, abrupt changes occur in the speed of running. Rats trained on small rewards suddenly run much faster when offered larger rewards, and those trained on large rewards suddenly run much slower when switched to a small reward.

Collins (1963) has done a study somewhat similar to that reported by Atkinson (1958). He used telephone operators as subjects in a laboratory experiment in which two different piece rates were offered. One group was offered 10 cents and the other 50 cents. Contrary to expectations, both groups produced about the same amount. Similar data are presented by Moore (1968). She found no significant productivity difference between groups paid 20 cents, 30 cents, and 40 cents a page to do proofreading, although there was a slight tendency for the higher-paid subjects to be more productive. Two other studies suggest that increasing the size of a piece rate does not necessarily increase productivity and motivation. Lawler and O'Gara (1967) and Andrews (1967) have reported studies in which subjects were paid different piece rates. The results of these studies are in perfect agreement: Increasing the size of the piece rate led to lower productivity but higher-quality work. Lawler and O'Gara ran two groups of subjects, one of which was paid 10 cents per piece, and the other 25 cents. The average productivity of the group paid 10 cents was 29.6, while that of the group paid 25 cents was 20. Andrews ran three groups of subjects who were paid 15 cents, 20 cents, and 30 cents, respectively. His data showed that the higher the pay, the lower the productivity and the higher the quality of the work.

The findings of the Atkinson study would appear to be in some disagreement with those of Collins (1963); Andrews (1967) Lawler and O'Gara (1967), and Moore (1968). Before we assume that Atkinson's findings are completely irreconcilable with the others and with our model, however, let us note one difference between the payment system used in the Atkinson study and the systems used in the others. In the Atkinson study the subjects were all competing for a prize, which was to be given to the one individual who performed best. In the other studies the subjects were operating under straight piece rate conditions so that, for each subject, the more he produced the more money he made. The two situations are quite different. In the Atkinson study, productivity was not related to performance in the sense that more work directly produced more money. Rather, in order to obtain any money at all, good performance (actually the best in the group) was necessary. Poor performance or even second-best meant no reward. From a psychological point of view, this is quite different from the straight piece rate situation where, as has been pointed out, large piece rates can lower the valence of pay and as a consequence decrease productivity. A piece rate system allows people to accumulate large amounts of money quickly, and because of feelings of equity and satiation, this can lead to a decrease in the valence of pay. Thus, the finding that large piece rates do not always lead to high productivity can be explained by our model, as can the data from Atkinson's study.

RESEARCH RELATED TO EXPECTANCY THEORY

Research on Beliefs About How Pay is Determined

A number of studies have examined the relationship between job performance and employees' attitudes or beliefs about what impact performing well will have on their pay. This particular line of research has its foundations in expectancy theory and directly tests several parts of our model. One of the clearest predictions that can be made from our Motivation Model concerns this very point. According to the model, the more strongly employees believe that effective performance will lead to financial rewards, the more motivated they should be to perform well. The studies that have tested the relationship between expectancy-type attitudes and job performance have provided an extensive amount of evidence that seems to support the model. They have consistently found a positive relationship between job performance and employees' beliefs about the degree to which pay is related to performance.

Probably the first study to consider this relationship systematically was done by Georgopoulos, Mahoney and Jones (1957). They found that 38 percent of those who perceived that productivity would lead to high pay in the long run were high producers, while only 21 percent of those who felt it would not were high producers. The one problem with this study was that it used self-ratings as measures of performance, and as has been shown (Lawler, 1967b), it is not always clear how self-ratings are related to other measures of performance. Also, when self-ratings are related to expectancy attitudes, two self-report measures are being related to each other, and this can sometimes lead to spuriously high relationships between two variables.

Two later studies, however, did find a relationship between expectancy attitudes and performance even when superiors' ratings and objective measures were used as criteria. Spitzer (1964) reports finding a low but significant ($r = .17$) correlation between employees' attitudes toward the degree to which contributing to cost reduction can be helpful in attaining more pay and the employees' actual contribution to cost reduction. The results of the second study, which looked at managers, are shown in Figure 7-3 (Lawler, 1964; Porter & Lawler, 1968a). As can be seen from the figure, in terms of both self- and superiors' ratings, stronger beliefs that performance influences pay are associated with both higher performance and higher effort. Note that the relationship between effort and expectancy attitudes is stronger (steeper slope to line) than the relationship between performance and expectancy attitudes. This should be expected if, as specified in our model, expectancy attitudes are deter-

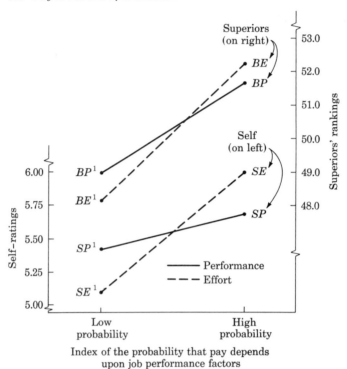

FIGURE 7-3. Relationship between degree to which pay is seen to be tied to performance and measures of effort and performance. (Porter & Lawler, 1968a)

miners of motivation. As the model illustrates, effort is a more direct indication of motivation than is performance. Performance is determined by a number of things besides motivation (e.g., ability, situational factors), while effort rather directly reflects motivation.

A number of recent studies have analyzed the relationship between job performance and expectancy attitudes toward a number of rewards, including pay (e.g., Evans, 1968; Hackman & Porter, 1968, Galbraith & Cummings, 1967; Lawler, 1968a; and Lawler & Porter, 1967a). None of these more recent studies, however, report separately the data for the relationship between performance and expectancy attitudes toward pay. Instead, they combine pay expectancy attitudes with attitudes toward the valence of pay and/or with expectancy attitudes toward various other rewards. These studies do, nonetheless, report data that support our model, and thus it is reasonable to assume that in most cases they show a positive relationship between pay expectancy attitudes and job performance.

Attitudes Toward the Importance or Attractiveness of Pay

A few studies have directly related employees' statements about the valence or importance of money to their performance and have obtained positive results. Our Motivation Model would lead us to expect just such a result, since the more employees say pay is important to them, the more valence they will attach to it, and the more motivated they should be to perform in a manner that will earn them more money. It is important to note however, that, from the model, one should expect importance attitudes to be related to performance only where subjects see some relationship between pay and performance. Thus, it is not surprising that in all the studies where importance attitudes have been found to be related to performance, the subjects have been paid on a piece rate basis.

Lawler and O'Gara (1967) report that in a laboratory study they found a correlation of .46 between subjects' statements about the importance of pay and their productivity. In a somewhat similar study, Lawler, Koplin, Young, and Fadem (1968) report a correlation of .70 between importance attitudes and productivity for subjects working on a six-hour interviewing job. Locke and Bryan (1967) report that in a laboratory situation, information about the strength of subjects' desires to make money is predictive of the kind of task subjects will choose to work on. Those who desire more money will select tasks that allow for higher productivity. The results from these laboratory studies fit quite well with some of the field observational research reported by Whyte (1955). This research rather clearly showed that the rate busters (high producers) in a piece rate situation are the people who value money the most (see Chap. 3). In a study of hospitals, Schneider and Olson (1970) have found evidence that attitudes toward the importance of pay are related to performance where good performance does, in fact, lead to pay, but not in situations where performance is not rewarded. The findings of these studies are also consistent with the great amount of research on animals that has shown a strong relationship between need strength and motivation. The more the animals desire a certain reward, the faster they will run and the harder they will work to obtain it (Osgood, 1953; Woodworth & Schlosberg, 1954).

Expectancy Attitudes Combined with Attitudes Toward the Valence of Outcomes as Predictors of Performance

Following the lead of expectancy theory, a number of studies have combined expectancy attitudes and attitudes toward the valence of outcomes in order to predict performance. Georgopoulos, Mahoney, and Jones

(1957) found (as might be expected from expectancy theory) that the relationship between performance and P→O beliefs was greater for workers who rated pay high in importance than for those who rated it low. This finding suggests that (as indicated by our model) P→O beliefs and valence do combine multiplicatively. Assuming a multiplicative combination of these factors, in fact, leads to the prediction that no relationship should be expected between P→O beliefs and performance when pay is unimportant or of low valence. This comes about because with importance at 0, it does not matter what P→O beliefs exist, since the product of the two will always be 0.

In a more recent study, Porter and Lawler (1968a) report findings that are similar to those reported by Georgopoulos et al. They found a stronger relationship between effort→reward beliefs and performance when pay was very important than when it was low in importance. Not fitting the multiplicative model are some data reported by Spitzer (1964). As stated Spitzer did find a correlation between expectancy attitudes and performance, but when he multiplied the expectancy measure by an importance measure, not only did it not increase the correlation, but it decreased it. If importance and expectancy attitudes combine multiplicatively to determine motivation, then their combination should be a better predictor of performance than should either alone. Thus, the data gathered by Spitzer do not support the multiplicative model.

Evidence collected by Galbraith (Galbraith, 1966; Galbraith & Cummings, 1967) does, however, fit the model. This evidence shows a significant interaction between importance attitudes and P→O beliefs when both are considered determinants of performance. This would, of course, be expected if they combine multiplicatively. Another study has shown that multiplying P→O beliefs by the importance of outcomes can increase the ability of the P→O beliefs to predict performance (Lawler & Porter, 1967a). A study by Hackman and Porter (1968) has also shown that P→O beliefs can predict performance when combined multiplicatively with importance attitudes.

All the studies discussed so far have related attitudes to performance, with both being measured at the same point in time. In a recent study, Lawler (1968a) has related attitudes measured one year earlier to current performance and found a stronger relation between them than between performance measured one year earlier and current P→O attitudes. This finding follows from the view that performance attitudes cause performance, rather than vice versa (Campbell & Stanley, 1963). This is an important point, because it provides the only real confirmation of the causal implications of the expectancy model. Thus, there is some evidence that supports the view that expectancy attitudes combine multiplicatively with importance attitudes to determine motivation and that they manifest themselves in performance. The one study that does not fit this conclusion is the one by Spitzer (1964). But the positive evidence available seems to overwhelm this one finding. Overall, the evidence on the relationship between expectancy attitudes, importance attitudes and performance provides rather impressive support for our model. Basically, it can be summarized in the following four points:

1. Beliefs about the degree to which pay depends upon performance are positively related to job performance.
2. Where pay depends upon performance, statements about the importance of pay are related to job performance.
3. Job performance is most strongly related to a multiplicative combination of importance attitudes and P→O beliefs.
4. P→O beliefs seem to be more strongly related to future performance than to either present or past performance.

Chapter 8
EQUITY
THEORY:
THE
RESEARCH
EVIDENCE

Undoubtedly, the most difficult data for our Motivation Model to handle are those gathered by Adams and others to test equity theory. On the surface, some of these data do not seem to fit the model, particularly if it is assumed that pay obtains valence only because of its ability to satisfy the needs mentioned in Chapter 2. This chapter maintains, however, that all the data can be explained by the Motivation Model (presented in Chapter 6), because it includes equity as one factor that influences the valence of rewards. In discussing the equity research, we must look at four payment conditions, because equity theory makes different predictions for the piece rate situation and for the hourly pay situation and because people in each of these situations can be overpaid or underpaid. Thus, piece rate overpayment, hourly rate overpayment, piece rate underpayment, and hourly rate underpayment will be discussed in turn.

OVERPAYMENT: PIECE RATE

Productivity

Perhaps the most interesting prediction that Adams (1965) has derived from equity theory is that, under a piece rate system, subjects who feel overpaid will produce less but do higher-quality work than subjects who feel equitably paid. Adams makes this prediction because he assumes that the overpaid subjects will try to raise the quality of their work, and because the negative correlation usually found between quality and quantity will lead to lower productivity. The data relevant to this aspect of the theory generally support the prediction of low productivity and high quality. Adams (1963b), Adams and Jacobsen (1964), and Moore (1968)

---

[1] Based in part on Lawler, 1968c.

have found that subjects who are made to feel unqualified for a job, and therefore to feel overpaid, produce less in a two-hour period than do equitably paid subjects. In addition, overpaid subjects produce higher-quality work than do equitably paid subjects. These studies, of course, do not establish whether the subjects' purpose was to increase quality (as suggested by Adams, 1965) or to reduce productivity. Unfortunately, the tasks employed in these studies do show a negative correlation between quality and quantity; as a result, it is difficult to tell whether the subjects were concerned about reducing production or whether it was low simply because of their desire to do high-quality work.

Wood and Lawler (1970) have recently tried to determine whether overpaid piece rate subjects will be low producers even when quality and productivity are unrelated. They paid subjects to read passages as part of a "linguistics study." The subjects were paid on the basis of the amount of time they actually read. Thus, they were on a piece rate, but in a situation in which trying for high quality did not necessarily interfere with high productivity. In this situation, overpaid subjects produced less than equitably paid subjects. This suggests that overpayment leads directly to reduced productivity. This is an important point since, as will be shown, many of the nonequity theory explanations of the data from the overpayment studies argue that subjects are motivated by factors not related to their feelings of pay equity to produce less in the overpayment situation. Adams, on the other hand, suggests that they are motivated by inequity to raise the quality of their work and that low productivity is a consequence of this.

Expectancy theory emphasizes that individuals will try to maximize their outcomes rather than try to balance their inputs and their outcomes. On the surface, it seems that the overpaid subjects who had low productivity in the Adams studies were not behaving in a way designed to maximize at least one positively valued outcome—money. In short, the subjects were not producing, even though there appeared to be a high probability that production would lead to a valued reward. Adams (1963a) makes this point rather clearly: "The results also suggest that the need to establish equity was a more potent motivation than the motivation to maximize economic gain."

It is not clear from these studies, however, that, in fact, equity did motivate the overpaid subjects. It has been argued that the results of these studies can be explained in several ways by expectancy theory, without using a concept of equity. The explanations rest upon the view that the equity manipulation used in the studies may, in addition to creating feelings of overpayment, affect the value of the rewards offered for productivity or the perceived probability that certain rewards depend upon the amount of effort directed toward producing. Unless such effects can be shown, of course, expectancy theory would have to predict no productivity differences between the overpaid and the equitably paid subjects, since, in both conditions, similar pay outcomes were offered for high production. We shall consider, first, those explanations of Adams's data which argue that his equity manipulation affects expectancies and, second, those explanations which argue that it affects the attractiveness of the rewards associated with performance.

EFFECTS ON EXPECTANCIES. It has been suggested that the overpaid, low-producing subjects in the piece rate situation are really not operating in a way that they think will lower their long-term economic gain. According to this view, telling subjects they are unqualified for the job arouses feelings of job insecurity (Evans & Molinari, 1970). The feelings of insecurity then lead subjects to believe that the best way to protect their jobs is to turn out a small amount of very-high-quality work. Evans and Molinari (1970) have in fact shown that when insecurity is induced by telling subjects that they may not be allowed to continue working, they do precisely this. Under a piece rate system, this kind of behavior should guarantee the employer that he is getting a fair return for his investment and thus protect the job of the insecure worker. In addition, the worker does not call attention to himself as a high producer and thereby does not risk the possibility that his piece rate will be cut. Given that, in the equity studies, the subject is told that he has low qualifications, a piece rate cut and dismissal certainly may be on his mind. In short, the induction may destroy the expectancy that high productivity will lead to high pay.

If it could be shown that the induction does indeed produce feelings of insecurity which lead to production restriction, then the results are directly predictable from expectancy theory. Many studies of workers on piece rates (see Chap. 7) show that employees will restrict their production, even though it hurts them financially for a short period, because they feel that in the long run it will lead to a greater number of positively valued rewards. Adams (1965) states that the results of one of his studies show that security about future employment cannot explain the results from the piece rate overpayment situation. In this study Adams and Jacobsen (1964) argue that insecurity should be an important determinant of productivity only when subjects feel that they will be rehired for another job. Thus, Adams and Jacobsen undertook to determine whether the equity manipulation would produce the same results when subjects were told there was little chance of additional work; they found that the equity effect of low productivity and high quality still appeared. Hence, the data from this study support the view that the insecurity explanation cannot account for the productivity effects that Adams ascribes to feelings of overpayment in the piece rate situation.

Before dismissing the insecurity argument entirely, however, we should note that the Adams and Jacobsen (1964) study does not represent an ideal test. The crucial comparison here is between the equitably paid and the overpaid subjects who were given the impression that the possibility of future work was negligible. The subjects were told, "Usually it isn't necessary to hire someone to proofread for us . . . the job will take a short time only." The overpaid subjects in this condition were also told that they were unqualified for the job, while the equitably paid subjects were told that they were qualified. Even though both groups knew that the probability of obtaining future work was low, it would seem that the overpaid subjects, by virtue of being told they were unqualified, would be more insecure about future work than would the equitably paid subjects. Even with this induction, it would seem that some subjects might still believe that more work would be available and as a result be concerned about obtaining it. In short, Adams's argument would seem to hold only if the subjects in both the over- and equitably paid groups were convinced that absolutely no future work was possible and that, as a result, both groups felt equally insecure; there is little indication that this condition existed in the study. Hence, there remains the possibility that the overpaid subjects were more insecure about future work than the equitably paid subjects and that this had some effect.

Lawler, Koplin, Young, and Fadem (1968) hired subjects for 3 two-hour sessions with the explicit understanding that they would not be rehired because of the nature of the job. Thus, there should be little problem here with insecurity arising from doubts about getting future work. But some insecurity in this study and in the Adams studies may arise from the possibility that unqualified subjects could be fired or have their pay cut during their short work period. Indeed, even though subjects might accept the fact that there would be no future work, they might feel insecure about keeping the job they have and getting paid for it at the high rate when their job qualifications are challenged. Interestingly, the data collected by Lawler et al. showed that the subjects did behave in the manner predicted by equity theory during the first two-hour session, but after that, they failed to behave as predicted by the theory. One explanation for this could be that, after the overpaid subjects were allowed to come back for the second session, they felt relatively secure about holding their job and maintaining their pay rate, and hence began to behave like the qualified subjects who had felt secure all along. Or to state the situation in terms of our model, they became convinced that indeed a high probability did exist that high productivity would be rewarded. Thus, it seems likely that two kinds of insecurity feelings may come into play in equity studies where subjects are told that they are unqualified. One kind exists when the possibility of long-term future employment is present and has to do with beliefs about being rehired or retained. The other exists when someone is told he or she is unqualified for a job, whether or not long-term job possibilities exist, and has to do with concern over immediate dismissal and a reduction in the agreed-upon wage rate.

The Adams and Jacobsen (1964) study included a third treatment condition that is a possible relevant test for the impact of the security dimension. Subjects in one group were told that they were unqualified and would therefore be paid at a lower rate. It has been argued that, if the security explanation is valid, these subjects and the overpaid unqualified subjects should experience similar feelings of insecurity and both groups should therefore be low producers. The data show that the productivity of this group—the low-paid unqualified—was not low, however. It was closer to the productivity of the equitably paid subjects than to that of the overpaid subjects. This has been interpreted by Adams as proving that the security argument is invalid. It is not clear, however, why the unqualified overpaid subjects and the unqualified subjects whose pay was reduced should have similar feelings of security. The subjects who had their pay reduced might very well have felt "safe" at the lower pay rate, since it was commensurate with their qualifications, while those who remained at the higher rate may have felt very insecure about receiving a higher pay than their qualifications warranted.

In summary, it seems unlikely that just telling the subject that he will work only X hours can ever completely eliminate the differential feelings of security and insecurity that exist between qualified and unqualified subjects. Admittedly, at this point, there is not conclusive evidence to suggest that the differences between the overpaid and the equitably paid groups can be accounted for by differential feelings of insecurity. In fact, there is some evidence that this explanation cannot account for all the differences. Andrews (1967) did pay subjects different amounts of money in order to produce feelings of overpayment. This would appear to be a manipulation that is not strongly confounded by the security issue and as pointed out earlier, his data do show a small difference between a high paid piece rate group and a lower or equitably paid piece rate gorup. This finding is difficult to interpret, because Andrews has little evidence to indicate that his ovepaid subjects actually felt overpaid. Moore (1968) also overpaid subjects, but she found no differences in either productivity or quality between them and an equitably paid group. Although this finding does not offer strong support for equity theory, the fact that the overpaid subjects did not produce more offers some support for it and indicates that the security explanation cannot account for all the effects found in the original equity experiments. As was pointed out in Chapter 7, if it is assumed that the larger the amount of money the greater its attractiveness, then in this situation it would follow that the higher-paid groups should have produced more. The fact that they did not suggests the need for some modification in traditional thinking about the utility of money.

It would appear that the way to find out how important the security factor is would be to conduct studies that induce feelings of overpayment by means other than just telling the subject he is unqualified. As long as one subject is told that he is qualified and another is told that he is unqualified, it is very likely that they will have differential feelings of security and different expectancies both with respect to long-term job possibilities and with respect to simply getting paid for the short-term work they are doing.

EFFECTS ON VALENCE OF PAY. According to our Motivation Model the second factor that influences a person's motivation to produce is the valence or attractiveness of the rewards associated with productivity. Clearly, in the piece rate inequity studies, the reward that appears to be most important is pay. Our model suggests that the valence of pay is influenced by its perceived equity. Thus, one possible explanation for the lower productivity of overpaid subjects is that, for them, money has a lower valence. The lower valence of pay should lead the subjects to be less motivated to produce. This explanation, like some of the previous ones, requires that the subjects' low production not be a side effect of their trying for high quality; hence the importance of the data from the Wood and Lawler (1970) study. Presumably, money takes on a lower valence because the subjects feel that the rewards are too high for their low job qualifications. Indeed, such an interpretation of the piece rate studies is directly suggested by Adams and Jacobsen's comment that "simple economic motivation is . . . subordinate to the motivation to achieve consonance between perceived inputs and outcomes" (1964).

Vroom (1964) and Lawler (1965a) have suggested that the low production of the subjects in the overpayment situation may only be transitory. Essentially, their argument is: the inequity due to overpayment can only briefly sustain the perception that a given amount of pay is less attractive than a smaller but more equitable amount. Rather quickly, the larger amount will be seen as equitable and thus more attractive. In the piece rate situation, this would be expected to lead to increased productivity.

Support for the view that the low productivity of overpaid subjects in the piece rate situation is only transitory can be found in the previously mentioned study by Lawler et al. (1968). After an initial two-hour work period, the productivity of the overpaid and the equitably paid subjects was the same. This would seem to suggest that feelings of inequity can only temporarily decrease the attractiveness of a given amount of money. The fact that feelings of inequity do seem to reduce the valence of pay initially, however, points to the importance of including the concept of equity in our Motivation Model. Without it, the model would have difficulty explaining the impact of piece rate overpayment on productivity.

Work Quality

So far, the discussion of the overpayment piece rate studies has dealt with the productivity data rather than the quality data. Adams and Jacobsen (1964) did find that there was a tendency for the overpaid subjects to turn out higher-quality work than the equitably paid subjects. Lawler et al. (1968) found a similar tendency in the first of three experimental work sessions but not in the last two. Adams explains the high quality as an attempt by the subjects to increase their inputs in order to align them more closely with their outcomes. These data can be explained, however, without employing the concept of equity.

One explanation that rests upon an already stated view is that the overpayment induction creates feelings of insecurity and thereby affects the subjects' expectancies. The basic point here is that an individual may react to feelings of insecurity by doing higher-quality work and, hence, try to safeguard his job. As noted in the discussion of productivity, Adams and Jacobsen have attempted to show that the insecurity argument is invalid. Just as they did not provide conclusive evidence with respect to productivity, however, they do not, for the same reason, provide conclusive evidence with respect to work quality. In other words, it does not seem to be possible to dismiss the insecurity argument entirely, nor will it ever be as long as studies induce feelings of overpayment by attacking an individual's qualifications. In fact, the data collected by Lawler et al. suggest that the insecurity argument may have validity. The data showed that, once the subjects proved they could ho high-quality work, they then slumped off, possibly because their expectancies changed, and they felt secure enough to lower the quality of their work. Also relevant here is the study by Moore (1968), which showed that a group which was actually overpaid did poorer quality work than did an equitably paid group. This suggests that it is the qualifications attack rather than the overpayment which is crucial in producing high quality.

A second explanation for the quality data rests upon the possibility that important motives other than equity and security become involved. Because of the induction used, feelings of self-esteem, prestige, and competence may be associated with good quality work. When a person is told that he is unqualified, he may become highly concerned about proving to himself and others than he is competent. Hence, his high-quality work may reflect his P→O belief that good performance will lead to feelings of self-esteem and competence.

At the moment, there is little evidence to indicate the degree to which this kind of phenomenon influences the results in the piece rate situation. It is congruent with the data presented by Moore but does not fit with the finding by Andrews (1967) that higher piece rates bring higher-quality work. The data collected by Adams and Jacobsen (1964) are also somewhat relevant here, particularly for the subjects who were told that they were unqualified and that their pay was being reduced. The competence of these subjects was challenged, and they did show a tendency to turn out better-quality work than the equitably paid subjects. Still, the quality of the work of this group was not as high as that of the unqualified overpaid group. This suggests that the explanation cannot account for all the work quality effects reported by Adams and Jacobsen (1964). At this time, all that can reasonably be concluded is that, unless a different manipulation is used to produce feelings of overpayment, this argument will continue to have relevance.

OVERPAYMENT: HOURLY RATE

Productivity

Adams and Rosenbaum (1962) have reported that if subjects are paid at an hourly rate, they will produce more when they feel overpaid than when they feel equitably paid. As in most of the other equity studies, the feelings of overpayment were induced in this study by telling the subjects they were unqualified for the job. Equity theory explains that the high productivity of overpaid subjects is a result of their trying to increase their inputs in order to bring them more into line with their too bountiful outcomes. As was true with the piece rate overpayment data, it is not immediately obvious how these data can be explained by our Motivation Model. Here, two groups perform differently even though they are paid at the same rate and in the same manner. According to our model, it would seem that there should be no difference in the performance of the two groups, since, presumably, they should see the same rewards attached to productivity. As with piece rate results, however, several factors operating here make it impossible for us to conclude that this study can only be understood by using equity theory.

The major complication rests upon the question, What outcomes are perceived to be associated with high productivity in the overpaid condition? On the surface, it would seem that the same rewards are offered for productivity in both the overpaid and the equitably paid conditions, since both groups are paid the same amount for their work. It is possible, however, that the two groups perceive the rewards for high productivity differently in at least two respects.

First, it may be that the overpaid subjects feel that high productivity will lead to greater job security, while the equitably paid subjects do not perceive job security as an issue. Naturally, if job security is an issue, then our model or any expectancy theory would predict the results found. One study has been done to determine whether insecurity can explain the results for the overpaid hourly subjects. Arrowood (1961) overpaid subjects under two conditions. In one, the "private condition," subjects were told that no one would know what their output was; in the other, subjects were told that their output would be known. In both conditions the overpaid subjects produced more than the equitably paid subjects. Adams (1963a) argues that if insecurity were an important determinant of the equity effect found, then no productivity effect should exist for the overpaid private condition subjects. This argument rests upon the assumption that the equitably paid and the private condition, overpaid subjects will feel equally secure in their jobs. It is hard, however, to believe that subjects who are told they are unqualified will feel as secure as those who are told they are qualified, even when output is supposed to be kept secret. It does not seem likely that subjects will accept both the statement that they are not qualified for the job *and* the statement that no one will check their work. In short, it seems that no matter how elaborate the manipulation, there will always exist the possibility that subjects who are told that they differ in their job qualifications will also differ in their feelings of job security and in their P→O beliefs.

The same explanation that was used to interpret the high-quality work turned out initially by the overpaid piece rate workers also seems to be able to interpret the productivity effects of hourly overpayment. That is, telling the subject that he is unqualified may very well bring into play such motives as self-esteem and recognition. In such a situation, high productivity would satisfy a number of higher-order needs (e.g., esteem) and hence have more valence for overpaid than for equitably paid subjects. Our model, of course, predicts that the greater the rewards for high productivity, the more motivated people will be to produce. Thus, if it could be shown that rewards like self-esteem and recognition were felt to be more closely associated with high productivity in the overpaid than in the equitably paid situation, the findings of Adams (1963b) and Adams and Rosenbaum (1962) could easily be explained by our model.

Some evidence suggests that the overpayment manipulation used by Adams does indeed affect the degree to which the satisfaction of needs such as esteem and recognition becomes associated with high productivity. In a very interesting study, Andrews and Valenzi (1970) obtained data which suggests that in fact subjects typically do see Adams' equity induction as an attack on their self image and self-esteem. Lawler (1968b) conducted a study that used two methods of inducing feelings of overpayment. Subjects in one overpaid group were told that they were unqualified for the job and those in the other were told that they were overpaid for a reason other than their low qualifications. Subjects in this "overpayment by circumstance" group were told that they were working on a grant and that the grant required that they be paid higher wages than were typically paid to workers like themselves. They were also told that workers like themselves were being paid considerably less elsewhere in the city. A third, or equitably paid, group of subjects was also included in the study. Subjects in the "overpaid by circumstance" group reported that they felt more overpaid than did either the unqualified overpaid subjects or the equitably paid subjects. Hence, the subjects who were overpaid by circumstance felt that they received too high an outcome (salary) relative to their inputs. Their productivity, however, was identical to that of equitably paid subjects and considerably below that of unqualified, overpaid subjects.

Adams (1968) has said that the subjects who were overpaid by circumstance may have seen the high pay as a "windfall" or "lucky break" and thus experienced no inequity. This interpretation does not seem to fit with the fact that these subjects reported feelings of overpayment. It also underlines the argument that equity theory should be more specific about when people will feel inequity. Adams (1968) seems to imply that people feel inequity only when they themselves are personally responsible for the inequitable rewards they receive. This point is not emphasized in his earlier writings and, if true, represents an important limitation on equity theory.

A possible reason for the higher productivity of the unqualified overpaid group can be found in data from a postexperimental questionnaire that was completed by each subject. The subjects in the unqualified, overpaid group indicated that doing well on the task was important to them because it would prove their competence to themselves and others. These data suggest that the unqualified, overpaid subjects' productivity was due not to their feelings of being overpaid, but to the way in which they were made to feel overpaid and, in particular, to the kinds of intrinsic and extrinsic rewards they felt would result from high productivity.

This interpretation is congruent with data from five other studies that have examined the hourly overpayment situation. Gordon and Lowin (1965) did a study in which subjects in one group were told they were unqualified and therefore their pay was being reduced, while those in another group were simply told they were unqualified. Interestingly, the first group reported no feelings of overpayment, yet they produced at a rate similar to that of the second group. When the results of this study are considered together with the results of the study by Lawler (1968b), the data show that, for the hourly situation, just feeling overpaid does not lead to high productivity, while having one's qualifications attacked does, even though feelings of overpayment are not aroused. This evidence would seem to suggest that here the attack on qualifications, rather than the overpayment, is crucial. A study by Friedman and Goodman (1967) also seems to support this point. These investigators were unable to replicate Adams's finding of higher productivity, but they did show that productivity could be predicted from the subjects' self-concepts of their qualifications. They explain this in terms of a self-consistency model that is similar to the self-esteem or challenge-to-competence view set forth here.

Valenzi and Andrews (1969) have presented results which are similar to those reported by Lawler (1968b). They overpaid subjects "because of a budget technicality" and found that overpayment had no effect on productivity. Anderson and Shelly (undated) made subjects feel overpaid by telling them they were unqualified in a nonthreatening manner; they found that feelings of overpayment had no effect on productivity. Finally, Wiener (1970) presents data which show that the qualifications attack leads to high productivity only when the subject's ego is involved in the task. This would seem to follow from the self-esteem argument (there is no reason that they should produce highly if an important part of their self-concept is not attacked) but not from equity theory.

In summary, it appears that simply feeling overpaid is not enough to make a subject try to raise his input. Subjects seem to raise their inputs only when they are attacked by the experimenter because of some personal inadequacy. Such a view is not, of course, congruent with equity theory as originally stated, since there is no indication in it that inequity must be induced in this manner before attempts will be made to reduce it. The data can be explained by our Motivation Model without using the concept of inequity. The model simply points out that people, when attacked, often are motivated to perform well because good performance leads to feelings of esteem and competence. Thus, at this time, it is not apparent that equity theory is needed to explain the results for the hourly rate overpayment situation.

Note that, in the overpaid piece rate situation, it was argued that threatening a person's feelings of competence leads to higher-quality work, while in the overpaid hourly situation, it leads to higher productivity. This may seem to be contradictory, but it is logical in light of the different demand characteristics of the two situations. In the hourly pay situation, high productivity is the clearest way for a person to establish his competence to himself and to others. But, in the piece rate situation, it is much less clear that high productivity is a mark of competence that will be accepted by all. Indeed, any worker in a piece rate system will point out that high productivity is often looked upon with suspicion by others. This situation is, of course, created by the fact that additional pay goes along with higher productivity in the piece rate situation.

Work Quality

According to equity theory, it would seem that overpaid hourly rate subjects should increase both their productivity and their work quality, since both are ways of increasing inputs. Adams has not, however, presented any data on the effects of hourly rate overpayment on work quality, despite the fact that quality could be measured for the tasks he had his subjects perform (Adams, 1963b; Adams & Rosenbaum, 1962). Part of the problem here undoubtedly is created by the negative correlation between quality and productivity that characterizes the tasks employed by Adams (e.g., interviewing). This would suggest that the high productivity of the overpaid group might have been achieved at the expense of work quality. The results of the study by Lawler (1968b) support this point. Similar data have also been reported by Valenzi and Andrews (1969) and by Anderson and Shelly (undated). These studies show that unqualified overpaid subjects did produce more than equitably paid subjects but that the quality of their work was, in fact, lower. These data do not appear to be congruent with equity theory. Indeed, considered together, the studies involving overpayment on an hourly rate do not suggest that equity theory is a particularly good explanatory concept where the effects of overpayment on productivity and work quality are concerned.

UNDERPAYMENT: PIECE RATE

Three studies have examined the effects of perceived piece rate underpayment (Andrews, 1967; Lawler & O'Gara, 1967; Moore, 1968). All these studies have produced the feeling of underpayment by actually paying a low piece rate wage, rather than by manipulating the perceived qualifications of the subjects. The results of the studies by Andrews and by Lawler and O'Gara are in general agreement with what would be predicted by equity theory. A low piece rate seems to lead subjects to produce a great number of low-quality products. This, of course, serves to raise their outcomes without demanding greater inputs. Apparently, the subjects in these studies had some conception of what a fair total hourly rate was, and they simply adjusted their inputs to obtain this amount of pay. For these underpaid subjects, fair total pay could be obtained only by having low work quality and high productivity. The study by Moore found no differences between underpaid and equitably paid subjects.

The productivity and work quality differences between the equitably paid and underpaid groups can be explained by our Motivation Model because of the assumptions it makes about what influences the valence of money. It has already been suggested in discussing piece rate overpayment situations that the valence of money may not be directly related to the size of the piece rate offered. Note that the valence of money may also be a function of the amount that the individual already has. Specifically, the more he already has, the less value he will attach to additional amounts. Thus, an individual who already has $3, may value an additional 25 cents less than an individual who has only $1, will value an additional 15 cents. Such reasoning can explain in expectancy theory terms why lower-paid piece rate subjects produce more than higher-paid piece rate subjects. The lower-paid subjects have to produce more in order to reach a point where additional money begins to have lower valence.

The results for piece rate underpayment can be explained by our model, because it assumes that equity influences the valence of money. The point to be remembered, however, is that equity theory gives some clues about what influences the valence of rewards. In the piece rate situation, equity theory leads to the prediction that a certain amount of pay will be seen as fair and that when someone has reached this point, additional amounts of money will not necessarily have a high valence. It could be argued that the same prediction can be derived from a satiation view of needs, but it does not seem to be as applicable here. It is hard, for example, to argue that the desire for money becomes satiated after subjects have earned $3 doing interviews. It would seem to be more logical to argue that they have reached an earnings level that they perceive as fair. At least in understanding the subjects' behavior in the underpaid piece rate situation, equity theory seems to be a helpful concept.

UNDERPAYMENT: HOURLY RATE

Two research studies have been specifically designed to test the predictions of equity theory about the effects of underpayment on an hourly rate. According to equity theory, subjects faced with underpayment might be expected to reduce their inputs in order to bring them into line with their outcomes, or they might be expected to raise their outcomes in order to bring them into line with their inputs. Presumably, if subjects lowered their inputs, this should appear in terms of lower productivity and lower work quality. Valenzi and Andrews (1969) have tested this prediction of equity theory. They found no differences in either productivity or quality between equitably paid and underpaid subjects. Similar data are reported by Heslin and Blake (1969). Both these studies actually underpaid the subjects.

A number of additional studies provide evidence relevant to the point that subjects will reduce their productivity and their work quality if they feel unfairly rewarded, although none of these studies was intended as a test of equity theory. For example, all the studies that have looked at the relationship between job satisfaction and job performance are relevant here. Many simply asked employees to indicate how satisfied they were with their job outcomes; others asked employees to indicate how fair their pay and other rewards were. It can be argued that feelings of satisfaction and feelings of equity are not identical conceptually. In fact, Adams (1965) argues that feelings of satisfaction come from feelings of equity. Empirically, they appear to be highly correlated, particularly where satisfaction is defined as the degree of congruity between what one feels one should receive and what one actually receives. Thus, it seems that, although not directly aimed at testing equity theory, the research on the relationship between satisfaction and performance is relevant because of the close relationship between feelings of equity and feelings of satisfaction.

There have been three major reviews of the studies concerned with the relationship between satisfaction and performance (Brayfield & Crockett, 1955; Herzberg et al., 1957; Vroom, 1964). None of the reviews has concluded that a substantial relationship exists between job satisfaction and job performance. Vroom, for example, reports a median correlation of +.14 in the studies he reviewed. This evidence would seem to suggest that the predicted relationship between feelings of equity and productivity also may not exist. Indeed, from the model of satisfaction that will be presented in Chapter 12, a strong relationship between either satisfaction and performance or equity and performance would not be expected. According to this view, job satisfaction is determined by the amount of the rewards received in the job and is more or less unrelated to many of the determinants of performance that are shown in our Motivation Model. Thus, in the hourly rate situation where pay is not dependent upon performance, there is little reason to believe that the perceived equity of the pay offered or the amount of the hourly rate would directly affect the subject's performance once he had decided to take the job. It might, however, affect his decision to take the job, as the amount of pay would influence the attractiveness of the job. From this point of view, satisfaction would never strongly affect performance, although the two might be related if good performers were consistently given higher rewards.

Some laboratory studies are also relevant to the predictions of equity theory with regard to the effects of insufficient rewards. Weick (1964), for example, found that subjects who were severely underpaid worked harder than subjects who were fairly paid. On the surface, at least, this would seem to be directly contrary to the predictions of equity theory. This study is particularly interesting, because Weick argues that his results are predictable from dissonance theory. He points out that, given a situation where subjects have agreed to do something for low rewards, they can best maintain cognitive consistency by upgrading their evaluation of the importance and interest of the job and putting a lot of effort into performing it. Equity theory, which is also based upon dissonance theory, suggests that subjects will respond to these conditions of low reward in just the opposite manner; that is, they will put forth less effort in order to maintain an equitable input-outcome balance. Clearly, additional research is needed to test the contrasting predictions of these two theories. Still, at this point, it seems reasonable to conclude that there is little evidence to indicate that equity theory is a good predictor of productivity and work quality for the hourly rate underpayment situation. The evidence seems to indicate that once an individual has taken a job, the perceived equity of his hourly pay (where underpayment is involved) has little effect on his output.

SUMMARY AND CONCLUSIONS

The data from the four situations discussed in this chapter suggest that different conclusions about the usefulness of equity theory are needed for the hourly and piece rate situations. When the hourly payment situation was considered, there was little-evidence the concept of equity was needed to explain either the work quality or the productivity data obtained by the studies that have dealt with this condition. Neither overpayment nor underpayment on an hourly rate appeared to affect work quality and productivity, as equity theory suggests they should. On the other hand, our Motivation Model does not predict that either overpayment or underpayment should affect output when pay is not related to performance. Thus, as far as the hourly over- and underpayment situations are concerned, it seems reasonable to conclude that our model can handle the data adequately without assuming that equity is one of the factors which influence the valence of pay.

An explanation of the results from the piece rate situations does seem to demand a concept of equity. On the one hand, the evidence suggests that perhaps the major determinant of productivity in a piece rate situation is the valence or attractiveness of money, as determined by the subjects' desire for money. This, of course, is congruent with the predictions of our model. On the other hand, the fact that output does not bear a simple relationship to the size of the piece rate offered suggests that equity may influence the valence of rewards, as shown in our model. There are two ways in which equity may come into play as a determinant of the valence of certain rewards. First, there is the possibility that increasingly large piece rate rewards may have a decreasing valence for subjects. That is, rewards that are seen as too large, and therefore inequitable, may have a lower valence than rewards that are perceived as equitable. Second, there is the possibility that the amount of the rewards received affects the valence of additional rewards. It seems reasonable to expect that, once a person achieves a level of rewards that he perceives as equitable, future rewards will have lower valences. Thus, as far as the piece rate situations are concerned, our Motivation Model can explain the research results best if it includes equity as one of the factors that influences the valence of pay.

Chapter 9
USING
PAY
TO
MOTIVATE
JOB
PERFORMANCE

The research evidence reviewed so far and the Motivation Model clearly indicate that under certain conditions pay can be used to motivate good performance. The required conditions are deceptively simple and obvious when they are drawn from the model. They are deceptively simple in the sense that establishing the conditions is easier said than done. Theory and research suggest that for a pay plan to motivate people, it must (1) create a belief among employees that good performance will lead to high pay, (2) contribute to the importance of pay, (3) minimize the perceived negative consequences of performing well, and (4) create conditions such that positive outcomes other than pay will be seen to be related to good performance. In this chapter, we shall consider some of the problems an organization confronts when it tries to set up a pay system that will satisfy these four conditions. We shall not, however, go into the second condition—the importance of pay—in detail, because we have already discussed it in Chapter 4. Of the other three conditions, the first is the most basic; it is the central issue around which any discussion of pay and motivation must revolve. We shall approach this issue by asking the following questions: To what degree is pay actually tied to performance in organizations? Do employees feel that pay should be tied to performance? Which of the various ways of tying pay to performance lead most directly to the establishment of the conditions that must exist if pay is to motivate job performance?

TYING PAY TO PERFORMANCE

One obvious means of creating the perception that pay is tied to performance is actually to relate pay closely to job performance and to make the relationship as visible as possible. Several studies have attempted to determine the degree to which this is done in organizations and have come up with some unexpected results. Their evidence indicates that pay is not very closely related to performance in many organizations that claim to have merit increase salary systems. Lawler and Porter (1966) show that pay is related to job level, seniority, and other non-performance factors. Svetlik, Prien, and Barrett (1964) show that there is a negative relationship between amount of salary and performance as evaluated by superiors. Lawler (1964) shows that managers' pay is relatively unrelated to superiors' performance evaluations. Meyer, Kay, and French (1965) show that managers' raises are not closely related to what occurs in their performance appraisal sessions.

Studies by Haire, Ghiselli, and Gordon (1967) and by Brenner and Lockwood (1965) also indicate that at the managerial level, pay is not always related to performance. The evidence in both these studies consists of salary history data; they point up some interesting tendencies. Haire et al., for example, have established that the raises managers get from one year to another often show no correlation with each other. If the companies were tying pay to performance, the lack of correlation would mean that a manager's performance in one year was quite different from his performance in another year. This assumption simply does not fit with what is known about performance: A manager who is a good performer one year is very likely to be a good performer the next. Thus, we must conclude that the companies studied were not tying pay to performance. Apparently, pay raises were distributed on a random basis, or the criteria for awarding raises were frequently changed. As a result, recent raises were often not related to past raises or to performance.

Overall, therefore, the studies suggest that many business organizations do not do a very good job of tying pay to performance. This conclusion is rather surprising in light of many companies' very frequent claims that their pay systems are based on merit. It is particularly surprising that pay does not seem to be related to performance at the managerial level. Here there are no unions to contend with, and one would think that if organizations were effectively relating pay to performance for any group of employees, it would be at the managerial level. Admittedly this conclusion is based on sketchy evidence, and future research may prove it to be wrong. It may be, for instance, that pay is indirectly tied to performance and that the tie is obscured by promotion policies. All the studies reviewed here looked at the relationship between pay and performance within one management level. Even though there is no relationship between pay and performance within a level, there may actually be a relationship if the better performing managers are promoted and because of this receive higher pay. There is little evidence, however, to suggest that this is true.

Failure to tie pay closely to performance in many companies could mean that pay is not motivating job performance. In order for pay to motivate performance, it must appear to be related to performance; and employees are not likely to believe that pay is related to performance if it actually is not. Lawler (1967b) has shown that in one instance where pay was not related to performance, managers were aware of this fact and, consequently were not motivated by pay. This study also showed that in a group of organizations where measurements indicated that pay was only marginally tied to performance, managers had a fairly high belief that pay was related to performance. Thus, the data suggest that, given some positive indicators, employees are willing to believe that pay is based upon performance. Often, however, the positive indicators are missing, and as a result, pay does not motivate the employees to perform effectively.

DO EMPLOYEES WANT PAY TO BE BASED UPON PERFORMANCE?

One reason pay is not closely related to performance in many organizations may simply be that employees object to this way of handling pay. If employees object to seeing their pay tied to their performance, there can be real problems in trying to implement any kind of merit pay system, since it could be and, in fact, would probably be undermined by the employees themselves. One of the clearest findings that comes out of the research on incentive systems like the Scanlon Plan is that these plans work best when the employees want the plan and when they trust management (Whyte, 1955). Thus, the issue of whether employees in general are favorably inclined toward incentive plans is a crucial one when consideration is given to using pay as a motivator.

Two studies have measured managers' attitudes toward how their pay should be determined, and both show that managers prefer to have their pay based upon performance. Lawler (1967b), for example, found that managers believe that performance should be the most important determinant of their pay, but feel that in fact it is not. There was a consistent tendency across all companies for there to be a large gap between how important managers felt performance was in determining pay and how important they felt it should be. This gap between what should be and what was reflects the inability of the companies to develop pay plans that fit the needs of employees. It also indicates that pay could be a much stronger source of motivation in these organizations. In one sense this gap represents a challenge to management to develop a more motivating pay system.

Andrews and Henry (1963) have also presented data to show that managers prefer to have their pay based upon performance. Perhaps the most interesting finding they reported was a tendency for educational level to be related to preferences. Less-educated managers were less in favor of having their pay based upon performance than more highly educated managers. This finding also is congruent with evidence that blue-collar employees are somewhat less enthusiastic about having their pay based upon performance than are managers. But before the studies concerned with blue-collar employees are discussed in detail, a study of salesmen should be mentioned. It shows that they, like the managers, prefer to have their pay based upon general performance and merit rather than upon such factors as seniority and market competition (Research Institute of America, 1965).

Studies done among blue-collar workers to determine their preferences with respect to pay plans, do not show overwhelming acceptance of merit-based plans. The studies are a little difficult to interpret, however, since many of them asked for reactions to specific pay plans, such as piece rate plans, rather than to the general idea of merit-based pay. Workers might, for example, object to piece rate plans but still favor other kinds of merit-based systems. Thus, it is hard to tell if the workers studied objected to the principle of merit pay or to the specific plans queried.

Two studies provide strong evidence that often workers are not favorably inclined toward incentive pay schemes. A large-scale study by the Opinion Research Corporation (1949) found that, although workers felt that incentive plans got the highest output per man, 65 percent of the respondents preferred hourly pay plans. Similarly, a study in Great Britain by Davis (1948) found that 60 percent of the workers sampled were opposed to a system of payment based on results. There is evidence that opposition to incentive plans is lower among workers who have been working on such plans. In the Opinion Research Corporation study (1949), for example, 59 percent of the workers who had been on incentive plans opposed them while 74 percent of the workers who had been on hourly wages opposed incentive plans. Other studies show that incentive plans are usually endorsed by workers already on them, and suggest that in some instances the majority of workers favor them. A study reported by *Factory* (1947), for example, reports that 59 percent of the workers sampled who were not paid on an incentive basis said "they would like to work under such a system if it were fairly run." This finding suggests that employees in general are not against pay based upon performance, although they might be against certain merit pay systems. The results of another study by the Opinion Research Corporation (1946) are presented in Table 9-1. They show the same pattern: Workers on merit plans prefer such plans, and workers on hourly rates prefer them. The data show, however, that overall only 36 percent of the workers studied prefer piece rate plans. It is possible that a far larger proportion would be in favor of merit pay in principle, but would not prefer the piece rate plan to an hourly pay rate.

TABLE 9-1. Replies to question: "On a job which could be paid by either piece rate or hourly rate, which would you rather work on?" (Opinion Research Corporation, 1946)

	No. of Mfg. Manual Workers	Percentage Who Prefer		
		Piece Rate	Hourly Rate	Do Not Know
Total	919	36	61	3
Paid by:				
Hourly rate	658	24	73	3
Incentive plan	131	57	39	4
Piece rate	130	75	22	3
Union status:				
No union where work	220	43	53	4
Have union	699	34	63	3
Members	597	33	65	2
Nonmembers	102	35	54	11

Beer and Gery (undated) have carefully analyzed what determines whether an employee will prefer merit-based pay. Their data suggest that individual preferences are influenced by a person's needs and by the situation in which he finds himself. Employees high in advancement and responsibility needs seemed to prefer merit systems; those with strong security needs did not. The more competent the individual, the better his past experience with the system and the better his relationship with his boss, the more he preferred merit-based pay. Jones and Jeffrey (1964) have found that in one plant workers strongly preferred incentive pay schemes, while in another they strongly rejected the idea of incentive pay. Considered together, this evidence suggests that workers are not necessarily opposed to incentive schemes, but that the situation in which they work and their work history may lead them to oppose them. Presumably in many situations opposition to incentive pay comes about because the employees feel they cannot trust the company to administer incentive schemes properly.

Overall, the studies indicate that workers are less favorably disposed toward merit pay plans than are managers; in fact, the majority of the work force in many organizations may be against them. This conclusion has important practical implications for management. Clearly, to install an incentive plan successfully at the worker level will be difficult. A lot of effort may have to be devoted to building up a relationship of trust between management and workers, and to explaining the particular plan to be instituted as well as the whole concept of incentive pay. To install an incentive plan at the management level may be much easier, since the value system of managers appears to be more congruent with the idea of merit pay.

No incentive pay plan will ever work at any level in an organization unless superiors are committed to the plan and are willing to see their subordinates paid different amounts of money based upon their performance. Superiors must provide a large part of the performance information upon which pay decisions are based. If superiors reject systems that reward people according to their performance, then they are unlikely to provide valid performance evaluations and it will be impossible to base pay upon performance. The evidence indicates, however, that, in general, at least in the United States, managers in business organizations are willing to base pay upon performance. There is some evidence to suggest that good managers are much more amenable to the idea than poor managers, but still, the generalization holds (Gruenfeld & Weissenberg, 1966). It is, of course, consistent with the research that shows managers generally in favor of basing pay on merit.

Some preliminary evidence indicates that there may be cross-cultural differences among managers in their attitudes and values concerning pay. My own research shows that English managers are less willing to distribute pay on the basis of performance than American managers. In making pay raise decisions, the English respondents seem to give much greater weight to nonperformance factors, such as seniority and family situation. Similar findings for other European countries have been reported by Bass (1968). If these preliminary findings are confirmed by future studies, the possibility of using pay to motivate people may be more limited than is frequently suggested. To base pay on performance in many countries, an organization would probably have to undertake a tremendous educational program among managers as well as workers. Even then they might find it ineffective because it conflicts with the basic values of the people.

METHODS OF RELATING PAY TO PERFORMANCE

There are virtually as many methods of relating pay to performance as there are organizations, and at times it seems that every organization is in the process of changing its approach. The R.I.A. (1965) study found, for example, that one out of every three companies has "recently" changed its method of paying salesmen. Campbell, Dunnette, Lawler, and Weick (1970) report that their survey of company personnel practices showed widespread dissatisfaction with current pay systems. Such dissatisfaction is hardly surprising in light of the previously reported finding that pay is not closely related to performance in many companies. It is doubtful, however, that the problems and the dissatisfaction can be corrected simply by changing the mechanics of the plan already in use. Many plans seem to fail not because they are mechanically defective, but because they were ineffectually introduced, there is a lack of trust between superiors and subordinates, or the quality of supervision is too low. No plan can succeed in the face of low trust and poor supervision, no matter how valid it may be from the point of view of mechanics.

Still, some types of plans clearly are more capable than others of creating the four conditions mentioned at the beginning of the chapter. Some plans certainly do a better job of relating pay to performance than others, and some are better able to minimize the perceived negative consequences of good performance and to maximize the perceived positive consequences. One of the reasons pay often is not actually related to performance is that many organizations simply do not have pay plans that are correctly set up in order to accomplish this. Often this comes about because the particular conditions in the organization itself may not have been taken into account when the plan was developed. No plan is applicable to all situations. In a sense, one may say that a pay plan should be custom-tailored. Companies often try to follow the latest fads and fashion in salary administration, not recognizing that some plans simply do not fit their situation (Dunnette & Bass, 1963). Let us stress again, however, that mechanical faults are by no means the only reason that pay plans fail to relate pay to performance. Many of those which fail are not only well designed mechanically but also appropriate to the situation where they are used.

In looking at the mechanics of various types of pay programs, we shall group them together according to the way they differ on three dimensions. First, pay plans distribute rewards on different bases: individual, group, or organizationwide. Second, they measure performance differently: The measures typically vary from admittedly subjective (i.e., based on superiors' judgments or ratings) to somewhat objective (i.e., based on costs, sales, or profits). Third, plans differ in what they offer as rewards for successful performance: salary increases, bonuses, piece rates, or—in rare cases—fringe benefits. Table 9-2 presents a breakdown of the various plans, following this classification system. This classification yields some eighteen different types of incentive plans. A more detailed classification system would, of course, yield more. The table shows where

TABLE 9-2. A classification of pay-incentive plans

	Performance Measure	Reward Offered	
		Salary Increase	Cash Bonus
Individual plans	Productivity Cost effectiveness Superiors' ratings	Merit rating plan	Sales commission Piece rate
Group plans	Productivity Cost effectiveness Superiors' rating		Group incentive
Organizationwide plans	Productivity Cost effectiveness Profit	Productivity Bargaining	Kaiser, Scanlon Profit sharing (e.g., American Motors)

the better-known plans fit in. It also shows a number of plans that are seldom used, and thus do not have a commonly known name. For example, companies do not typically base salary increases to individuals on the cost effectiveness of their work group. This does not mean that such a plan is a bad approach to distributing pay; it just means that it is not used very often.

EVALUATING THE DIFFERENT APPROACHES TO MERIT-BASED PAY

It is possible to make some general statements about the success of the different merit pay plans. We shall evaluate the plans in terms of how capable they have proved to be in establishing three of the conditions that are necessary if pay is to motivate performance. Such an evaluation must, of course, reflect actual experience with the different approaches in a number of situations. Here we are ignoring for the moment the effect of situational factors on the effectiveness of the plans in order to develop general ratings of the plans.

Table 9-3 lists the different types of incentive plans and provides a general effectiveness rating for each plan on three separate criteria. First, each plan is evaluated in terms of how effective it is in creating the perception that pay is tied to performance. In general, this indicates the degree to which the approach actualy ties pay closely to performance, chronologically speaking, and the degree to which employees believe that higher pay will follow good performance. Second, each plan is evaluated in terms of how well it minimizes the perceived negative consequences of good performance. This criterion refers to the extent to which the approach eliminates situations where social ostracism and other negative consequences become associated with good performance. Third, each plan is evaluated in terms of whether it contributes to the perception that important rewards other than pay (e.g., recognition and acceptance) stem from good performance. The ratings range from +3 to −3, with +3 indicating that the plan has generally worked very well in terms of the

TABLE 9-3. Ratings of various pay-incentive plans

Type of Plan	Performance Measure	Tie Pay to Performance	Minimize Negative Side Effects	Tie Other Rewards to Performance
SALARY REWARD				
Individual plan	Productivity	+2	0	0
	Cost effectiveness	+1	0	0
	Superiors' rating	+1	0	+1
Group	Productivity	+1	0	+1
	Cost effectiveness	+1	0	+1
	Superiors' rating	+1	0	+1
Organizationwide	Productivity	+1	0	+1
	Cost effectiveness	+1	0	+1
	Profits	0	0	+1
BONUS				
Individual plan	Productivity	+3	−2	0
	Cost effectiveness	+2	−1	0
	Superiors' rating	+2	−1	+1
Group	Productivity	+2	0	+1
	Cost effectiveness	+2	0	+1
	Superiors' rating	+2	0	+1
Organizationwide	Productivity	+2	0	+1
	Cost effectiveness	+2	0	+1
	Profit	+1	0	+1

criterion, while −3 indicates that the plan has not worked well. A 0 rating indicates that the plan has generally been neutral or average.

A number of trends appear in the ratings presented in Table 9-3. Looking just at the criterion of tying pay to performance, we see that individual plans tend to be rated highest, while group plans are rated next, and organizationwide plans are rated lowest. This reflects the fact that in group plans to some extent and in organizationwide plans to a great extent, an individual's pay is not directly a function of his *own* behavior. The pay of an individual in these situations is influenced by the behavior of others with whom he works and also, if the payment is based on profits, by external market conditions.

Bonus plans are generally rated higher than pay raise and salary increase plans. Under bonus plans, a person's pay may vary sharply from year to year in accordance with his most recent performance. This does not usually happen with salary increase programs, since organizations seldom cut anyone's salary; as a result, pay under the salary increase plan reflects not recent performance but performance over a number of years. Consequently, pay is not seen to be closely related to present behavior. Bonuses, on the other hand, typically depend on recent behavior, so that if someone performs poorly, it will show up immediately in his pay. Thus, a person under the bonus plan cannot coast for a year and still be highly paid, as he can be under the typical salary merit pay program.

Finally, note that approaches which use objective measures of performance are rated higher than those which use subjective measures. In general, objective measures enjoy higher credibility; that is, employees will often grant the validity of an objective measure, such as sales or units produced, when they will not accept a superior's rating. Thus, when pay is tied to objective measures, it is usually clear to employees that pay is determined by their performance. Objective measures such as sales volume and units produced are also often publicly measurable, and when pay is tied to them, the relationship is often much more visible than when it is tied to a subjective, nonverifiable measure, such as a superior's rating. Overall, then, the suggestion is that individually based bonus plans which rely on objective measures produce the strongest perceived connection between pay and performance.

The ratings with respect to the ability of pay programs to minimize the perceived negative consequences of good performance reveal that most plans are regarded as neutral. That is, they neither contribute to the appearance of negative consequences nor help to eliminate any which might be present. The individual bonus plans receive a negative rating on this criterion, however, This negative rating reflects the fact that piece rate plans often lead to situations in which social rejection, firing, and running out of work are perceived by individuals to result from good performance. Under a piece rate system, the perceived negative consequences of good performance may cancel out the positive motivational force that piece rate plans typically generate by tying pay closely to performance.

With respect to the final criterion for pay plans, tying nonpay rewards to performance, the ratings are generally higher for group and organizationwide plans than for individual plans. Under group and organizationwide plans, it is generally to the advantage of everyone for an individual to work effectively. Thus, good performance is much more likely to be seen to result in esteem, respect, and social acceptance, than it is under individual plans. In short, if a person feels he can benefit from another's good performance, he is much more likely to encourage his fellow worker to perform well than if he will not benefit, and might even be harmed.

It should be clear from this short review that no one pay plan presents a panacea for a company's job motivation problems. Unfortunately, no one type of pay program is strong in all areas. Thus, no organization probably ever will be satisfied with its approach, since it will have problems associated with it. It is therefore not surprising to find that companies are usually dissatisfied with their pay programs and are constantly considering changing them. Still, the situation is not completely hopeless. Clearly, some approaches are generally better than others. We know, for example, that many of the approaches not mentioned in the table, such as stock option plans, across-the-board raises, and seniority increases, have no real effect on the performance motivation of most employees. In addition, the evidence indicates that bonus-type plans are generally superior wage increase plans and that individually based plans are generally superior to group and organizationwide plans. This suggests that one widely applicable model for an incentive plan might take the following form.

Each person's pay would be divided into three components. One part would be for the job the employee is doing, and everyone who holds a similar job would get the same amount. A second part of the pay package would be determined by seniority and cost-of-living factors; everyone in the company would get this, and the amount would be automatically adjusted each year. The third part of the package, however, would not be automatic; it would be individualized so that the amount paid would be based upon each person's performance during the immediately preceding period. The poor performer in the organization should find that this part of his or her pay package is minimal, while the good performer should find that this part of his or her pay is at least as great as the other two parts combined. This would not be a raise, however, since it could vary from year to year, depending on the individual's performance during the last performance period. Salary increases or raises would come only with changes in responsibility, cost of living, or seniority. The merit portion of the pay package would be highly variable, so that if a person's performance fell off, his or her pay would also be decreased by a cut in the size of the merit pay. The purpose of this kind of system is, of course, to make a large proportion of an individual's pay depend upon performance during the current period. Thus, performance is chronologically closely tied to large changes in pay.

The really difficult problem in any merit pay system, including this one, is how to measure performance. A valid measure of performance must meet several requirements. Not only must it be valid from the point of view of top management, but it must lead to promotion and pay decisions that are accepted by people throughout the organization: Supervisors, subordinates, and peers must all accept the results of the system. Without this wide acceptance, pay raises will not be seen to reflect merit. Employees gain much of their knowledge about how pay systems operate by watching what happens to other people in the organization. If people whom they feel are doing good work get raises, then they accept the fact that a merit pay system exists. On the other hand, if workers they do not respect get raises, their belief in the system breaks down. Obviously the more the appraisal system yields decisions that are congruent with employee consensus about performance, the more the employees will believe that a merit system exists. The performance measure should also be such that employees feel that their contributions to the organization show up in it very directly. They must feel that they have control over it, rather than feeling that it reflects so many other things that what they do has little weight. This point relates to the first part of our Motivation Model (E→P). Finally, the performance measure or measures should be influenced by all the behaviors that are important for the job holder to perform. People perform those behaviors that are measured, and thus it is important that the measure be sufficiently inclusive.

The performance appraisal systems that are actually used by organizations range all the way from superiors' subjective judgments to the complicated "objective" accounting-based systems that are used to measure managers' effectiveness. The problems with the simple, subjective, superiors' judgments are obvious—the subordinates often see them as arbitrary, based upon inadequate information, and simply unfair. The more objective systems are appealing in many ways. Where they can be installed, they are the best, but even they often fail to reflect individual efforts. Stock option plans are a good example. With these plans, pay is tied to the price of the stock on the market, and this presumably motivates managers to work so that the price of the stock will go up. The problem with this approach is that for most managers the connection between their effort and the price of the stock is very weak.

Plans that base bonuses or pay increases on profit centers or on the effectiveness of certain parts of the business may work, but all too often much of the profitability of one part of the organization is controlled more by outside than by inside forces. Another problem with this kind of system is illustrated by the fate of most piece rate incentive plans used at the worker level. They give the false illusion that objective, highly measurable rates can be "scientifically" set and that trust between superiors and subordinates is not necessary, since the system is objective. Experience has shown that effective piece rate systems simply cannot be established where foremen and workers do not trust each other and have a participative relationship. No completely "objective" system has ever been designed, nor will one ever be. Unexpected contingencies will always come up and have to be worked out between superiors and subordinates. Such events can be successfully resolved only when trust based upon mutual influence exists. Where poor relationships exist, workers strive to get rates set low and then they restrict their production, because they do not believe that good performance will in fact lead to higher pay in the long run.

Thus the answer in many organizations must rest in a reasonable combination of the simple, superior-based rating system and a system which uses more objective measures. First, we must accept the fact that no system can ever be 100 percent objective and that subjective judgments will always be important. Second, we must realize that the key to general acceptance of the decisions that the appraisal system yields lies in having as broad as possible participation in the system.

What would such a system look like? It would be based upon superior-subordinate appraisal sessions where subordinates feel that they have a real oportunity to influence their boss. Obviously, such a system cannot operate, nor can any other for that matter, unless superior-subordinate relations are such that mutual influence is possible. In the first appraisal session the superior and subordinate would jointly decide on three things. First, they would decide on the objectives the subordinate should try to achieve during the ensuing time period. This period might last from three months to several years, depending on the level of the job. Second, they would decide on how the subordinate's progress toward these objectives will be measured. Objective measures might be used as well as subjective ratings by peers and others. Third, they would decide what level of reward the subordinate should receive if he accomplishes his objectives. A second meeting would be held at the end of the specified time period in order for the superior and subordinate to jointly assess the progress of the subordinate and decide upon any pay actions. Finally, a few weeks later the whole process would begin again with another objectives-setting session. The advantages of this kind of system extend far beyond pay administration. It can create a situation where superiors and subordinates jointly become much more certain of what the subordinate's actual job duties and responsibilities are. Some recent studies suggest that there is often greater than 70 percent disagreement between superior and subordinate about what constitutes the subordinate's job, so agreement on his score would not be an insignificant step forward. The fact that the subordinate has a chance to set goals and that he commits himself to a certain level of performance may have an impact on his motivation that is independent of rewards like pay. There is evidence that when people commit themselves to challenging goals, needs like esteem and self-realization can come into play and motivate them to achieve the goals.

This system also offers the subordinate a chance to become involved in important decisions about his own future and thereby encourages a kind of give and take that seldom exists between superiors and subordinates.

Despite the fact that it is possible to state some general conclusions about the effectiveness of different pay plans, perhaps the most important conclusion arising from the discussion so far is that it is vital to fit the pay plan to the organization. What might be a wonderful plan for one organization may for a whole series of reasons be a bad plan for another. Thus, although it is tempting to say that X approach is always best, it is wiser to turn now to a consideration of the factors that determine which kind of plan is likely to be best in a given situation.

FACTORS INFLUENCING THE EFFECTIVENESS OF DIFFERENT PAY PLANS

In selecting a plan for a particular organization, what situational factors must be considered? This question will be dealt with here and again in Chapter 16, where organizationwide factors will be considered. One factor that must be considered when an organization is deciding what type of pay plan to use is the degree of cooperation that is needed among the individuals who are under the plan. When the jobs involved are basically independent from one another, it is perfectly reasonable to use an individual-based plan. Independent jobs are quite common; examples are outside sales jobs and certain kinds of production jobs. In these jobs, employees contribute relatively independently to the effectiveness of the total group or organization, and thus it is appropriate to place them on an incentive scheme that motivates them to perform at their maximum and to pay little attention to cooperative activities.

As organizations become more complex, however, more and more jobs demand that work be done either successively (i.e., work passes from one person to another) or coordinately (i.e., work is a function of the joint effort of all employees) (Ghiselli & Brown, 1955). With successive jobs and especially with coordinate jobs, it is doubtful that individual incentive plans are appropriate. For one thing, on these jobs it is often difficult to measure the contribution of a given individual, and therefore difficult to reward individuals differentially. The organization is almost forced to reward on the basis of group performance. Another problem with individual plans is that they typically do not reward cooperation, since it is difficult to measure and to visibly relate to pay. Cooperation is essential on successive and coordinate jobs, and it is vital that the pay plan reward it. Thus, the strong suggestion is that group and organizationwide plans may be best in situations where jobs are coordinate or successive.

A related issue has to do with the degree to which appropriate inclusive subgoals or criteria can be created for individuals. An example was cited earlier of an individual pay plan that motivated salesmen to sell but did not motivate them to carry out other necessary job activities such as stocking shelves. The problem was that pay was tied to the most obvious and most measurable goal in the job, and some of the less measurable activities were overlooked and unrewarded. This situation occurs frequently; for many jobs, it is quite difficult to establish criteria that are both measurable quantitatively and inclusive of all the important job behaviors. The solution to the problem with the salesmen was to establish a group incentive plan. Indeed, inclusive criteria may often be possible at the group and organizational level but not at the individual level. It is quite easy to think of jobs for which a criterion like productivity might not be inclusive enough when individuals are looked at, but might be inclusive enough when a number of jobs or employees are grouped together. The point, of course, is that in choosing an incentive plan, an organization must consider whether the performance measures that are related to pay include all the important job activities. One thing is certain: If an employee is not evaluated in terms of an activity, he will not be motivated to perform it.

The point has often been made that, wherever possible, objective performance measures should be used. There are, however, many situations where objective measures do not exist for individual or even group performance. One way of dealing with such situations is to measure performance on the basis of larger and larger groups until some objective measures can be found. Another approach is to measure performance on the individual or small group level and to use admittedly subjective measures. This is possible in some situations but not in others. The key factor in determining whether this approach is feasible is the degree of superior-subordinate trust. The more subjective the measure, the higher the degree of trust needed, because without high trust there is little chance that the subordinate will believe that his pay is really fairly based upon performance. Figure 9-1 illustrates the relationship between trust and the objectivity of the performance criteria. Note that it indicates that, even with the most objective system, some trust is still required if the individual is going to believe in the system. It also shows that unless a high degree of trust exists, pay plans based on subjective criteria have little chance of success.

One further issue must be considered when an organization is installing a pay plan: will the individuals under the plan actually be able to control the criteria on which they will be evaluated? All too often the criteria are unrelated to the individual worker's efforts. A good example of this is the American Motors Corporation profit-sharing plan: The indi-

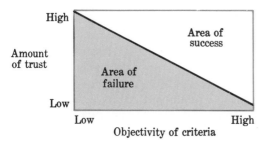

FIGURE 9-1. Relationship of trust and the objectivity of performance criteria to success of the program.

vidual worker is not in a position to influence the profits of the company, yet this is a criterion upon which part of his pay is based. If a pay system is going to motivate employees, the criteria must be such that the employees can directly influence them. The criteria must, in short, be within the employees' control. This point, of course, argues for the use of individual criteria where possible, since they best reflect an individual's efforts.

Pay systems may also be results or process-oriented; that is, they may reward employees chiefly for results (e.g. actual production) or for the way the task or job is carried out. There are usually problems with any system that rewards process only, just as there are problems with systems that reward results only. Perhaps the ultimate example of what can happen in the process-oriented system can be seen in the large bureaucracies that grow up in many civil service and other large organizations. In these bureaucracies people seem motivated to follow the rules, and not to accomplish the objectives for which the organization was established. On the other hand, a salesman may be motivated only by a short-term desire to maximize results. His behavior may lead to a sale, but it may be such that his organization never makes another sale to that buyer. A pay system must be designed to reward both process and results. This may be difficult in many situations; process is particularly difficult to measure objectively, and thus subjective measures may have to be used. As has already been pointed out, subjective measures can only be used effectively where a high degree of trust exists.

SHOULD PAY BE USED TO MOTIVATE?

Although we have not said so explicitly, it is clear that there are many situations in which pay should not be used to motivate job performance. In many jobs, it is impossible to develop adequate criteria for relating pay to performance. There may be no objective measures of performance, so that very subjective measures are needed but cannot be used because of the low level of trust between superiors and subordinates. On the other hand, the problem may be that objective measures are available but the level of trust is not even sufficient to allow their use. As was illustrated in Figure 9-1, there are situations where it simply may not be wise to measure performance for the purpose of relating it to pay. As has already been pointed out, it may be possible to measure some but not all of the relevant aspects of performance. A number of new problems can be created if pay is tied only to those aspects of performance that are measurable: The measurable aspects may receive all the employee's attention, while the others are neglected. In this situation it may well be better not to try to use pay to motivate performance.

Often, profit-sharing plans are used where individual performance measures are not appropriate, and the organization desires to use pay to motivate performance. There is some doubt whether this is worthwhile in large organizations. The larger the organization, the less likely it is that a companywide profit-sharing or cost effectiveness plan will work. The reason for this is simple: The larger the organization, the less influence any one individual has over companywide results, and the less an individual feels that his pay is related to performance. Thus, where individual-based pay plans are not possible, it is not always advisable to use an organizationwide plan. It may in fact be better to have no incentive pay plan at all. Often when organizationwide plans are installed in large organizations, they produce no extra motivation but do produce quite a few extra costs for the company: thus, the suggestion that the cost effectiveness of each plan should be considered.

Finally, motivating people with financial rewards is not a piker's game. Large amounts of money must be given to the good performers if employees are to place a high value on good performance and the raises to which it leads. A company must be willing and able to give certain employees very large raises and/or bonuses if pay is to motivate performance. If a company cannot afford to do this or is not willing to, it should probably forget about using pay to motivate performance. Even if they are willing to spend large amounts of money it may be that pay is not important to the employees and because of this not a possible source of motivation. In this case some other reward may be more appropriate. For example, in one factory that employed large numbers of unmarried women, time off the job was more important than money so when the women were told they could go home after a certain amount of work was done productivity increased dramatically. Several earlier attempts to use pay to motivate high productivity had failed.

In summary, serious thought should be given to *not* using pay as an incentive in organizations where:

1. The trust level is low.
2. Individual performance is difficult to measure.
3. Performance must be measured subjectively.
4. Inclusive measures of performance cannot be developed.
5. Large pay rewards cannot be given to the best performers.

PAY SECRECY

Secrecy about pay rates seems to be an accepted practice in organizations, regardless of whether they use individual or group plans, bonus or salary increases, objective or subjective performance measures. Secrecy seems to be particularly prevalent with respect to management pay (Lawler, in press). Some research suggests that one of the effects of secrecy may be to reduce the ability of pay to motivate (Lawler, 1965a; Lawler, 1967c). As noted in Chapter 4, the argument that has been presented against secrecy is that it makes accurate social comparisons impossible (Festinger, 1954). Secrecy thus makes it difficult to conclusively and visibly establish that pay is tied to performance. Further, it is argued that because social comparisons are difficult, employees often get incorrect feedback about their own performance.

One of the findings that has consistently appeared in the research on pay secrecy is that managers tend to have incorrect information about the pay of other managers in the organization. Specifically, there is a general tendency for them to overestimate the pay of managers around them. For example, in one organization the average raise given was 6 percent, yet the managers believed that it was 8 percent, and the larger their raise was, the larger they believed other people's raises were (Lawler, in press). This had the effect of wiping out much of the motivational force of the differential reward system that was actually operating in the company. Almost regardless of how well the individual manager was performing, he felt that he was getting less than the average raise. This problem was particularly severe among the high performers, since they believed that they were doing well yet receiving a minimal reward. They did not believe that pay was in fact based upon merit. This was ironical, since their pay *did* reflect their performance. What actually existed did not matter as far as the motivation of the managers was concerned; they responded to what they thought existed. Thus, even though pay was tied to performance, these managers were not motivated because they could not see the connection.

There is another way in which pay secrecy may affect motivation. Several studies have shown that accurate feedback about quality of work is a strong stimulus to good performance (Vroom, 1964). People work better when they know how well they are doing in relation to some meaningful standard. For a manager, pay is one of the most meaningful pieces of feedback information. High pay means good performance. Low pay is a signal that he is not ·doing well and had better improve. The research shows that when managers do not really know what other managers earn, they cannot correctly evaluate their own pay and the feedback implications of it for their own performance. Since they tend to overestimate the pay of subordinates and peers and since they overestimate the raises others get, the majority of them consider their pay low; in effect, they receive negative feedback. Moreover, although this feedback suggests that they should change their work behavior, it does not tell them what type of change to make. When managers are not doing their jobs well, negative feedback is undoubtedly what they need. But it is doubtful that it is what managers who are working effectively need.

Note that one recommendation that appears in the discussion of factors affecting the importance of pay as well as in the discussion of factors affecting the belief that pay depends upon performance is that pay information should be more public. Unless this condition exists, pay is not likely to motivate performance, because it will be seen neither as an important satisfier of higher-order needs nor as something that is obtainable from good performance. Making pay information public will not itself establish the belief that pay is based upon merit or ensure that people will get accurate performance feedback. All it can do is clarify those situations where pay actually *is* based upon merit but where it is not obvious because relative salaries are not accurately known. This point is apparent in some unpublished data collected by the author. An organization was studied that had a merit-based plan and pay secrecy. At the beginning of the study, the data collected showed that the employees saw only a moderate relationship between pay and performance. Data collected after the company became more open about pay showed a significant increase in the employees' perceptions of the degree to which pay and performance were related. The crucial factor in making this change to openness successful was that pay was actually tied to performance. Making pay rates public where pay is not tied to performance will only serve to emphasize more dramatically that it is not, thereby further reducing the power of pay to motivate.

MAKING MEN RICH

Gellerman (1968) has argued that if pay is to motivate performance, very large amounts of pay must be involved. He also quite correctly points out that these large amounts of pay must be perceived to be dependent upon performance. This argument is basically in agreement with the emphasis of this book. It is clear from the material on motivation presented in Chapter 6 that increasing the value of the rewards that are tied to performance should increase motivation, since it will lead to an increase in the size of the second factor in the motivation model (the attractiveness of the performance). The model also stresses, however, that it is possible to offer rewards that are too large and, as a result, depress the motivation to perform. This can come about in two ways.

First, because of the operation of a concept of equity in many people, a very large amount of additional pay might be seen as unfairly large and thus not as attractive as a smaller amount. Jaques (1961) has stressed the point that amounts of pay that are unfairly large can produce anxiety on the part of the employee; therefore, employees often do not seek very large amounts. Jaques, in fact, implies that people will actually go out of their way to avoid making amounts of money that they feel are unfairly large. All this strongly suggests that, when very large raises are considered, it is important to determine what the employees feel a fair raise would be. This estimate will probably be conservative, since as the equity theory research suggests, people can quickly raise their perceptions of what a fair pay rate is. But seriously violating people's perceptions of what a fair raise or pay rate is can have harmful effects on motivation because of its effects on the importance of pay. Thus, pay raises can be both too high and too low.

A second reason that very high pay raises or salaries can be harmful was discussed in Chapter 4: The accumulation of large amounts of money will affect the way a person views a given amount of pay. Because the needs upon which pay depends are satiable, it seems likely that once a certain amount of money is acquired, money will begin to have a lower valence. Once it loses its value, it ceases to motivate behavior. Thus, one of the effects of "making men rich" may be to make them disinterested in pay. When this happens, pay cannot motivate them. Very few people ever reach a level where pay ceases to be important. Nevertheless, the issue does present a potential problem for the type of pay administration strategy that emphasizes very large raises and pay based upon performance. It is quite possible that this strategy could, paradoxically, destroy the extrinsic motivation of the good performer because of the great amounts of money he can acquire over time. This rarely happens, since it requires that a person be operating almost wholly on the self-fulfillment need level, and as Maslow and others have pointed out, few people ever reach this level.

SELECTION

The Motivation Model indicates that there are some relatively fixed individual difference factors that determine how employees will see the relationship between pay and performance. Specifically, it suggests that people vary in the degree to which they believe in external versus internal control of the events that affect them. People high in external control essentially feel that they have little control over what happens to them and that they have little ability to influence their environment. People high in internal control feel that they can influence their own destiny. It has been suggested that high external control people are not likely to feel that they can influence their pay, regardless of what they do and regardless of the kind of pay system an organization uses. On the other hand, people high in internal control are likely to believe that they can influence their pay—if the pay system gives them any reason to hold this belief.

It is quite likely that a person's position on the continuum from high internal control to high external control is rather fixed; thus, selection decisions may play an important role in determining the success of pay programs. If an organization is populated entirely by people who are high in external control, a merit pay system may be doomed to failure almost from the beginning. On the other hand, if it is populated by people who believe in internal control, then it is an excellent position to use pay as an incentive. This suggests two points. First, before organizations decide what kind of pay system they are going to use, they might wish to determine what kind of employees they have. Second, in selecting people for jobs where pay is supposed to be an incentive, organizations should look for high internal control people. Rotter (1966) has developed a test to measure the degree to which people believe in internal control, and it is likely that in the near future more such measures will appear. This raises the possibility that people can be tested and selected initially on the basis of the degree to which they are likely to accept a merit pay system. Or, to state the issue more broadly, it might be possible to identify, at the time of hiring, those people who can be motivated by extrinsic rewards.

Chapter 10
PAY
AS A
SOURCE OF
MOTIVATION
FOR JOB
ATTENDANCE

So far the discussion of pay and motivation has focused upon the role of pay in motivating good job performance. Pay can also play an important role in motivating job attendance. Some writers have indicated (e.g., Bass, 1965) that it may influence a worker's decisions about job attendance more than his decisions about how hard he will work. Table 3-1 shows that pay is indeed an important factor in job attendance decisions, but it does not seem to be any more influential in these decisions than in others. Some investigators (e.g., Haire, 1956) have suggested that today many organizations pay only for attendance and that, as a result, pay serves only to motivate attendance. These points and a number of others will be considered in the next two chapters, which will be devoted to a discussion of the role of pay in motivating job attendance. Theory and research will be emphasized in this chapter, and implications for practice will be considered in the next.

The theoretical work used to explain the role of pay in motivating performance is also relevant in this discussion. The only thing that has changed is the kind of behavior that is being motivated. In one instance, it is good performance (e.g., high productivity), and in the other, it is job attendance. A theory or model of motivation should be able to explain both kinds of behavior, as well as many others, since it seems likely that there are some general principles or laws of motivation that apply to all kinds of behavior. Therefore, in this chapter, we shall consider the usefulness of our Motivation Model in explaining job-attendance behavior.

The behavior of a person actually going or not going to his or her specific job on a particular day is influenced by decisions made in several job-related situations. These decisions can be grouped for discussion purposes into three categories. First, there are the decisions that determine what occupation is chosen. Next, there are the decisions that determine which company or organization is joined in order to pursue the chosen occupation. Then there are the decisions that determine whether a person will go to work on a given day once the job has been obtained. Admittedly, every person may not consciously make all three types of decisions, because various situational factors may decide one or even two of them for him. For many people the decisions overlap and feed back to one another. Many people, for example, start by making the second decision, and that decision automatically settles the first. We shall treat these decisions separately, however, since there is a separate body of research that is relevant to each.

OCCUPATIONAL CHOICE

Occupations vary tremendously in the rewards they offer and in the difficulty of entry. Still, somehow, millions of people sort themselves out into different occupations, and at the same time are being sorted out by the representatives of those occupations which limit admission (e.g., medicine, law). Even unskilled workers in most societies have many possible occupations or jobs to which they can aspire. What determines which specific job or occupation a person will choose? Is money a crucial determinant?

Our Motivation Model indicates that a number of factors influence occupational choice. Probably the most crucial factor is suggested by the second term of the model, which is concerned with the factors that influence the attractiveness of different behaviors. If the term "job performance" is broadened to include "entering an occupation," then the model indicates that the attractiveness of entering an occupation is determined by the degree to which a person feels that this occupation will provide the rewards or outcomes he values. Thus, the model suggests that to determine the attractiveness of a given occupation for a person, we must know all the outcomes that the individual perceives to be attainable from that occupation and the valence he attaches to all the outcomes. The more that positively valued rewards are seen to be attainable by choosing a given occupation, the more desirable membership in that occupation will be.

For those people to whom money is highly important, the differential opportunities of making money in various occupations should have a strong influence in determining which occupation is most attractive. This is because of the multiplicative relationship between valence and instrumentality that is specified in the model. The degree to which each occupation is seen to lead to high pay is multiplied by the valence (V) figure for pay. Thus, for people who assign a high valence to pay, a slight difference in the degree to which an occupation is seen to lead to high pay can have a strong influence on the attractiveness of the occupation. For these people small differences in pay can outweigh large differences in factors that for them have a lower valence. On the other hand, for people who do not value pay highly, small differences in the degree to which occupations are perceived to lead to high pay will have little effect. In summary, the attractiveness of an occupation is an important influence in career choice decisions. Attractiveness is determined by a combination of the individual's subjective probabilities with respect to the outcomes that the occupation will lead to and the valence or value the individual assigns to these outcomes.

If attractiveness were the only factor that determined which occupations people were motivated to enter, then a few very attractive occupations would be overwhelmed with applicants. This does not happen, although some occupations certainly have more applicants than there are positions available. One reason more people do not try to enter the occupations that are most attractive to them is indicated by the first term in the Motivation Model (E→P). When the E→P term is zero, there will be no motivation, since to determine motivation it is multiplied by the attractiveness, or second term in the model. It is, in effect, a reality factor. It indicates that people will not be motivated to enter an occupation if they see no probability of entering it. Thus, no matter how attractive an occupation may be seen to be, a person will not try to enter it unless he feels that there is some probability of success. This accounts for the fact that many people choose occupations that are not, in their eyes, the most attractive. It does not mean that they will always abandon trying to join their most preferred occupation just because they feel it is difficult to gain entry to it. As long as a person believes that there is some probability that he can gain entry into his most attractive occupation, he may be motivated to try to join it. The model is a comparative one that predicts the person will try to enter that occupation which has the highest score based upon the combination of the first two terms. This suggests two conditions that may lead a person to seek entry into an occupation that he feels is very difficult to enter. (1) The occupation is much more attractive to him than any other occupation, and (2) his second or third choice is also seen as difficult to enter. When these conditions exist, then it is likely that the most attractive occupation will have the highest score when the first two factors in the model are combined. This, of course, should lead the person to choose the most attractive occupation and direct his efforts toward entering it.

VALENCE OF PAY AND OCCUPATIONAL CHOICE: RESEARCH EVIDENCE

A considerable amount of evidence indicates that the valence people attach to such outcomes as pay can predict the occupations they choose. A large number of studies have shown that the more people value economic outcomes, the more likely they are to prefer, to choose, and to take jobs in business organizations. Stone (1933) found that students who preferred business and banking scored high on the economic scale of the Allport-Vernon Study of Values. Vernon and Allport (1931) reported that people working in economics and business had the strongest economic values. Cantril and Allport (1933) found that male commercial students rated economic values very highly. Rosenberg (1957) developed an extrinsic reward index to indicate the degree to which people prefer outcomes like money. Data collected from 3,905 students showed that students choosing business occupations consistently scored highest on this index. Other data showing the high valence of money for people in business occupations have been reported by Allport, Vernon, and Lindzey (1951), Conrad and Jaffe (1960), and Strong (1943).

On the whole, the research evidence indicates that people who value money highly are more likely to choose business careers than other careers. Presumably, the explanation for this propensity can be found in the perceived instrumentality of business occupations for the attainment of money. If it is assumed that business occupations are generally seen to be very instrumental for the attainment of money, then the data from these studies make good sense in terms of our model. As indicated earlier, when money is regarded as very important, the individual's perception of the amount of money available in different careers becomes the vital perception in terms of career choice. Thus, people who value money highly should pick that career which they feel will yield the greatest economic return. It is hardly surprising that they choose business careers. Although there is little direct research evidence to support the point, in the United States business is generally regarded as the career to choose if you want to make money.

One study (LIAMA, 1967) provides some data to support this interpretation of why people who attach a high value to money choose business careers. It found that careers in banking, manufacturing, and merchandising were seen by students as more likely to lead to a good income than were jobs in education and government. It is also interesting to note in the LIAMA data that business occupations were not rated very highly in terms of their ability to lead to rewards other than money. This, of course, means that a business career may have little appeal for someone who does not value money highly. Given the perception that a business career is instrumental for obtaining money, but not other rewards, the model would predict that business occupations would be largely filled by people who value money highly. It follows from this that nonbusiness occupations should be composed of people who value most highly other outcomes. This point has a number of implications, perhaps the most important of which is that the same incentive system probably will not work in both business and nonbusiness organizations because different kinds of rewards will be valued in each.

Vroom (1964) has reported a study that provides general support for the view that occupational choice is influenced by the valence of the outcomes that are perceived to be obtainable in the occupation. Vroom asked college students to rank five occupations according to their ability to provide fifteen outcomes and to indicate the attractiveness of the five occupations. The data show that the more instrumental an occupation is for attaining desired outcomes, the more attractive it is. Wanous (1969) was able to replicate Vroom's finding. In addition he found that students' perceptions of the instrumentality of occupations for obtaining money were fairly accurate. A somewhat similar study was done by Englander (1960) except that he included only one occupation. His data showed that people who had chosen the occupation in question said it was more instrumental in satisfying their needs than did people who had not chosen the occupation. Finally, data collected by the Organization for Economic Cooperation and Development (1965) show that the supply of manpower for different occupations varies partially as a function of the expected wages of the occupation. Taken together, the data from these four studies offer fairly good support for the view of occupational choice that has been put forth in this chapter.

Korman (1966) has done a study that is directly relevant to the reality factor in our Motivation Model. As was pointed out earlier, people do not always choose the occupation that is most attractive to them because they frequently feel that it is beyond their abilities. According to the model, one of the variables that influences a person's belief about the likelihood that his effort will lead to successful performance is his self-esteem. It is argued that the higher his self-esteem, the more likely a person is to have a realistic view of his chances to perform successfully. People who are low in self-esteem seem to be particularly prone to understating the likelihood that they will be successful. Translating this to the career choice situation, we can argue that the higher a person's self-esteem, the more likely he should be to choose the occupation that is most attractive to him. Thus, people high in self-esteem should be more likely to believe that if they try they can enter X occupation, even though X is such an attractive occupation that "everyone" is competing for entry into it. In other words, for the person who is high in self-esteem, the so-called reality factor often will not be a significant influence on occupational choice be-case he will typically see a high likelihood of success across occupations. For the person low in self-esteem, just the opposite condition should exist; the reality factor will always be operative and may discourage him from trying to join many occupations that are attractive to him. This means that people high in self-esteem will be more likely to base their occupational choice simply upon the degree to which certain occupations are seen to fulfill their needs. Thus, the degree to which an occupation is seen to offer high pay is likely to be directly related to the occupational choice of a person high in self-esteem, while it may not be related to the choice of a person low in self-esteem. The latter, even though he values money highly, may reject occupations that offer the most money, because he does not feel that he can succeed in gaining entry into them. This effect may serve to destroy the simple relationship between the attrac-tiveness of occupations in terms of their financial rewards and the career choices of persons low in self-esteem.

Korman's data (1966) support the view that self-esteem is an im-portant determinant of whether an individual will choose the occupation which is, in fact, most attractive to him. His data show that persons who esteem themselves highly are more likely than others to choose occupa-tions that they feel will satisfy their important needs. Thus, for people high in self-esteem, occupational attractiveness is predictive of choice, while it is not for persons low in self-esteem. Although Korman does not present the data for pay separately, it follows that the attractiveness of the occupation in terms of pay would be predictive of the choices of per-sons high in self-esteem but not of persons low in self-esteem. Somewhat less direct evidence on this issue is contained in a study by McArthur and Stevens (1955). They found that the expressed vocational preferences of private school students correspond more closely to their final occupations than do the expressed preferences of public school students. If it is as-sumed that the public school students had lower self-esteem, then this finding is easily interpretable in terms of the model. Thus, although there has been very little research on the impact of self-esteem on career choice, the available evidence is consistent with the view that self-esteem mediates choices by affecting the degree to which people feel they can successfully participate in different occupations.

In summary, pay plays an important role in motivating people to enter certain occupations, but there are large individual differences in just how important its role is. Clearly, for those people who value money highly, pay has a very significant influence; it typically leads them to choose business careers because these are perceived to offer the greatest economic rewards. On the other hand, for people who do not value money highly, pay probably plays a crucial role only when two occupations are seen to be relatively similar in other ways. When this occurs, a person's perception of the economic outcomes provided by the two occupations may be crucial in occupational choice. Such a situation is probably the exception rather than the rule, however, so it seems best to conclude that for people who do not value money highly, their perceptions about the ability of occupations to lead to high pay probably are not important influences on their occupational choices.

The data also suggest that people will not necessarily choose the occupations that are most attractive to them if their own assessment of their abilities presents a constraint. Even though a person may value pay highly and feel that it can be obtained in a certain occupation, he will not choose the occupation if he feels that his abilities, age, sex, race etc., prohibit access to it. In short, then, pay is one of a number of outcomes that directly influence the attractiveness of occupations; but its influence on the career choice decision is strongly mediated by its relative importance and by the degree to which people feel they can actually enter higher paying occupations.

Finally, note that the model presented here suggests a number of interesting research studies that need to be done. As Vroom (1964) has said, particularly needed are experimental studies that manipulate the instrumentalities of occupations and examine the effect on the attractiveness of occupations. Unfortunately, most of the existing studies are correlational, and as a result, it is difficult to assess the causal basis for the relationships reported between attractiveness and choice. Correlational data are always open to the criticism that people are merely saying that their chosen occupation is attractive and highly instrumental in order to justify their choice. Experimental studies can go a long way toward establishing just which comes first: the instrumentalities and the attractiveness, as has been assumed, or the choice, which is then justified in terms of attractiveness and instrumentalities. Also of interest would be further research on the accuracy of the instrumentalities that people associate with different occupations. It is quite possible that people typically base their choices on inaccurate information and, in fact, consider only a few of the many possible consequences of choosing a particular occupation. In short, they may be operating on a limited view of the situation and using erroneous data as well.

ORGANIZATION AND JOB CHOICE

Once the decision to enter a particular occupation has been made, a job seeker must then decide which organization he will work for. Although a person makes this decision at the beginning of his work career, it is in one very important sense constantly being made by every employee. People are constantly choosing among jobs; in some cases it is among jobs they do not have, while in others it is between the one they presently hold and one that is being offered to them. Vroom (1966) has described how a job choice decision is made by a business school graduate student:

> He begins to search for possibilities and eventually discovers a series of alternatives. He then concentrates on evaluating these alternatives in terms of the degree to which they will permit attainment of each of his goals. Through visits to the organization, brochures prepared by its personnel or public relations staff, and conversations with friends, teachers, or parents he forms judgments of the likelihood that he will be able to attain particular goals through a given organizational membership (p. 214).

Presumably, the student then joins the organization that he feels will offer the best opportunity to attain his goals.

Vroom's description of the job choice decision is in some ways similar to our explanation of the way people make occupational choice decisions. The reason for the similarity is quite simple: There is reason to believe that the two decisions are based on the same kind of decision-making process.

The major difference between the two is that career decisions are often made first, and they seem to be more permanent. The career decision is a higher-order first-screening decision that tends to limit the number and range of job openings an individual considers. In the occupational choice decision, the behavior is that of choosing a career, while in job choice, the behavior is that of choosing among organizations in which to work and among specific jobs in the chosen organization.

Vroom's description of the job choice decision may be misleading in one sense. It pictures a decision based on relatively complete information; further it shows the person conducting an organized, rational search for alternatives. Although this may typify some people's job choice behavior, many decisions seem to be made on the basis of inaccurate and incomplete information (Simon, 1957).

The Motivation Model predicts that a person will try to obtain that job which he perceives as most instrumental for the attainment of his goals. Just as in occupational choice, a reality factor comes into play, since presumably a person will not try to obtain a very attractive job if he feels that he cannot. Vroom (1966) designed a study to test this approach to explaining job choice decisions. He asked students to rate the organizations they were considering in terms of their perceived instrumentality for the attainment of fifteen goals, one of which was a high salary. The students were also asked to rank the goals in order of importance.

His data showed that the students were most attracted to those organizations which were seen as instrumental for the satisfaction of their most important needs. They rated the highly instrumental organizations as more attractive, and they actually joined these organizations a few months later when they left school.

Vroom's study did not measure the subjects' E→P beliefs. They were not crucial here since the students were choosing among a number of jobs that were offered to them. As a general rule, E→P beliefs may not be relevant as often in job choice decisions as in occupational choice decisions. Frequently, a person is choosing between jobs that are offered to him, and E→P beliefs are not relevant; but in occupational choice, they usually are relevant, since people usually have to gain admission to occupations through some effort of their own. Admittedly, one may be offered admission to an occupation in the sense that he is offered a job in that occupation. In such situations, the distinction between job choice and occupational choice becomes blurred.

Unfortunately, there are very few other studies that can be used to test the thinking presented here about how people make job choices. Much of the research has looked at the effect of economic variables (on turnover and labor supply), but has not directly examined the psychological processes that underlie job choice decisions. Still, the research is of interest, and several findings seem to fit particularly well with the present approach to explaining job choices (see Organization for Economic Cooperation and Development, 1965; Yoder, 1956). These data show that:

1. Organizations that pay higher than average wages seem best able to attract and retain high-quality labor.
2. Turnover is high in organizations where wages are low relative to other organizations in the area.
3. The stimulus to leave an organization is greatest when employees in other organizations seem to be making more money.
4. Turnover is low in time of recession or depression.

The first three findings indicate that people tend to gravitate toward higher-paying jobs, particularly if the jobs are local and highly visible. These three findings are perfectly interpretable in terms of our model, since they show that people choose jobs that they perceive to have the highest instrumentality for one goal—pay. If it is assumed that the perceived differences between working as an X in company Y and working as an X in company Z are very small, then slight differences in wages may have a great influence on the decision about where to work. This could be true even for people who do not value money very highly, because the one clearly visible difference between the two companies is the salary. Thus, in choosing between the companies, a person is faced with a situation where things are equal in most respects except that one company has offered more money. Even though money is not of high importance to him, he will take the higher-paying job. The tendency for people to take the jobs that are the most instrumental for attaining their goals leads one to expect that people who value money highly will almost always gravitate toward high-paying companies. This holds whether the people are choosing a job for the first time or are choosing between their present job and one in another company. It would not hold if the low-paying company were seen to offer desirable nonpay rewards that the high-paying company did not.

Pay may typically have a stronger influence on job choice decisions than on occupational choice decisions. The same types of jobs in different organizations often seem equally attractive, so a small difference in pay can tip the scales toward the higher-paying job. On the other hand, occupations differ on a large number of variables, so that a difference in pay instrumentality is just one of the factors that is likely to be a basis for deciding between them. Even small differences in starting salary may be particularly potent influences on the job choice of a new job seeker. For one thing, the new seeker probably is not as sharp as the more experienced worker in assessing the instrumentality of jobs for providing noneconomic outcomes, so he is more likely to feel that the starting salary is the only clear difference between two jobs. This speculation leads to the prediction that most new college graduates will accept the highest-paying job they are offered in their chosen field. On the other hand, it would seem that the experienced worker would be relatively unlikely to change jobs for only a small salary increase. For one thing, he considers other instrumentalities; also he may envision a number of costs associated with leaving his present job: giving up long-term friendships and adopting new behavior patterns, for example. Thus he may not feel that the costs are worth the small difference in pay. The new job seeker has no such costs and thus he can give more weight to a small difference in starting salary.

The fourth finding mentioned above illustrates that a reality factor operates in job choices. Turnover is undoubtedly lower in times of recession, because people realize that, although another company may pay more, there is a low probability of getting a job there. Thus, they decide to hold onto the jobs they have.

THE DECISION TO GO TO WORK

Absenteeism is a major problem in many organizations. In some, it averages over 10 percent a day. It disrupts schedules, creates the necessity of overstaffing, and is quite expensive. Absenteeism reflects the fact that people have to be motivated to go to work each day. They do not just show up automatically. As the model indicates, they decide whether or not to go to work each day by comparing the perceived consequences of other behaviors they are considering with those associated with going to work. People will be motivated to go to work only when they feel that this behavior will lead to more positively valued outcomes than any alternative behavior. Thus, it is not surprising to find that a factor like being a member of a closely knit social group seems to motivate people to go to work regularly (Whyte, 1948). People who belong to such groups presumably associate more rewards with going to work than do people who are not group members. For example, the former feel that going to work will lead to the satisfaction of social needs. Group members also see some negative consequences associated with not going to work that do not operate for nongroup members. They often say that other people will have to work too hard if they do not go to work and they say that they feel bad about this (Whyte, 1948). In short, it is not surprising that people who belong to a cohesive social group are more likely to go to work, since job attendance is more attractive to them than staying away.

Pay is, of course, one of the factors that people consider when they are debating whether or not to go to their job, but it is only one of many influences. Employees are often absent even though it means less pay. The influence of pay on job attendance is partially dictated by the importance of pay to the individual. Unless pay is somewhat important, it will not play a deciding role in determining job attendance. This is because of the multiplicative relationship between valence and instrumentality. When the valence of an outcome is low or 0 it drops out of the equation. Pay may also not influence job attendance if the person sees no connection between going to work and getting paid. It is unlikely that anybody could feel that there was no relationship between long-term attendance and pay, but it is perfectly possible to feel that the relationship on a given day is nil. That is, a person may well feel that he will get the same amount of pay whether he goes to work on a particular day or not. In such a situation, pay will not influence his job attendance decision, even though pay is very important to him.

Haire (1956) has pointed out that some organizations pay people for attendance rather than for performance. But do they really pay even for attendance? Given the amount of leave a person can have without losing any pay, it seems that many organizations pay not so much for attendance as for membership. That is, they make pay contingent upon the person remaining on their membership roles and meeting the organization's minimal attendance requirements. The effect of all this is to allow a person to decide a number of times during a year not to show up for work without losing any money. In terms of the model, it has the effect of reducing the perceived positive consequences of going to work on certain days and because of this, it leads to lower attendance.

There is surprisingly little research on the way different pay systems affect absenteeism. A recent study by Lawler and Hackman (1969) does, however, provide strong support for the points that have been made in this chapter. Lawler and Hackman worked with a company that had been experiencing high absenteeism among part-time janitorial employees. A plan was developed that offered a cash bonus to workers who showed up regularly. The plan was designed to directly affect the perceived consequences of going to work and not going to work. The plan was developed participatively in three work groups. Figure 10-1 shows the results for these three groups. The bonus plan did lead to higher job attendance. This, of course, suggests the importance of tying pay to the kind of behavior that is to be motivated. The data clearly show that relating pay closely to attendance had the effect of increasing attendance.

Further data from the study illustrate a second important point about pay plans. The pay plan that was participatively developed by the groups involved in the study was imposed upon two similar work groups elsewhere in the organization. The data show that the plan was not as effective where it was imposed as where it was developed. The

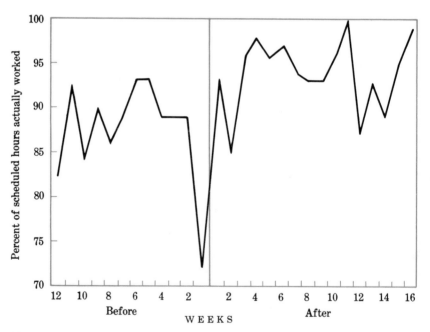

FIGURE 10-1. Impact of pay plan on attendance. (Lawler & Hackman, 1969)

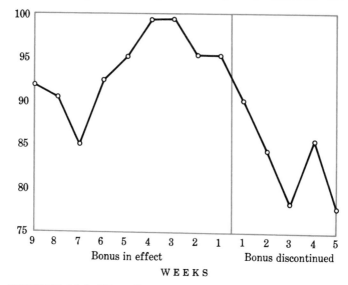

FIGURE 10-2. The effect on attendance of eliminating the bonus plan. (Scheflen, Lawler, & Hackman, 1969)

reason for this, undoubtedly, lies in the fact that the groups that developed the plan saw it as their plan and were committed to seeing that it was successful. The other groups saw the plan more as a management tool to get them to come to work, which, of course, it was. These data emphasize the frequently made point that the mechanics of a pay plan alone do not determine its success. Success is also very much influenced by how it is introduced, how it is accepted, the workers' initial experience with it, and the superior-subordinate trust levels.

In a followup study of the bonus plan, Scheflen, Lawler, and Hackman (1970) collected data on the impact of the plan after one year. Attendance had risen in the groups in which the plan had been imposed. In two of the three groups where the plan had been participatively developed, it had been discontinued by management. Figure 10-2 shows what happened when the plan was discontinued. Attendance dropped significantly, indicating that the plan did have an effect on attendance. In the other participative group attendance remained high. The researchers attribute the dropping of the plan to their own failure to obtain the commitment of management to the new plan.

Tardiness and early leaving are similar in many ways to absenteeism. They involve decisions about when to arrive at work and when to leave, rather than whether to go. All these decisions are presumably made in the same way. Thus pay should influence decisions about tardiness and early leaving only if it is important to the person and is seen to be affected by time of arrival and departure.

Pay will not motivate a person to show up on time if he is paid the same regardless of whether he is tardy or not. Thus, if pay is to affect tardiness and early leaving, it must be closely tied to the specific behavior involved. The time clock was designed to make this close relationship possible. It does not always succeed, because informal norms develop about punching other people in and out, and resentment often develops over having to "clock in." There is some reason to believe that time clocks do help to cut down on tardiness if pay is reduced when people check in late, but they may not be worth the resentment they produce and the mistrust they communicate. Furthermore, there is no evidence to indicate that they are necessarily the best way to solve the problem. There is no reason why a foreman, for example, could not reduce the pay of people who show up late. The important psychological principle necessitates tying an employee's pay to being on time, and there is no reason to believe that a time clock is the best or only way to accomplish this.

Just as in considering the role of different pay plans in motivating performance, it is important to consider whether using time clocks ties other positive outcomes to showing up on time and its effect on any negative outcomes that might be associated with coming to work on time. It has been suggested that because people resent punching time clocks, their use can cause the behavior of being on time for work to lead to certain negative outcomes (e.g., a feeling of dependency), and that they do not contribute to other positive outcomes being tied to being on time.

Also, some other motivation—acting as either a reward or punishment—may be more effective than using a time clock and cutting employees' pay. Besides the obvious organizational sanctions that can be invoked for lateness (e.g., dismissal, suspension), there are other sources of motivation—such as superior and work-group disapproval, getting a very difficult work assignment, and losing overtime—which can be used in addition to or instead of pay cuts. Of course, these methods will be effective only to the extent that they affect the perceived relative advantages of getting to work on time over arriving late. This can be done by offering some reward for coming on time or by tying more punishment to not coming on time, so that alternative times of coming to or leaving work look less attractive. In summary, then, pay is one of the factors that can influence absenteeism, tardiness, and early leaving. It can influence these behaviors only to the extent that it seems to be related to the behaviors and is important to the employees. When pay is seen to depend upon attendance, it increases the positive outcomes associated with attendance and thereby makes attendance more attractive and likely. It can be similarly related to arriving and leaving on time.

Chapter 11
USING
PAY
TO
MOTIVATE
JOB
ATTENDANCE

The research reviewed in Chapter 10 shows that pay can motivate job attendance. What is more, it clearly points up the psychological conditions that must exist if pay is to be effective in motivating attendance. This chapter will show how knowlege of these psychological conditions can, in turn, give organizations an insight into the impact of different pay practices on job attendance.

HOURLY PAY VERSUS SALARY

A number of books and articles have debated the relative advantages of paying workers on an hourly basis versus paying them a straight salary (see Bass, 1965; Kaponya, 1962). The arguments used generally hinge upon the effects these pay programs have on job attendance. It is generally conceded that workers prefer to be salaried and, all other things equal, will choose a salary job over an hourly job. This point makes good sense in terms of our model. A salary offers more security than hourly pay, and hence should be more positively valued. Further, the model predicts that people will pick that job which appears most likely to be instrumental in attaining positively valued outcomes.

It is also argued that salaries are cheaper to administer and that, therefore, it makes sense to put all workers on a salary schedule (Kuriloff, 1966). The critics of salaries, however, stress that salaries tend to encourage absenteeism and tardiness. The basis for this claim seems to be that, with no time clock to punch, workers will be less motivated to show up for work on time because pay is not closely tied to attendance. This point is probably valid if a well-administered hourly program is being compared with a poorly administered salary system. It is not valid, however, to say that all salary-based pay programs are worse in this respect than all hourly pay systems. Pay can be reduced for excessive absenteeism and tardiness under a salary system just as it can under an hourly system. Further, under a salary system the threat of dismissal for nonattendance or tardiness can be more meaningful than under an hourly system, because salary jobs are typically valued more than hourly jobs.

The basic argument, therefore, is that job attendance is a function of the outcomes that are seen to depend on it and that there is no necessary difference between hourly and salary pay systems in the degree to which they tie outcomes to job attendance. If properly administered, both approaches can tie positive rewards to coming to work and negative outcomes to not coming to work. Thus, it is hardly surprising to find that when companies switch from an hourly to a salary pay system, they often find little change in job attendance behavior. Absenteeism and tardiness do not increase as the experiences of several companies (e.g., Alcan, I.B.M., and Gillette; MacGregor, 1970) have shown. There is, in fact, evidence that eliminating time clocks and putting employees on salaries can sometimes lead to better job attendance. When some workers in Cannon Electric were switched to salaries, they showed better attendance records than did other workers (Kaponya, 1962). MacGregor (1970) reports that when Motorola eliminated time clocks and switched to an all-salary pay plan, attendance was at least as good as before and perhaps better. The better attendance of salaried workers probably reflected the trust the company showed in them and their desire to live up to it by coming to work on time and regularly (Bass, 1965). For them, coming to work regularly and on time seemed to lead to a number of intrinsic rewards (e.g., feelings of self-esteem). It is not clear, however, that just switching to an all-salary pay system will always have this effect. It may have to be accompanied by a general change in management style if this is to happen.

Perhaps the only conclusion about the relative advantages of hourly pay and salaries that can be reached is that there is no necessary difference between them in terms of motivating job attendance. If one is more convenient than the other for some other reason (e.g., cost), it probably should be used. Or if one is more attractive to prospective employees and can be used in recruiting, it should be used. Either system, when properly used, can motivate job attendance. The crucial question to ask when considering a change from one to the other is, What effect is the change likely to have on the perceived consequences of job attendance? Unless the new system changes the outcomes tied to job attendance in a given situation, it is not likely to lead to differences in job attendance. Just changing the pay system from hourly to salary may have no direct effect on the perceived consequences of coming to work in most organizations. One clear implication of this conclusion is that organizations should not expect to solve job attendance problems simply by switching either to or from an hourly pay system. Job attendance problems are solved by tying positive outcomes to job attendance and negative ones to nonattendance, and it is not at all clear that the most effective way to do this is to change either to an hourly system or a salary system.

As we shall see, the best ways to motivate attendance may lie in the areas of high-order need satisfaction, job involvement, and overall job satisfaction rather than in the area of pay and pay systems. To some extent, changes in the pay system (e.g., moving to a salary pay system) may support changes in these other areas, but as isolated events they should not be expected to have much effect.

OVERTIME PAY

One of the most effective means of motivating job attendance may well be overtime pay. Workers apparently will go to great lengths to earn the time-and-a-half and double-time pay that is usually given for overtime work. The expectation of overtime leads employees to show up regularly so that they will be in a position to collect overtime pay if it is available. Unless an employee has been coming in regularly and has thus put in his normal work week, he will be in no position to earn any overtime that might be available. For the worker who has not come in regularly and has not put in his forty hours, Saturday work or night work may not bring in any overtime pay. Therefore, the availability of overtime work may reduce absenteeism, because it creates the perception that in order to really cash in on the overtime money, an employee must come to work regularly. In effect, it clearly ties large amounts of money to coming to work regularly, and as a result, good attendance is seen to be rewarded.

The possibility of earning overtime pay may have the positive effect of motivating employees to come to work, but it may also have the negative effect of discouraging high productivity. There is little evidence on the effects of overtime pay on per hour productivity, but what there is suggests that overtime tends to suppress productivity (Ghiselli & Brown, 1955; Viteles, 1953). Physiological factors, such as the fatigue caused by longer hours, may in part account for the lowered productivity. But observational evidence suggests that more than simple physiological factors may be to blame. When overtime work is used to supplement regular productivity, employees' perceptions about the consequences of good performance are affected. Employees working under overtime systems come to believe that good performance and high productivity result in less pay. In short, if productivity is low, they get lucrative overtime pay, but if productivity is high, they get only their regular wages. Because of this, organizations that give overtime pay often place themselves in the position of financially rewarding poor performance. This problem does not arise where overtime is not available.

Some observational data I have collected show quite clearly that workers pace their productivity in order to obtain overtime pay. In one particular situation the workers perceptibly slowed down during weeks in which it appeared that they might be able to put in some overtime because of the higher work load. During weeks in which it was obvious that there was not enough work for even forty hours, they went ahead and did their work in a businesslike manner so that they could relax at the end of the week. This illustrates the point that overtime pay may be a disincentive, because it is seen as a reward for poor performance. The answer to this problem lies in reducing overtime work where possible. When overtime work cannot be avoided, it should be offered first to the high producers. If it is offered only to these individuals, it may be seen as a reward for good performance rather than as a reward for poor performance.

PAY SECRECY

Job choice decisions are often influenced by perceived rather than actual pay rates. All other things equal, a person will choose to work for the company that pays the highest rates. The problem is that, because of the secrecy surrounding pay, many employees do not have an accurate idea of what other people earn and what other companies pay (Lawler, in press). Thus, it is difficult for employees to make accurate comparisons between what they are being paid by their organization and what they might be paid by another. In short, they have poor information upon which to base a comparison. This means that sometimes they will feel they can do better in another organization when in fact they cannot. Since managers typically overestimate what others like themselves earn, it would not be surprising to find that some employees leave their present organization, expecting to find a better situation elsewhere, only to find that they have misperceived the situation they moved to. This, of course, is the old "greener grass" phenomenon. Secrecy about salaries contributes to such misperceptions and, indirectly, to personnel turnover.

A single organization can do little to solve this problem by itself. Making public its own salaries may help a little by showing an employee exactly where he stands in his own organization. It may even be important, since the evidence shows that managers typically think they are worse off in comparison with their peers and subordinates than they actually are. It should also counteract the tendency of employees to under-estimate what higher-level employees earn. If they knew just what kind of salary increase a promotion entailed, they might be less inclined to move to a different organization (Lawler, 1966c). It would not, however, prevent people from looking outside the organization and making erroneous comparisons there. Only if every organization made its salary schedule public would this problem be solved. It could, of course, be dangerous for one company to publicize its salary information if no other companies did. Employees might think that their company paid the lowest salaries and, as a result, look for work elsewhere. This might happen even if all companies were paying the same wages. One thing a single company can do is to make public the results of salary surveys so that its employees will have some accurate information about what other organizations are paying.

SALARY SURVEYS

Organizations make salary surveys of their leading competitors in order to determine if their own salaries are in line with those paid by other companies. The purpose of this, of course, is to minimize the chance that employees will leave their organization because they can get more pay elsewhere. The salary survey approach to administering salaries has been criticized as tending to create a kind of noninnovative sameness among corporation salary systems and as encouraging faddishness and "me too" behavior which fails to take into acount the very real differences that exist between organizations (Dunnette & Bass, 1963). The major criticism of salary surveys, however, is that organizations seldom try to determine which other companies or groups their employees use for comparison purposes. Westinghouse, for example, might do a salary survey that includes General Electric and Sylvania, and then peg their salaries according to the salaries paid by these national competitors. But how many Westinghouse employees actually look to General Electric and Sylvania when they make their pay comparisons? No one really knows, but there is good reason to believe that not very many do. Some research evidence suggests that they are more likely to compare their pay with that of friends who work for local companies or with that of other members of their craft or profession who work in a variety of companies (Patchen, 1961).

The simple fact is that salary surveys are useless unless they include data on the people with whom a company's employees actually compare themselves. All too often no research is done to determine who the reference groups are. One way to prevent the salary survey from being misdirected and to increase its validity in the eyes of employees is to have employees participate in planning the survey. They may not be sophisticated in survey techniques, but they do have valuable information about what companies should be surveyed. All too often a personnel manager or wage and salary administrator decides that it is appropriate to compare the salaries his company pays with those paid by some of its leading competitors. He does not attempt to determine if the companies represent the actual comparison groups for his own employees, and he is honestly shocked to find that his best people are leaving to work for XYZ down the street, which makes another kind of product. After all, his salary survey established that the company's salaries were in line with those of its competitors! The moral is that it is dangerous to make untested assumptions. Salary surveys that are based on inaccurate assumptions about which comparison groups are used are worse than useless. They are positively dangerous, since they can give a company a false sense that everything is all right when, in fact, it is not.

CAFETERIA-STYLE PAY PLANS

It has been suggested that organizations can greatly profit from introducing cafeteria-style wage plans (Lawler, 1966c; Mahoney, 1964; Nealey, 1963; Schuster, 1969; Taylor, 1968). These plans allow employees to select the combination of cash and fringe benefits that they want. Every employee is assigned X amount of compensation, which he can divide up among a number of fringe benefits and cash. This guarantees that each employee will get only the fringe benefits that he desires. Research evidence has established that there are large individual differences among people in the value they attach to various fringe benefits. Some value dental insurance highly, for example, while others do not. This means that in most organizations many workers are given fringe benefits that they do not value in proportion to what they cost the company. Thus, many companies are spending money on fringe benefits and getting a low return in terms of the value employees place upon the outcomes.

Cafeteria plans can solve this problem since they ensure that people get only those fringe benefits which they value. In addition, such plans impress on employees just how much the company is spending to compensate them. Under most pay plans the typical employee has no idea how much money the company is spending on his fringe benefits, and if asked, he would probably underestimate. Thus the company is not getting full value for its fringe benefits investment.

Cafeteria-style plans are particularly relevant to the topics of turnover and job choice. It can be argued that one of the effects of this approach to salary administration should be to increase the employee's perception of the value of his pay package, since the package would contain only valued benefits. If this argument is correct, then using the cafeteria approach should not only reduce turnover but make more people choose to work in the organization that uses it. Compared with other organizations, it will be seen as offering more outcomes that are positively valued. In other words, the cafeteria-style wage package will be more valued and so will membership in the organization offering it.

PAYING HIGH SALARIES

By paying high salaries, organizations can attract people and retain them. This follows logically from our Motivation Model. It also follows from the model that the people who are attracted to organizations which pay high salaries will be different from the people attracted to organizations that pay average or low salaries. High-paying organizations, like businesses, are more likely to attract those people who place a high value on money. As was pointed out earlier, people who value money highly are particularly likely to base job choice and turnover decisions on the amount of salary offered; furthermore, they are particularly likely to take the highest-paying job available. On the other hand, people who value money less may not be so ready to take the job offering the highest pay because they are equally or more interested in other outcomes. The more people value money and the less they value other outcomes, the more likely they are to make choices solely on the basis of money. This means that an organization which offers high salaries will be likely to end up with people who value money highly and perhaps are less concerned with other aspects of the job. This would seem to be particularly true for organizations that have little to offer besides high pay.

It may be advantageous to an organization to employ people who value money highly. They can be motivated by pay incentive systems, and they can be retained as long as the organization continues to pay high salaries. It can, however, also cause problems, particularly if the organization itself does not recognize that it is made up of such people. In an organization such as this, incentives other than money might not be effective in motivating behavior. This could be a problem particularly when financial incentives simply cannot be used to motivate all the kinds of behavior that are needed if a person is to perform his job effectively. On the other hand, organizations that are low-paying may find it difficult to motivate with money because their employees do not value money highly. This would come about because the job choice process is such that people who value money highly are not likely to come to work for low-paying organizations. This point would seem to have important implications for the possibility of using pay to motivate employees in such places as government organizations, social welfare agencies, and hospitals.

Employees who value pay above all else probably do not develop the same kind of loyalty as employees who choose an organization for nonpay reasons. Their commitment to the organization presumably would end as soon as someone else offered more money. Because of this, many organizations say that they refuse to "buy" people; in other words, they do not want people to come to them solely for monetary reasons. This is probably a reasonable policy from a motivational point of view, and it is certainly a prudent one from an economic point of view.

STOCK OPTIONS AND DEFERRED-BONUS PLANS

Stock option and deferred-bonus pay plans are often used by companies to attract and hold managerial talent. In this respect these plans are very similar to high salaries. Like high salaries, they attract a certain kind of person, and because of this, their use entails the same kinds of problems that the use of high salaries entails. There is one important way, however, that the stock option and deferred-bonus plans differ from the simple paying of high salaries. This approach postpones payment for present performance to some time in the future. A good example of this is the kind of bonus plan used by some automobile companies. A manager earns a performance bonus based upon his year's work, but this bonus is paid to him over the next five years. After the individual has been in the organization for a few years, he is owed bonus money for several previous years' performance, and for higher-level managers, this may amount to hundreds of thousands of dollars. All the manager has to do to receive this money is to remain a member of the organization. Clearly, this creates a strong financial motivation for him to stay put. Much the same situation can develop with stock option plans, since the receipt of the stock usually depends upon a manager staying in the company.

There has been very little research on the effectiveness of deferred-compensation plans, but it is reasonable to assume that they probably do lock many managers into organizations. The real question from the point of view of organization effectiveness, however, concerns who is locked in. There are some indications that these plans may lock in the wrong people. They may retain only the less effective and less desirable managers. As has been illustrated time and again, when companies want a good manager badly enough, they are willing to pay off or buy out any bonuses or stock options that he might have built up in another company. No company is going to be willing to buy off the options of a poor manager, even though they may be somewhat less than those held by a good manager. Thus, the poor performer is in no position to leave the organization, while the good performer is, just as he would be if there were no plan to lock him in. Thus, these plans can create a situation in which voluntary turnover may still take place among the good performers, while the desirable voluntary turnover of poorer performers is sharply reduced. This same problem can obviously occur where high salaries are paid to poor performers, although it may be less severe because guaranteed future bonuses and stock are not involved. High salaries can be reduced. Many of the problems that occur with bonus and stock option plans could be mitigated if organizations were willing to give sharply different rewards to good and poor performers. If poor performers received no bonuses, then they would not be locked in; but organizations are seldom willing to make such differentiations, just as they are unwilling to give salary cuts.

Part III
SATIS-
FACTION
WITH
PAY

The difference between $70,000 and
$75,000 is a difference only in the ego
of the player. I had made that clear
from the beginning.
If they didn't want to make me feel
happy, fine. But they were showing me
exactly what they thought of me. I
was an employee and they were my
employers. I could call them "mister"
when we passed in the hallway and,
presumably, tug at a forelock.

(Koufax, 1966)

Chapter 12
DETERMINANTS OF PAY SATISFACTION

It is estimated that between two thousand and four thousand studies concerned with job satisfaction have been published during the last thirty years. Psychologists' interest in job satisfaction was stimulated by the publication during the 1930s of two classic works: Roethlisberger and Dickson's *Management and the Worker* (1939) and Hoppock's monograph on *Job Satisfaction* (1935). Both works emphasized the strong feelings of satisfaction and dissatisfaction that workers have with respect to their jobs and suggested that these feelings might affect job performance. In addition these writers demonstrated the possibility of doing quantitative research on job satisfaction. The result has been a flood of studies that have correlated job satisfaction with just about every conceivable factor that might cause it, be caused by it, or for some other reason be related to it.

Despite the volume of this research, a number of critics have complained that our understanding of the causes of job satisfaction has not substantially increased during the last 30 years (see, e.g., Locke, 1968, 1969). There are a number of reasons why the research on job satisfaction has not contributed to our understanding, but two reasons stand out. The research has typically been atheoretical and correlational. Since it has not been guided by theory, a vast array of unorganized, virtually uninterpretable facts have been unearthed. For example, several studies have found a curvilinear relationship between age and job satisfaction, but others have not. There undoubtedly are explanations for this disparity, and it should be possible to say why age and job satisfaction are related in some situations, but not in others. At the moment, however, we are in no position to explain the different findings because we lack a theory of satisfaction to guide our thinking. One thing the research on job satisfaction has done is to demonstrate the validity of the statement that "theory without data is fantasy; but data without theory is chaos!"

Further, since the research has not been guided by a theory that states causal relationships, it has consistently tended to be correlational. Therefore, we know a great deal about what factors are related to satisfaction but very little about the causal basis for the relationships. This is, of course, a serious problem when one attempts to draw implications for practice from the research. It also increases the difficulty of testing and developing theories of satisfaction. Perhaps the best example of the dilemma concerns the relationship between satisfaction and performance. If satisfaction causes performance, then it seems clear that high satisfaction is good and that organizations should try to see that their employees are satisfied. If performance causes satisfaction, however, then high satisfaction is not necessarily good (Porter & Lawler, 1968b), and there is much less reason for organizations to try to see that their employees are satisfied.

The solution to these problems is quite simple to state but difficult to implement. We need studies guided by theory that test the causal basis for the many relationships found between satisfaction and other variables. We must discover which variables cause satisfaction and why they cause it. Similarly, we must try to determine which factors are influenced by satisfaction and why they are influenced. We should start, it seems, with a theoretical analysis of what satisfaction is. We need to understand the concept of satisfaction before we can really explain why certain factors cause it and others are caused by it. Thus, in looking at the topic of pay satisfaction, we shall place heavy emphasis on developing a model of pay satisfaction that will help us understand the research.

Psychologists concerned with learning, development, and other topics have not been particularly interested in satisfaction. In contrast, a number of motivation theories have been proposed. These theories were used as a starting point in developing the Motivation Model. Unfortunately, no such starting point exists in the area of satisfaction. There simply is not very much theory upon which to draw. What little there is comes almost entirely from the research of industrial psychologists. In some cases this theory is not explicit, but may be implied from the way satisfaction is measured. For example, although Porter (1961) has never presented a formal theory of satisfaction, implicit in his approach to measuring pay satisfaction is a way of thinking about what satisfaction is. His approach clearly indicates that he sees satisfaction as the difference between what one thinks one should receive and what one feels one actually receives.

In addition to Porter's view, several others have been proposed. At this time, three fairly well-developed ways of thinking about the meaning of satisfaction are current in the organizational psychology literature. Perhaps the best known of these is the discrepancy view, as exemplified by the work of Porter. A number of psychologists in addition to Porter have presented discrepancy views of satisfaction. Among the more prominent are Katzell (1964), Locke (1968), and Rosen and Weaver (1960).

Considerable attention has recently been given to two equity theory approaches to understanding pay. Perhaps the better developed of these is the approach of Adams (1965), which was discussed in Chapters 5 and 8. The second equity theory approach, which was developed by Jaques (1961), has received a good deal of attention in Europe. Finally, some psychologists have tended to see satisfaction in terms of fulfillment. Vroom's (1964) approach can probably be said to fit here, since Vroom equates satisfaction with valence and says it can be thought of as the attractiveness of the job to the person. He also notes that the attractiveness or valence of a job is determined by the kinds of positive outcomes it provides: in other words, the fulfillment or need satisfaction it produces.

As a first step in developing a model of pay satisfaction, we shall critically consider each of these different approaches to satisfaction. Perhaps they will provide at least a partial basis upon which to build a model or theory of the determinants of pay satisfaction.

DISCREPANCY THEORY

Katzell (1964) and Locke (1968, 1969) have probably presented the two most completely developed theoretical explanations of satisfaction. According to Katzell, $\text{Satisfaction} = 1 - \dfrac{(|X - V|)}{V}$ where X equals the actual amount of the stimulus and V equals the amount of the stimulus desired. Like many discrepancy theorists, Katzell sees satisfaction as the difference between what there actually is and some desired amount. But unlike most discrepancy theorists, he assumes that this difference should be divided by the amount of the stimulus that is desired. This means that the more a person wants of a stimulus the less dissatisfied he will be with a given discrepancy. This is roughly analogous to the psychophysical concept that, the more of something one has, the more it takes for him to notice a given discrepancy. Katzell offers no evidence for this assumption, and on a logical basis it is hard to make a compelling argument for it. A discrepancy from what is desired would seem to be about equally dissatisfying regardless of how much is desired. In his model, Katzell also speaks of "actual" discrepancies, while most discrepancy theorists talk of "perceived" discrepancies. Note also that in Katzell's model, getting more than the desired amount should produce less satisfaction than getting the actual amount desired.

Locke (1968) has stated a discrepancy theory that differs from Katzell's in several ways. First, Locke emphasizes that it is the perceived discrepancy that is important and not the actual discrepancy. He does not argue that the discrepancy should be divided by what the person either wants or has. Instead, he argues that satisfaction is determined by the simple difference between what the person wants and what he perceives he has. Locke says, "Job satisfaction and dissatisfaction are a function of the perceived relationship between what one wants from one's job and what one perceives it as offering." This definition indicates that, in order to determine satisfaction, Locke, like Katzell, feels that one must consider what a person wants and not what he expects or feels he should receive.

A few researchers have argued that satisfaction is determined by what one expects to receive rather than by what one wants. As Locke (1968) points out, this approach is hard to defend. Admittedly, getting what is not expected may lead to surprise, but it hardly need lead to dissatisfaction. What if, for example, it exceeds expectations? What if it exceeds expectations but still falls below what others are getting?

Porter (1961), in measuring pay satisfaction, asked managers how much pay there should be for their job and how much there was, and considered the discrepancy between the two pay satisfactions. This discrepancy approach has been the most widely used. It differs from Locke's approach since it sees satisfaction as determined, not by how much a person wants, but by how much he feels he should receive. There is a difference between asking a person how much pay he wants and how much he thinks he should receive for what he is doing. In a sense they help us understand different aspects of a person's feelings toward his present pay. A person's satisfaction with the fairness of the pay for his present job would seem to be more influenced by what he feels he should receive than by what he ultimately aspires to. What the person aspires to or wants tells more about his satisfaction with his present pay relative to his long-term aspired to or desired pay level.

If satisfaction is conceptualized as the difference between what one wants and what one presently receives, then it becomes difficult to talk meaningfully about pay satisfaction with respect to one's present job. It also becomes difficult to study pay satisfaction meaningfully if it is measured and conceptualized in this way; such an approach partially removes satisfaction from the context of the job and the situation. The question, How much do you want? is an individual difference variable that does not seem to be closely related to the job situation, since it is a statement of personal goals. In effect, this approach opens a Pandora's box of variables and makes it difficult to talk about or to meaningfully study the pay satisfaction level for a given job. Part of the satisfaction measure is made independent of the situation being studied. Locke apparently also recognizes the difficulty of doing situational research on pay satisfaction if the measure of how much a person wants is used. In some of his research on pay, he has not in fact asked subjects how much pay they want;

he has asked them how much they feel they should receive and has compared this with what they perceive they do receive. He calls this "should" measure their "practical ideal" (minimum adequate) and then goes on to argue that pay satisfaction is influenced by this measure and by how much the person wants (his ideal maximum).

Some data that I have recently collected show that employees consistently give higher answers to the "how much do you want" question than to the "how much should there be" question. Further, the "should be" responses seem to be more closely related to the actual job held by the person. They vary systematically, for example, with job level. Data gathered by Hulin and Smith (1965) show only a weak relationship between direct statements by subjects of how satisfied they are with their pay and the difference between their present pay and the pay they desire. My own data on blue-collar employees show that direct statements of pay satisfaction correlate about equally with the "want" and "should be" discrepancy measures. Apparently, when asked how satisfied they are with their pay, these workers responded both in terms of the fairness of their present pay and their long-term aspirations.

Conceptually, it seems clear that people can feel satisfied with the fairness of their present pay and yet want more. In research, we must therefore look at both what a person wants ultimately and what he thinks is fair in the present situation. In addition, we must consider the difference between both of these measures and what the person presently receives. It seems most logical to call the discrepancy between a person's present pay and what he feels it should be his "satisfaction with the fairness of his present pay," or simply his "pay satisfaction level." The difference between a person's desired pay level and his perception of his present situation could be called his "pay desires satisfaction." Pay desires satisfaction would seem to be particularly important in the study of careers, since it might help explain why a worker who is satisfied with his present pay quits his job to take up a new, higher-paying job or career.

The main focus in this chapter is on pay (fairness) satisfaction, since we are interested in understanding how a person comes to feel that he is being fairly paid on his job and what the consequences of this feeling are. The assumption is that this is the crucial feeling a person has about his pay as far as organizational pay research is concerned. This feeling about pay fairness is strongly influenced by organizational variables and, in turn, influences such things as turnover and absenteeism. Much of the research on pay satisfaction has specifically focused on this feeling, while the rest has focused on general pay satisfaction, which is probably influenced by both pay fairness feelings and pay desires satisfaction. This general pay satisfaction research can contribute to our understanding of pay fairness satisfaction, however, because the two are highly correlated.

Some researchers have conceptualized satisfaction as the difference between a person's fulfillment in some particular respect and the importance to the person of that particular kind of fulfillment. This approach has been used by Beer (1966), Kuhlen (1963), Ross and Zander (1957), and Glennon, Owens, Smith, and Albright (1960), to name a few. In a sense it is a discrepancy approach, since it looks at the difference between two perceptions that a person holds. Evans (1969) has stated that conceptually this approach is meaningless, and indeed there would seem to be good support for his position. Where pay is concerned, it is also operationally meaningless. Let us consider what some of the problems might be of measuring pay satisfaction with this approach. First of all, how is the person classified who says he has a great deal of pay, but it is very unimportant to him. There is a large discrepancy. Should we assume, then, that he is dissatisfied with his pay? On the other hand, is the person to whom pay is of moderate importance and who receives very little always going to be less satisfied than the person to whom pay is very important but who receives a moderate amount? The answer obviously is no; it depends on the person's perception of what his pay should be, and this probably is determined by the job the person holds and a number of other things. In summary, then, it does not seem to be particularly useful to think about pay satisfaction as the difference between the importance of pay to a person and the amount of pay he receives.

In most discrepancy theories it is possible for a person to say he is receiving more pay than he should receive (Lawler, 1965a) or more than he wants. This point has not been stressed by most discrepancy theorists, and in one sense it presents some problems for them. They have not been clear on how to equate dissatisfaction due to overpayment with dissatisfaction due to underpayment. Are they produced in the same way? Do they have the same results? Do they both contribute to overall job dissatisfaction? These are some of the important questions that discrepancy theory has yet to answer. Equity theory, which will be discussed next, has dealt with many of them.

In summary, it has been argued that in considering the broad issue of pay satisfaction, one should focus on how satisfied people are with the fairness of the pay they receive for their present job. It has been argued that this is determined by the difference between the pay a person feels he receives and what he feels he should receive for his job. The Model of the Determinants of Pay Satisfaction developed later in this chapter states the determinants of this type of pay satisfaction; and from this point on, the term "pay satisfaction" will be used to refer to this type of pay satisfaction.

EQUITY THEORY

Adams's version of equity theory has been discussed in the chapters on motivation and will not be covered in detail here. Other, similar, equity theories have been presented by Patchen (1961), Homans (1961), and Sayles (1958). Adams (1965) argues that satisfaction is determined rather directly by a person's perceived input-outcome balance: The perceived equity of a person's pay is determined by his input-outcome balance, and equity, in turn, influences satisfaction. Satisfaction is seen to result when equity exists and dissatisfaction to result when perceived inequity exists. This means that satisfaction is determined by the perceived ratio of what one receives from the job to what one puts into the job.

There is a strong emphasis in equity theory on the importance of other's input-outcome balance in determining how a person will judge the equity of his own input-outcome balance. Equity theory argues that people evaluate the fairness of their own balance by comparing it with their perception of the balance of their comparison other. This emphasis does not enter into discrepancy theory as it is usually stated. Although there is an implied reference to other in the discussion of how people develop their feelings about what their pay should be, discrepancy theory does not explicitly state that this perception is based upon perceptions of what others receive and what they contribute. This points up a strength of equity theory relative to discrepancy theory. Equity theory rather clearly states how a person assesses his inputs and outcomes in order to develop his perception of the fairness of his input-outcome balance. Discrepancy theory, on the other hand, is very vague about how people decide what their outcomes should be or what they presently are. Thus, equity theory is more complete and for that reason leads to more testable predictions.

Jaques (1961), like Adams, emphasizes the importance of social comparisons in determining people's feelings about their jobs. He notes, "All industrial disputes about payment are at source differential disputes; that is to say, disputes about the pattern of distribution of . . . income among the members of the population." Jaques argues that he has uncovered in the history of his research "an unrecognized system of norms of fair payment for a given level of work, unconscious knowledge of these norms being shared among the population." He goes on to point out the consequences of paying someone a rate that is not in agreement with the norms:

If the actual salary bracket for a person's role coincides with equity, he expresses himself as being in a reasonably paid role. If his actual payment bracket has fallen below the equitable bracket, he expresses himself as dissatisfied with the financial recognition for his role. If, on the other hand, his actual payment bracket has risen above the equitable bracket, then he reacts with a sense of discomfort over being paid within a higher range than he can ever hope to maintain. The intensity of his reaction varies with the size of the discrepancy between the actual and equitable bracket. [1961, p. 132]

Unfortunately, Jaques does not say exactly how these informal norms develop or how people become "unconsciously" aware of them. Nor does he say whether equity is determined by taking the difference between what is seen to be equitable pay and the person's actual pay (à la discrepancy theory), or whether it is determined by the kind of ratio equation stated by Adams. He does, however, say something about what the norms of fair payment are related to. They are, he says, related to the "time span of discretion" that operates in a job. Time span indicates the "period of time during which marginally substandard discretion could be exercised in a role before information about the accumulating substandard work would become available to the manager in charge of the role" (1961, p. 99). Jaques sees time span as closely related to organization levels, and he states that people holding jobs with similar time spans report that the same pay is equitable for their jobs. From this he argues that people holding similar jobs share common perceptions about what is fair pay. The longer the time span, the higher the pay that is seen to be equitable. Since time span is related to job level, this leads to the prediction that higher-level employees will feel that their pay should be higher than that of lower-level employees. Jaques, in fact, has drawn graphs that relate time span to perceived equitable payment. They show a gradual increase in equitable payment from time spans of less than a day to time spans up to six months, with a much sharper rate of increase from six months to ten years.

Jaques's theory has proved to be very attractive to many people. If valid it would, for example, make job evaluation much simpler, since it would mean that one would only have to know the time span of a job in order to set the appropriate pay rate. The theory has, however, been subjected to a considerable amount of criticism. Vroom (1964) has been critical of Jaques's work, since, as he points out, Jaques presents very little empirical evidence to support his theory. He does not, for example, report how he measures satisfaction, who his subjects were, or any quantitative analyses of his data.

Gordon (1969) has also criticized Jaques for his failure to present scientifically acceptable data to support his theory. Compared with the equity theories of Patchen (1961) and Adams (1965), Jaques's theory comes off second best, according to Gordon: Although it is similar to the others in many ways, it is less inclusive than Adams's and has less support in the research literature. Finally, in a study designed to test some of the points made by Jaques's theory, Goodman (1967) failed to find support for the points Jaques has made about how time span should operate. Goodman states, however, that part of the problem here may be the difficulty of successfully operationalizing Jaques's concept of time span. Goodman did not, for example, find a strong relationship between time span and management level or between time span and satisfaction. Probably the most reasonable conclusion that can be reached about Jaques's work is that it is interesting and potentially quite important, but that it is untested and has proved difficult to operationalize.

FULFILLMENT THEORY

Schaffer (1953) has argued that ". . . job satisfaction will vary directly with the extent to which those needs of an individual which can be satisfied are actually satisfied. . . ." Morse (1953) also views satisfaction in terms of perceived need fulfillment. Vroom (1964), too, seems to see job satisfaction in terms of the degree to which a job provides the person with positively valued outcomes. It is important to note the difference between this approach and that which characterizes the discrepancy theory view. Discrepancy theorists like Porter do measure fulfillment, but they subtract it from what the person feels he should receive. The fulfillment approach is essentially to stop short of this last operation and simply to assume that satisfaction is determined by fulfillment. The fulfillment approach would seem to be less helpful in thinking about satisfaction with pay. There is a great amount of research which shows that people's satisfaction with their pay is a function not only of how much they feel they receive, but also of how much they feel they should receive (Locke, 1968; Lawler & Porter, 1963). As has been noted, a foreman can be satisfied with a salary of $12,000, while a president can be dissatisfied with $100,000, even though the president perceives that he has higher need fulfillment. The obvious point here is that satisfaction is determined by what one perceives he receives and what one thinks he should receive. What the person thinks he should receive seems to be influenced by a number of factors, and a theory of pay satisfaction must make some attempt to deal with them.

EQUITY THEORY AND/OR DISCREPANCY THEORY

The discussion so far seems to indicate that equity theory and discrepancy theory are the two strongest theoretical explanations of satisfaction. Either one could clearly be used as a basis for developing our Model of the Determinants of Pay Satisfaction. The present approach, however, is not to choose between them, but to capitalize on the strong points of each in building a new model. In many ways, the theories are quite similar. Both stress the importance of a person's perceived outcomes from his job and their relationship to a second perception. In discrepancy theory, the second perception is how much the outcomes should be, while in equity theory it is what the subject's perceived inputs are. Clearly, it could be argued that the two theories are not talking about such different things when they talk about perceived inputs and the subject's feeling about what his outcomes should be. Presumably, a person's perception of what his outcomes should be is partially determined by what he feels his inputs are.

Equity theory and discrepancy theory also differ in that equity theory places explicit emphasis on the importance of social comparison theory, and discrepancy theory does not. Obviously, this is a plus for equity theory, although discrepancy theory can be altered to include this emphasis. Finally, discrepancy theory talks in terms of a difference, while equity theory argues in terms of a ratio. Thus, equity theory would have to say that a person with 8 units of inputs and 2 of outcomes will be the same in satisfaction as a person with 16 units of inputs and 4 of outcomes. Although discrepancy theory does not talk in terms of inputs, if we consider inputs as one determinant of what outcomes should be, then discrepancy theory would not go along with the equity view. It would argue that the person with 16 units of inputs will be more dissatisfied than the person with 8. On purely logical grounds this would seem to be more defensible. It does seem that people think more in terms of differences than in terms of ratios, although there is little evidence to support this view. The two views also suggest a different type of relationship between feelings of what pay should be and dissatisfaction. Discrepancy theory would predict a linear relationship such that with pay held constant, as "should be" increases, so should dissatisfaction. Equity theory, on the other hand, would predict a nonlinear relationship [where satisfaction = $(\frac{\text{is getting}}{\text{should be getting}})$] such that if a poor ratio exists, a further increase in "should be" will have little effect on satisfaction.

In building our Model of the Determinants of Pay Satisfaction, we will use the difference approach rather than the ratio approach. This choice is one of the few either/or choices that must be made between the two views. The major elements of both can be used in building our model.

A MODEL OF PAY SATISFACTION

Figure 12-1 presents the proposed Model of the Determinants of Pay Satisfaction. It stresses the importance of social comparisons, and it gives inputs and outcomes a prominent role, as does equity theory. It argues that satisfaction is basically determined by the difference between perceived pay (*b*) and the person's belief about what his pay should be (*a*). It indicates that when the subject's perception of what his pay is and his perception of what it should be are in agreement, that he will be satisfied with his pay. When his pay outcomes fall short of what they should be, he will feel dissatisfied with his pay. When his pay outcomes exceed what he feels they should be, however, he will have feelings of guilt and inequity and perhaps some discomfort (Adams, 1965; Jaques, 1961).

Present wage rate is the key influence on a person's perception of what his pay is, but his perception is also shown to be influenced by his pay and work history and by his perception of what his referent others receive. Presumably, the higher his previous pay has been, the lower his present pay outcomes should look. Similarly, the higher the pay of his referent others, the lower his pay will appear. Thus a person's psychological view of how much pay he receives is said to be influenced by more than just its dollar and cent amount. Its perceived size is influenced by several other factors. Because of these factors, the same amount of money often can be seen quite differently by two people. To one it can be a large amount of money, while to another it can be a very small amount.

The model also shows that a person's perception of what his pay

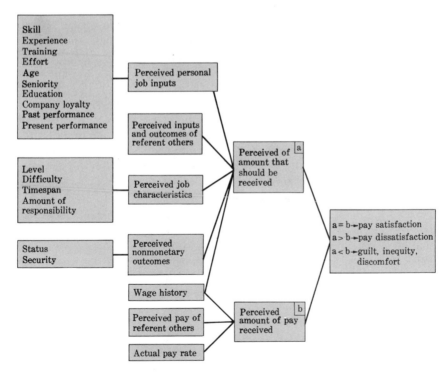

FIGURE 12-1. Model of the determinants of pay satisfaction.

should be is influenced by a number of factors. Perhaps most important is his perceived job inputs. These include all the skills, abilities, and training he brings to the job as well as the behavior he exhibits on the job. Clearly the greater he perceives his inputs to be, the higher will be his perception of what his pay should be. Because of this, people with high job inputs will have to be paid more, or they will be dissatisfied with their pay. The model also shows that a person's perception of what his pay should be is influenced by his perception of the job demands. The greater the demands made by the job, the more he will perceive he should be paid. Job demands include such things as job difficulty, responsibilities, and organization level. If salaries do not rise along with these factors, the clear prediction of the model is that the people who perceive they have more difficult, higher-level jobs will be more dissatisfied.

The model also shows that a person's perception of what his pay should be is influenced both by what the person perceives others' pay rates to be and what he perceives their inputs to be. This aspect of the model is taken directly from equity theory. It is included to stress the fact that people look at the inputs and outcomes of others in order to determine what their own should be. The higher others' outcomes are relative to their inputs, the more a person will feel he should receive for performing his own job. The model also shows that a person's wage history may influence what he thinks his pay should be. The suggestion is that people develop, as a part of their self-concept, a view of what they are "worth," and this influences what they feel they should be paid on a given job. Presumably people who have a history of being paid highly will have a high view of their worth and therefore expect more pay.

Finally, the model shows that a person's perception of what his pay should be is somewhat influenced by the nonmonetary outcomes he receives from his job. Probably this is typically not a very strong influence, but in some cases it can be crucial. The model stresses the point that some nonpay outcomes can partially substitute for pay outcomes and that, because of this, the number of other outcomes received can affect what a person feels his pay should be. The more nonmonetary outcomes a person receives (if he considers them a substitute for pay), the lower his view will be of what his pay should be (see Chap. 2). This aspect of the model can explain the fact that some people are satisfied with their pay even though it is relatively low and their job is demanding in every sense. According to the model, they are satisfied because they get other rewards that substitute for pay, and pay reduces their perception of what their pay should be.

Note that the model does allow for the possibility that people will feel that their pay outcomes exceed what they should be. The feelings produced by this condition are quite different from those produced by underpayment. Because of this, it does not make sense to refer to a person who feels overpaid as being dissatisfied. Although not explicitly stated in the model, there are a number of reasons to believe that very few people at any point feel overpaid. For one thing, the social comparison aspect of pay satisfaction means that people can quickly look around and find someone to compare themselves with who is doing equally well. Also, a person tends to value his own inputs much higher than they are valued by others (Lawler, 1967a). Because of this, his perception of what his pay should be often is not shared by those administering his pay and is above what he actually receives. Thus, it is to be expected that many people will be dissatisfied with their pay.

Let us briefly list some conditions that, according to the model, should lead to pay dissatisfaction. Other things being equal:

1. People with high perceived inputs will be more dissatisfied than those with low perceived inputs.
2. People who perceive their job to be demanding (e.g., high level, difficult) will be more dissatisfied than those who perceive their jobs as undemanding.
3. People who perceive that they receive few attractive nonmonetary outcomes from their jobs will be more dissatisfied than those who feel they receive many.
4. People who perceive similar others as having a more favorable input-outcome balance will be more dissatisfied than those who perceive their own balance as similar to or better than that of others.
5. People who are paid a low wage will be more dissatisfied than those who are paid a high wage.
6. People with a wage history of high salaries will be more dissatisfied with their present salaries than will people with a history of low salaries.
7. The more salary a person perceives his referent other as receiving, the more dissatisfied he will be with his own present pay. This should be particularly true when other is seen to hold a job that demands the same or fewer inputs.

RESEARCH ON THE DETERMINANTS OF PAY SATISFACTION

Probably the first two questions that occur to anyone interested in pay satisfaction are: How satisfied are employees with their pay? How does a person's pay satisfaction compare with his satisfaction with other job factors? Not surprisingly, a number of researchers have struggled with these questions.

Many studies in the literature report data on the percentage of employees who are actually satisfied with their pay or on the extent to which they are satisfied. Some of the studies go on to compare these data on pay with the satisfaction employees express concerning other job factors. In fact, this topic has been researched almost as heavily as the topic of how important pay is. It might also be noted that it has been researched with the same disappointing results. The methodological problems confronted in trying to determine what percentage of the work force is satisfied with its pay or how satisfied workers are with their pay are overwhelming. All the problems that are relevant to determining the importance of pay reappear here: the problems of social desirability, item wording, and sample characteristics. For example, if people are simply asked whether they are satisfied with their pay (yes or no), a much higher percentage generally report that they are satisfied than if a 5-point scale running from dissatisfied to satisfied is used.

It does not matter whether the findings are reported as the percentage of workers who are satisfied or as the average satisfaction score of employees, the same methodological problems exist. Both approaches demand as basic data the measurement of individual pay satisfaction, and this is where the difficulty is located. Further complications arise when attempts are made to compare the employees' pay satisfaction and their degree of satisfaction with nonpay factors. Here, problems of scaling become severe, since people may, for example, use a rating scale differently when they respond to a satisfaction with pay question and a satisfaction with security item. Only if the scales are used in a similar manner does it make sense to compare the levels of satisfaction with different job factors.

Because of the many methodological problems involved in making statements about what percentage of the population is dissatisfied with its pay or how pay satisfaction compares with other kinds of satisfaction, it is not particularly helpful to review the literature extensively. It may, however, be worth noting the general finding of the research work. Not surprisingly, studies have varied greatly in their reports of how many employees are satisfied with their pay. They are in agreement on one point: Pay is usually the job aspect with which the greatest number of employees express dissatisfaction. More employees seem to be dissatisfied with their pay than with any other job factor. Porter (1961), for example, reported that 80 percent of a sample of managers were dissatisfied with the present pay for their jobs. A content analysis of the interview data gathered in the Western Electric studies showed that pay was the most frequently mentioned employee gripe. It was mentioned more than twice as often as the second most frequently mentioned problem area. Carlson, Davis, England, and Lofquist (1962) also reported that pay is the greatest source of dissatisfaction to a group of employees. Lawler (1965a) reported that 86 percent of a sample of government managers and 67 percent of a sample of industrial managers were dissatisfied with their pay. Finally, Centers and Cantril (1946) reported that 20 percent of the people they sampled who made more than $100 per week were dissatisfied with their pay. Among lower-income groups, the percentage of dissatisfied employees was much higher, ranging up to 72 percent.

The studies cited clearly indicate the widely varying results of attempts to determine the percentage of employees dissatisfied with their pay. This wide range of figures undoubtedly reflects the fact that studies used different measuring instruments and tested different populations. Perhaps the only conclusion that can be drawn from these studies is that, when asked, a majority of employees usually say they are dissatisfied with their pay. By stretching the data a little, it is probably also reasonable to conclude that typically more employees express dissatisfaction with their pay than with any other aspect of their job. What this means raises another issue. It may mean nothing more than that it is easier and more socially acceptable to express pay dissatisfaction than to express other kinds of dissatisfaction. On the other hand, it may mean that the workers do feel the greatest dissatisfaction with respect to pay. There is some justification for believing that this may be true. As was pointed out in the discussion of the Model of the Determinants of Pay Satisfaction, there are some reasons (e.g., high self-evaluations, unrealistic social comparisons) to expect that a large number of employees will be dissatisfied with their pay.

Determining what percentage of the work force is satisfied with its pay is not particularly important for the testing of our model, because it makes no specific predictions about this subject. The key research questions, as far as testing the model is concerned, relate to who is satisfied with their pay and what the correlates of pay satisfaction are. In other words, to test the model, it does not matter whether 30 percent or 70 percent of the work force is satisfied with its pay. It does matter, however, when other things are held constant, if highly educated workers are more dissatisfied than poorly educated workers. The model attempts to predict the relationships between variables such as educational level and pay satisfaction. It does not attempt to predict what the absolute levels of variables will be. Because of this, problems concerned with absolute measurements (i.e., whether workers are satisfied or not) are not relevant to testing the model.

The question remains, Is it methodologically feasible to measure the relative satisfaction with pay of different groups? Is it possible, for example, to measure the pay satisfaction of people accurately enough so that the satisfaction of highly educated employees can be compared with that of poorly educated employees? The answer is probably yes, even though some methodological problems still exist when this level of comparison is attempted. But let us look briefly at why this kind of comparison is more methodologically defensible than the statement that x percent of the population is satisfied with its pay. The argument here is essentially the same one that was stated in Chapter 3 with respect to measuring the importance of pay. There it was pointed out that many of the problems encountered in making statements about whether pay is first or second in importance are not involved when statements are made about the relative importance of pay to different groups. The problems of social desirability become less severe (assuming that social desirability is similar in all the groups tested), and the problem of item wording disappears (everyone is given the same item to respond to). Similarly, when we make comparative statements about pay satisfaction, problems with respect to item wording or social desirability are reduced if data from one group are compared with data from another group where the same item was used for both. The same bias should appear in both populations and because of this, any difference between the two groups should reflect a real difference in satisfaction even though the absolute scores by themselves are meaningless.

Some problems remain even when comparisons are made between the relative satisfaction of different subject populations. For one thing, the population groups may use the scale differently. To continue the example of two groups that are different in educational level, it might be that a scale describing different degrees of satisfaction would have different meanings for the groups. Thus, they could end up at the same place on the scale even though they had quite different feelings about their pay, simply because they interpreted or used the scale differently. It is also possible that what is socially desirable for one group might not be for the other, and because of this, differences could appear that were not real. Highly educated managers may feel it is not proper to express pay dissatisfaction while poorly educated ones may feel it is. This can lead better educated managers to express less pay dissatisfaction even though they do not actually feel this way. Thus, in reviewing the research evidence on pay satisfaction, keep in mind that some of the differences that appear between groups may be due to social desirability and scaling problems rather than to real differences in the subjects' feelings of pay dissatisfaction and that some actual differences may be obscured by these problems.

Note also that the Model of the Determinants of Pay Satisfaction is a causal one: Certain factors are said to cause pay satisfaction. Unfortunately, most of the research has been correlational rather than experimental in approach. For example, typically, researchers either have correlated the level of a factor (e.g., pay) with pay satisfaction, or have divided the subjects into groups that are high or low on a variable (e.g., age), and then compared the satisfaction of the two groups. There are many reasons why there have been few experimental studies. For one thing, many of the factors that have been studied do not lend themselves to experimental manipulation. Nevertheless, this limitation in the evidence means that the model can be only partially tested. If correlations do not appear where predicted by the model, it will serve to disprove the model; but if they do appear, it will not prove that they occur for the causal reason stated by the model.

Perhaps the major limitation of the studies of pay satisfaction, as far as testing the model is concerned, is that typically the studies have looked at the relationship between only one variable and pay satisfaction. They have not controlled for the effects of other variables. Thus, in many instances it is impossible to tell whether the relationship found between a variable and pay satisfaction is due to the effect of the variable studied or another variable. For example, a number of studies have related pay satisfaction to organization level and have found that higher-level managers are more satisfied. This may or may not be due to the effects of job level. Along with higher organization level go a number of other outcomes (e.g., higher pay), and it is quite possible that the higher satisfaction of the higher-level employees may reflect, not the impact of job level, but of other variables. The way to deal with this is, of course, to compare the pay satisfaction of people who differ only in management level. Unfortunately few studies have done this, and thus the results of many studies must be interpreted cautiously.

The model makes predictions about the way in which a number of factors influence pay satisfaction. Basically, the factors are grouped according to whether they are personal input factors, job factors, nonmonetary outcome factors, social comparison factors, or pay outcome factors. In the following pages we shall review the research evidence concerned with the relationship between each of these types of factors and pay satisfaction.

PERSONAL INPUT FACTORS

Education

A clear prediction is derivable from the model with respect to the relationship between educational level and pay satisfaction. Other things equal, the higher the educational level of the person the greater should be the pay dissatisfaction. This should come about because the person with a higher educational level has higher perceived inputs than the person with a lower educational level. Five studies have specifically focused on the relationship between educational level and pay satisfaction, and four report findings that are in accord with the predictions of the model. Andrews and Henry (1963) report that in a sample of managers, those with postgraduate training were least satisfied of all. Centers and Cantril (1946) report a similar relationship between educational level and pay dissatisfaction. Cantril (1943) suggests, in accord with our model, that the higher a person's social class (and presumably his education) the more likely he is to feel that his income is less than he deserves.

Probably the best study on educational level was done by Klein and Maher (1966). They report finding a strong relationship between educational level and pay dissatisfaction. It is interesting to note that they controlled for some other factors (e.g., pay) and still found the relationship. Klein and Maher initially suggested that the higher dissatisfaction of the better educated people might be due solely to their feelings that they should be able to get better jobs and more money elsewhere. This is in disagreement with the model, since it suggests that such comparisons are only one of the factors that influence pay satisfaction. There is no reason, from the model, to believe that these comparisons can account for all pay dissatisfaction or that a more highly educated person should be equal in satisfaction to a less highly educated person, even when he sees no better job opportunities. Klein and Maher tried to test their prediction by controlling for perceptions of other job possibilities and found that these perceptions could account for only about one-third of the variance in pay satisfaction. Thus, as is predictable from the model, even with perceived other job possibilities equal, better educated people are more dissatisfied. Lawler and Porter (1966) have also looked at the relationship between pay satisfaction and educational level. They found no relationship between the two for a group of managers; nevertheless, there probably is enough positive evidence to conclude that usually educational level and pay satisfaction are related as predicted by the model.

Skill

Much of the research on equity theory is relevant to the prediction that people with higher skills will usually be more dissatisfied with their pay than will less-skilled people. It is hardly necessary to review all this research again. It probably is appropriate, however, to repeat the finding that when a person with low skills receives high wages, he feels overpaid. That is, as predicted by the model, when people have high outcomes but low inputs, they feel their pay is higher than it should be. The data also show that people who are paid the same wages as the unqualified people, but are told they are qualified (higher inputs), are much more likely to feel their pay is satisfactory or too low. Thus, perceived skill level does seem to be related to subjects' feelings about the adequacy of their pay.

The finding that the combination of high pay and low skill yields feelings of overpayment is important because it represents one of the few findings in the literature to support the predictions of the model with respect to feelings of overpayment. It would seem to suggest that people can feel overpaid when their pay is high and their skills are low. But as has been pointed out, there probably are not too many people outside the laboratory who actually feel overpaid for any extended length of time.

Job Performance

The model suggests that unless pay rises according to performance, people who perceive themselves as better performers will be more dissatisfied with their pay than will people who perceive themselves as poor performers. This is to be expected because the better performers will have higher expectations about what their pay should be. Porter and Lawler (1968a) report data that directly support this prediction. They show that as people raise their self-evaluation of their performance, they also raise their estimation of what their pay should be.

These data also illustrate the importance of a person's rating of his performance. People's expectations about what their pay should be were much more closely related to their self-rating of performance than to their superior's rating of their performance. Penner (1966) has related self-ratings of performance directly to pay satisfaction and has found a strong relationship. Managers who perceived themselves to be high performers were much less satisfied with their pay. This is particulary interesting since Penner did not try to compare only people receiving the same pay, yet he found a strong negative relationship. This suggests either that, in the company studied, pay was not related to rated performance or that the relationship between satisfaction and self-rated performance is so strong that it appears even when better performers get somewhat greater amounts of pay. Overall, the data available would seem to support the prediction of the model that higher performers, unless they are paid more, will be more dissatisfied with their pay than poor performers.

Age and Seniority

A few studies have examined the relationships among seniority, age, and pay satisfaction. If it is assumed that age and seniority are input factors that influence people's perception of what their pay should be, then high seniority and old age should be associated with high pay dissatisfaction. A study by Morse (1953) provides the most support for this view. Pay satisfaction decreased with both age and length of service. Lawler and Porter (1966) have reported generally insignificant relationships between these variables and pay satisfaction. Hulin and Smith (1965) found only weak relationships between age and tenure and pay satisfaction. If anything, their results seem to show a positive relationship rather than the negative one that might be predicted from the model. Overall, the research evidence does not justify a conclusion that age and seniority are related to pay satisfaction. Part of the problem here may be due to the fact that the studies did not typically hold pay and other factors constant while they studied the relationship between pay satisfaction and age and seniority. Another explanation for these data may be that age and seniority are not seen as important input factors and because of this they do not influence employees' perceptions of what they should be paid.

Sex

Three studies—Hulin and Smith (1964), Morse (1953), and Stockford and Kunze (1950)—have shown that female workers are usually more satisfied with their pay than males. This finding is strongest when females are paid approximately the same as males for doing the same work, but there also is some indication that females are more satisfied even when they are paid slightly less for doing the same work. This finding is interpretable in terms of the model if it is assumed that both men and women perceive that sex is a relevant job input factor and that being a male is a greater input than being a female. This seems to be a valid assumption in the American culture, since females have been downgraded as far as most kinds of employment are concerned. This situation is clearly changing; and as it does change, the relationship between sex and pay satisfaction probably will disappear.

Summary

Overall, the data on personal job input factors fit the model quite well. Perceived high job inputs seem to be consistently associated with high pay dissatisfaction. High inputs do not seem to lead to high dissatisfaction when high pay is given to those people who perceive their inputs to be high. We cannot comment here on a number of the factors listed in the model (e.g., company loyalty) because of lack of data. These aspects of the model remain to be tested. Nevertheless, the available data provide substantial support for the model. Further research also clearly needs to be done on what job inputs people consider important when they judge their inputs (Weick, 1966). It may well be that there are some which are not explicitly stated in the model. Lawler (1966a) and Adams (1966) have looked at this issue but their work only begins to come to grips with it. Their data suggest that there are wide individual differences and that these may influence the degree to which an individual feels that a particular factor should be treated as an important input.

JOB FACTORS

Organization Level

The model shows that job level is one factor that influences a person's feelings about what his pay should be. The higher the level, the more pay people feel they should receive. Thus, unless pay increases sharply with job level, it should be expected that higher-level managers will be more dissatisfied with their pay than lower-level managers. Several studies support this view. Lawler and Porter (1963, 1966) report that when managers who earn the same amount are compared, higher-level managers are more dissatisfied with their pay than are lower-level managers. Lawler and Porter (1963) show that this is due to the fact that the higher one's job level, the higher one feels his pay should be. A foreman making $12,000 is better satisfied with his pay, for example, than a company president making less than $49,000 because the company president has a much higher perception of what his pay should be. Morse (1953) also reports data which show that higher-level employees are more dissatisfied with their pay than lower-level employees.

Andrews and Henry (1963) and Rosen and Weaver (1960) report that higher-level managers are more satisfied with their pay than lower-level managers. They point out, however, that the higher-level managers are paid much more. Andrews and Henry (1963) also report that in one company where only small pay differences existed between management levels, no relationship existed between job level and pay satisfaction. Porter (1961) presents data that show a very slight tendency for lower-level managers to be more satisfied than higher-level managers. It should be noted that Rosen and Weaver, Porter, and Andrews and Henry did not compare the pay satisfaction of managers at different levels while holding pay constant. That is, they did not compare similarly paid managers from different levels. Thus, their data do not provide a good test of our model. Still, the indication from data they report is that if they had held pay constant the results would have supported the prediction that higher-level managers would be more dissatisfied. Overall, the data support the point that as job level increases, pay satisfaction will decrease if pay is held constant.

Time Span

Jaques's work (1961) has looked extensively at the relationship among time span, pay expectations and satisfaction. His data clearly suggest that the longer the time span the more that the person feels he should earn. Thus, unless people holding jobs with a long time span earn more, they should be more dissatisfied with their pay. Jaques's data suggest that this is true. As was pointed out earlier, there are some methodological problems with the data that Jaques has gathered. Thus, at best we can only tentatively conclude that time span is related to pay satisfaction. Still, when Jaques's evidence is combined with the data on job level, it provides fairly good support for the prediction of the model that unless higher pay goes along with greater job demands, people who hold demanding jobs will be more dissatisfied with their pay than people holding less demanding jobs.

NONMONETARY OUTCOMES

Penner (1966) has reported a relationship between the nonmonetary outcomes received and pay satisfaction. Basically, his data supoprt the prediction of the model that people who receive large amounts of certain positive nonmonetary outcomes will be more satisfied with their pay than will people who receive lesser amounts. He finds that the more autonomy people feel they have in their job the more satisfied they are with their pay. He also finds that the better the relationship a person has with his boss and the greater his chances for promotion, the higher will be his pay satisfaction. Thus, his data seem to support the view that receiving nonmonetary outcomes can affect pay satisfaction. One note of caution should be interjected in interpreting these results, however. Penner did not control for amount of pay, and the higher satisfaction of the more autonomous managers may merely reflect the fact that they were being paid more.

The data presented in Chapter 2 on the instrumentality of pay for the satisfaction of certain needs are also relevant here: Pay, it was said, is just one of the outcomes that can satisfy such needs as security and esteem. If this is true, then satisfaction with pay may be related to the degree to which one receives other outcomes that satisfy the same needs as pay. The data presented in Chapter 2 showed that pay satisfaction was correlated with security and status satisfaction. If we assume that status and security satisfaction are partially determined by the amount of security and status received, then it follows that, the more status and security received, the greater pay satisfaction should be. Much of this is, of course, speculative, and further research is needed to fully test this aspect of the model. Perhaps all that can be concluded now is that the data suggest that it may be valid.

SOCIAL COMPARISON

The Model of the Determinants of Pay Satisfaction emphasizes that social comparisons are relevant at two points. (1) The perception of what others receive relative to their inputs influences what an individual feels he should receive, and (2) the perception of what others receive influences what he feels he actually receives. The more he perceives that others receive, the less he may feel he receives and consequently the less satisfied he may be with his pay. Also, the greater the outcomes he perceives that others receive, the higher will be his perception of what he should receive, and hence, the greater the chance he will be dissatisfied with his pay. Thus, both a person's inputs and outcomes are evaluated relative to others' inputs and outcomes. Patchen's study (1961) was the first to focus extensively on the importance of social comparisons in determining pay satisfaction. His study was largely concerned with finding out what determines a person's choice of a comparison other. The data suggest that relative wage position, mobility chances, and feelings of responsibility for present stature are important determinants of who will be chosen for comparison purposes. Andrews and Henry (1963) have also pointed out that as educational level rises, managers are more likely to choose people outside their organization for their pay comparisons.

Patchen states that people who compare their pay with that of others who earn more than they do will be dissatisfied with their pay unless the other person has higher inputs. This is, of course, congruent with the model's emphasis on looking at both inputs and outcomes as determinants of pay satisfaction. Andrews and Henry report that, of those managers who were dissatisfied with their pay, 87 percent said that the downward pay differential was too small (subordinates' pay was too close to theirs). These managers obviously felt that lower-level managers had a better input-outcome balance than they did (lower inputs, but similar pay), and this led them to be dissatisfied with their own pay. Lawler (1965a) has also shown that when managers see the downward pay differential as too small, they are likely to be dissatisfied with their own pay. Thus, although the evidence is sketchy, it indicates that social comparisons do influence pay satisfaction. Social comparisons seem to lead to dissatisfaction when a person compares himself with someone who is seen to have a more favorable input-outcome balance. It may be more favorable for a number of reasons (e.g., same inputs, higher pay; lower inputs, same pay), some of which have not been fully researched (Weick, 1968).

The social comparison aspect of the model is particularly interesting because of some of the effects of pay secrecy that have already been discussed. Secrecy makes accurate comparisons difficult and can thus influence satisfaction. It is particularly likely to lead to increased dissatisfaction when it causes people to overestimate the pay of their comparison others and to underestimate their inputs. As we shall see in Chapter 14 there is some evidence that this does happen.

PAY FACTORS

Amount of Pay

There is a very large amount of evidence to show that, other factors equal, the more pay a person receives the more satisfied he will be with his pay. The model suggests that this should come about because the highly paid person will feel that his outcomes are high. Data presented by Lawler and Porter (1963) and Porter and Lawler (1968a) show clearly that, with increasing pay, people's perceptions of what their pay actually is rise, but their perceptions of what it should be do not necessarily rise. Figures 12-2 and 12-3 present data from the study by Lawler and Porter (1963). They show perceptions of pay going up with income, but not perceptions of what pay should be. Figure 12-2 shows this for vice-presidents, and Figure 12-3 shows it for lower managers. The decreasing distance between the lines in both figures shows that higher pay does bring higher satisfaction.

So many studies have shown a strong relationship between pay and pay satisfaction that it is not necessary to review all of them to establish the validity of this aspect of the model. A few illustrative examples should suffice. Locke (1968) has pointed out that in his laboratory studies pay satisfaction is directly related to amount of pay received, Morse (1953) has reported the same finding for white-collar workers, and Centers and Cantril (1946) have reported the same finding for a more heterogeneous sample.

Anticipated Future Earnings

Andrews and Henry (1963) were the first to relate managerial pay satisfaction to feelings about the possibility of future raises. They report that managers who expect large increases in pay tend to be more dissatisfied with their present pay than do managers who do not expect raises. There is no reason to predict from the model that this relationship should be found. If anything, one might expect that those with strong expectations of future raises might be more satisfied with their pay: The knowledge of

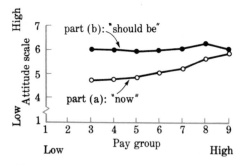

FIGURE 12-2. Responses of vice-presidents to questions asking how much they are paid and how much they should be paid as a function of actual pay. (Lawler & Porter, 1963)

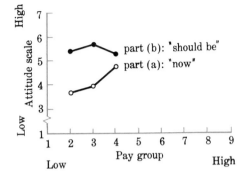

FIGURE 12-3. Responses of lower-level managers to questions asking how much they are paid and how much they should be paid as a function of actual pay. (Lawler & Porter, 1963)

money to come might serve as an outcome itself, thereby decreasing dissatisfaction with present pay. Klein and Maher (1966) found data to support just this point: Employees who expected large raises were more satisfied with their pay. In my own research on managers, I have typically found no relationship between pay satisfaction and raise anticipation. Thus, one study shows a positive relationship, one a negative relationship, and one no relationship. Therefore, it is hardly possible to reach any kind of conclusion at this time. Further research will probably show that situational factors dictate the kind of relationship that exists between pay satisfaction and raise anticipation.

Perceptions of How Pay Is Determined

Penner (1966) has reported that employees who feel their pay is based upon performance are typically more satisfied with their pay than employees who do not feel their pay is performance-based. Lawler (1966b) reports a similar finding, but notes that the relationship does not hold for those employees who feel pay should not be based upon performance; they are more satisfied with their pay if it is based upon nonperformance factors. From these studies, it would seem that pay satisfaction increases when pay is perceived to be based upon the criteria that employees feel it should be based upon. This conclusion does not directly challenge the conclusion of Penner that pay satisfaction will be higher when pay is based upon performance since, as has been shown, most employees believe pay should be based upon performance. From this it would be expected that on the average more people will be satisfied when pay is based upon performance than when it is not. For maximum pay satisfaction to exist, however, each individual's pay would have to be decided as he feels it should be.

It is not difficult to see why people who feel that their pay is determined in the way they think it should be are more satisfied. First, as has been noted, people generally feel that their pay should be based upon the personal input factor or factors on which they stand relatively high. Thus, when a person says his pay is being determined on the correct basis or on merit, he more often than not is saying that it is reflecting correctly his high inputs in an area. When he says it is not being determined correctly, he is in effect saying that it is not reflecting his high inputs in certain areas. Thus, it would follow directly from the model that the person who perceives that his pay is correctly determined would be more satisfied with his pay, since his pay outcomes should be seen to more clearly reflect his perceived inputs.

THE RESEARCH EVIDENCE AND THE MODEL: SUMMARY AND CONCLUSION

A great deal of the evidence that has been reviewed is congruent with the predictions of the model. Particularly impressive is the large amount of evidence which shows that, as personal inputs increase, pay satisfaction typically decreases. Similarly, there is fairly good evidence to indicate that, as job demands increase, pay satisfaction decreases. There is strong evidence to support the view that as pay increases so does pay satisfaction. Although there is evidence to support the view that social comparisons are important in determining pay satisfaction, it is not very complete. Clearly more research is needed on the social comparison aspects of pay satisfaction. There also is relatively little research on the effect of nonmonetary rewards on pay satisfaction. Although people have long said that pay dissatisfaction is just a sympton or scapegoat for other kinds of dissatisfaction, few hard data are available to support this view. Also missing is research on the effects of wage histories on people's perceptions of their present pay. Finally, there is a dearth of studies on perceived overpayment. The model states that overpayment will lead to feelings of guilt and discomfort, yet few field studies have even considered overpayment. Thus, it remains to be proved that overpayment produces a feeling that is qualitatively different from that produced by underpayment. Although logically it seems legitimate to argue that the dissatisfaction caused by overpayment is not similar to that experienced from underpayment, more research is needed to establish this point.

Chapter 13
THE CONSEQUENCES OF PAY DISSATISFACTION

In the literature, pay dissatisfaction is said to be responsible for everything from poor job performance to strikes. Figure 13-1 shows some of the most frequently mentioned consequences of pay dissatisfaction. Despite the fact that pay satisfaction is often credited with the power to influence a large number of factors, there is no theory or view of why dissatisfaction with pay should affect all these variables. There are some mini-theories that try to explain why it affects one or two (Brayfield & Crockett, 1955), but most researchers have simply not tried to explain the relationships they have reported. It is likely that pay dissatisfaction affects such things as job performance and job satisfaction for somewhat different reasons. Because of this, we must—at least partially—work at the mini-theory level and deal separately with some of the variables shown in Figure 13-1.

It is not necessary, however, to state a separate theory of why pay dissatisfaction influences turnover, absenteeism, strikes, etc. There are some common elements here, and we must try to recognize them. There are common elements in that many of these consequences of pay dissatisfaction are influenced by the same feelings or reactions that people have when they are dissatisfied with their pay. Many of the behaviors shown in Figure 13-1 are behavioral outcroppings of the same kind of employee feelings, feelings that are influenced or affected by feelings of pay dissatisfaction. Figure 13-2, which is a Model of the Consequences of Pay Dissatisfaction, illustrates this point; it shows that two important kinds of feelings people have about their job are influenced by pay dissatisfaction. First, it shows that people's desire for money increases as pay dissatisfaction increases (see Chap. 2; Alderfer, 1969). Second it shows that the attractiveness of the job decreases as pay dissatisfaction increases. This simply reflects the fact that when a person says that he is dissatisfied with his pay, he is also saying that he regards the pay rewards associated with holding his job as too low. As was pointed out in Chapter 11, people

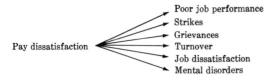

FIGURE 13-1. Some consequences of pay dissatisfication.

are not attracted to jobs that have low rewards attached to them (Graen, 1969).

The model shows that it is the impact of pay dissatisfaction on the attractiveness of the job and on the person's desire for more money that relates pay dissatisfaction to such behaviors as absenteeism and turnover. Feelings of dissatisfaction, because of their impact on people's desire for money, lead to those behaviors which are likely to result in more money—joining a union, searching for a new job, performing better, presenting grievances, and striking. Because feelings of pay dissatisfaction lower the attractiveness of a job they lead to turnover, absenteeism, and job dissatisfaction. Thus, the model agrees with the frequently stated view that pay dissatisfaction is related to a number of variables (Herzberg, Mausner, Peterson, & Capwell, 1957). The model also argues that there are common underlying reasons that cause these various factors to be related to pay dissatisfaction. This approach is different from the usual approach, which treats the relationship between pay dissatisfaction and each of the variables separately (Brayfield & Crockett, 1955) and does not examine the reasons for the relationships. The model clearly points out the reason these diverse variables are related to pay dissatisfaction: that is, they are partially or wholly influenced by one or both of the important feelings or reactions that result when people are dissatisfied with their pay.

TURNOVER

The model shows that pay dissatisfaction can be a determinant of turnover. The emphasis here is on voluntary turnover, since the expectation is that pay dissatisfaction can affect only the employee's decision to change jobs, and this is what is reflected in voluntary turnover figures. Pay dissatisfaction should not be related to employer-initiated terminations. Chapter 11 focused on the decision to stay in the same job versus taking another job. It emphasized that a person will be motivated to accept another job and to quit his present one when he perceives that the valence of the outcomes associated with taking the new job are more positive than those associated with holding his present job. Since pay is one of the positively valued outcomes that a person gets for holding a job, and since the valence of pay generally increases with the amount, it follows that, the higher the pay, the higher the valence of the job. Thus, other things equal, people will gravitate toward higher-paying jobs. It follows from this that turnover should be associated with pay dissatisfaction and job dissatisfiction. As has been stressed, when a person says he is dissatisfied with his pay he is also saying that he wants more money and that holding his job does not lead to highly valued pay outcomes (Graen, 1969). A person who says he is satisfied with his pay, on the other hand, is saying that holding his job does lead to highly valued pay outcomes. Clearly, the person who perceives that his job leads to highly valued rewards is more likely to hold onto his job than one who perceives that his job does not lead to such rewards. The former is less likely to search for other jobs and to see other jobs as more attractive than his present one.

It is not realistic, however, to predict that pay dissatisfaction should be perfectly correlated with turnover. First, pay is just one of the rewards that influences the attractiveness of a job. A person may be dissatisfied with his pay but satisfied with other job aspects, and because of this, he may feel that his present job is more desirable than any alternative one. He may also remain on his job even though he is dissatisfied with the pay if he feels that there is a low probability of obtaining a better-paying job. This would seem to be a particularly important influence in times of high unemployment. Thus, in such periods one might expect pay dissatisfaction to be quite unrelated to turnover; even though a person has a low-paying job, the probability of his finding a better one is low, and he therefore would not quit his present job. Note, too, that pay desires satisfaction may influence turnover. A person may quit a job even though he is satisfied with his pay if he feels that his career pay objectives cannot be satisfied on it, but can be satisfied elsewhere. In summary, the thinking outlined so far suggests that turnover should bear

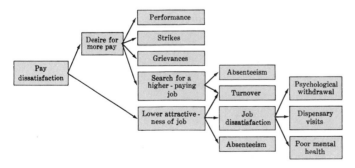

FIGURE 13-2. Model of the consequences of pay dissatisfaction.

a strong, but far from perfect, relationship to pay dissatisfaction and that the relationship should be strongest in periods of full employment.

Data from two studies generally support the view that people who are dissatisfied with their pay will be more likely to think about leaving their present job than people who are satisfied with their pay. Penner (1966) reports that employees dissatisfied with their pay were twice as likely to consider changing jobs as those who were satisfied. Similar data have been reported by Haire (unpublished) on the basis of a study of M.I.T. Sloan fellows.

There is also evidence that employees who are dissatisfied with their pay are not only more likely to think about leaving their jobs, but are actually more likely to leave in greater numbers than satisfied workers. As might be expected, many studies have shown that total job satisfaction is related to turnover (for reviews of this literature see Brayfield & Crockett, 1955; Herzberg, Mausner, Peterson, & Capwell, 1957; Schuh, 1967 and Vroom, 1964). In general the studies have found that pay dissatisfaction is a good predictor of turnover but that it is not as good a predictor as total job satisfaction. Hulin (1966) found a good relationship between overall satisfaction and turnover among female clerks, but little relationship between pay dissatisfaction and turnover. Hulin points out that this finding may be due to the fact that the female employees studied had low economic needs. This follows from the view presented in Chapter 10, which stressed that pay will not influence turnover unless it is important. Wickert (1951) has also presented data which show that pay dissatisfaction is not necessarily the best predictor of turnover. Hulin (1968) has recently reported a follow-up study on his original sample of clerks. It shows that when pay satisfaction increased among the employees, turnover dropped substantially. This, of course, provides evidence that pay satisfaction has the power to influence turnover even when pay is relatively unimportant. It is also in agreement with the point that turnover and pay dissatisfaction should be strongly related during periods of full employment, since the data were collected when employment was high. Some data collected by Weitz and Nucklos (1953) are in agreement with those reported by Hulin. They show that 83 percent of the employees who reported that their pay was adequate were still with the company at the end of a year, while only 67 percent of those who reported it was too low were still with the company. Thus, although the data are skimpy, they generally support the view that under most conditions pay dissatisfaction leads to turnover among employees to whom pay is important.

Three studies have presented data that indirectly support the view that pay dissatisfaction will be more strongly related to turnover in times of full employment than in times of unemployment. Behrend (1953) found evidence that in periods of unemployment very little voluntary turnover takes place. Similar data have been reported by Brissenden and Frankel (1922) and by Woytinsky (1942). This evidence does not, of course, provide direct support for the view that pay dissatisfaction and turnover will be more strongly related under conditions of full employment. In order to test this directly, one would need to compare the correlation of pay dissatisfaction and turnover during a period of full employment with the correlation of the two in a period of high unemployment, and this has not been done. The data suggest, however, that the correlation may be higher under full employment, since they support part of the reasoning that led to this view. The data show that a "reality" factor influences turnover decisions and that, because of this, in times of unemployment people are likely to hold onto their jobs even though they are dissatisfied with them. This condition undoubtedly comes about because no viable alternatives are available during periods of unemployment. Thus, in times of high unemployment, it is unlikely that pay dissatisfaction would bear a strong positive relationship to turnover. On the other hand, in the full-employment situation where a number of people are changing jobs, pay dissatisfaction has been shown to be positively related to turnover by several studies.

In summary, the data generally support the view that pay dissatisfaction is related to turnover; they clearly indicate, however, that the two are not always highly related. The relationship seems to be strongly affected by general employment conditions, by the person's satisfaction with other aspects of his job, and by the importance the individual attaches to pay.

ABSENTEEISM

The model in Figure 13-2 shows that absenteeism may be affected by pay dissatisfaction. It is not necessarily true, however, that a strong relationship should be expected, as a brief look at why they might be expected to be related should explain. The discussion in Chapter 10 of the job-attendance decision emphasized that the decision is based upon a comparison of the valence of the outcomes associated with going to work and the valence of those associated with not going. A number of the outcomes involved here are not monetary, and for this reason pay factors can never predict absenteeism perfectly. People might decide to go to work to see their friends, regardless of the financial outcomes. But even where pay dissatisfaction comes into play, it is a rather indirect influence. As the model shows, it influences the attractiveness of the job, which, in turn, is one factor that influences absenteeism. Job attractiveness can influence absenteeism because in many organizations high absenteeism can lead to loss of job. Where this is true, it would stand to reason that people will go to work regularly to protect the job they hold if and only if the job is attractive to them. Thus, high job attractiveness should lead to low absenteeism where absenteeism means loss of job.

Pay dissatisfaction should also be related to absenteeism if a person will lose his pay for not showing up for work. The more dissatisfied the person is with his pay, the less he tends to value the amount he will lose by not showing up. Because of this attitude, the person who is dissatisfied with his pay will be less likely to show up than the one who is satisfied. Thus, low pay satisfaction can be a cause of absenteeism when absenteeism means loss of money. When absenteeism does not mean loss of pay or loss of job then the previously stated reasons to expect pay dissatisfaction to be related to absenteeism do not appear to hold.

The model shows that searching for a new job might also lead to high absenteeism. This reflects the fact that employees are sometimes absent from their job in order to look for a new job. Since looking for a new job is often motivated by pay dissatisfaction, it follows that pay dissatisfaction can potentially cause absenteeism even when absenteeism is not likely to cause loss of pay or job. This factor is likely to operate only when other possible jobs are available. Equity theory would also predict that pay dissatisfaction would lead to absenteeism. According to equity theory, underpayment should lead employees to try to reduce their inputs, and certainly one way to do this is to be absent. In short there are a number of different reasons for predicting that pay dissatisfaction will lead to high absenteeism, but most of them apply only under certain conditions. Thus, although in most situations it might be expected that pay dissatisfaction and absenteeism will be related, the reason for the relationship will vary, depending on such factors as whether or not absenteeism is perceived to result in loss of pay or loss of job and whether or not alternative jobs are available locally.

One of the difficulties in doing research on absenteeism is that absenteeism is not a unitary trait. A simple measure of how many days a person is absent from work reflects absences due to a number of causes. People can be absent because of sickness and injury and because they simply have decided not to make the effort to come to work. There is no reason to believe that pay dissatisfaction can strongly influence absences that are due to many kinds of sickness or disability. It is possible, however, that it can influence absences that are due to certain kinds of mental and psychosomatic illnesses. What is needed, of course, is a measure of absenteeism that reflects a person's tendency to go to work when he is physically able. On this measure, the record of a person who loses thirty days a year because of actual sickness should look different from that of a person who loses thirty days a year because he is not motivated to go to work. Unfortunately, there is no direct way to establish why a person missed work on a given day. Metzner and Mann (1953) have suggested that data on frequency of absence best reflect how motivated the person is to go to work. A measure of total days absent seems to be more heavily weighted by illness-caused absence. Illness tends to lead to long periods of absence. A record of many one- or two-day absences, on the other hand, usually reflects lack of motivation to appear for work. Thus, number of seperate absence periods probably is a better measure of a person's motivation, although it is far from a perfect measure.

Despite the difficulties of measuring absenteeism, several studies have reported significant relationships between overall job satisfaction and absenteeism. Kerr, Koppelmeir, and Sullivan (1951) have reported a relationship of −.44 between absenteeism and job satisfaction, and Fleishman, Harris, and Burtt (1955) have reported a correlation of −.25 between morale and absence rates. Two studies have looked specifically at the relationship between absenteeism rate and pay dissatisfaction. Metzner and Mann (1953) report that only 43 percent of white-collar workers who were absent four or more times in six months were satisfied with their pay while 69 percent of those who were absent once or not at all were satisfied. Van Zelst and Kerr (1953) report that pay satisfaction correlates −.17 with number of days absent. This is a low correlation, but not surprising in light of the fact that this study used number of days absent as its measure of absenteeism. As was pointed out, this measure is not very sensitive to the kind of absenteeism that is expected to occur because of pay dissatisfaction. Overall, there is not a great deal of evidence to support the view that absenteeism can result from pay dissatisfaction; but what data there are, are consistent with this view. Clearly, research is needed to determine how different factors affect the relationship between absenteeism and pay dissatisfaction.

PERFORMANCE

In the last twenty years, the relationship between job satisfaction and job performance has been given much research attention. It is beyond the scope of this book to treat in detail the history of this research (see Porter & Lawler, 1968a). It is appropriate, however, to point out that initially the researchers expected that job satisfaction should be related to job performance, because of the strong influence of job satisfaction on job performance (Brayfield & Crockett, 1955). The evidence has not supported this view. Most studies have found only weak relationships between job satisfaction and performance. Vroom (1964) reports a median correlation of .14 between the two. As he points out, some researchers have reported strong positive relationships, while others have reported strong negative relationships. Lawler and Porter (1967b) have stressed that job satisfaction, rather than being a cause of performance, may be caused by performance. They point out that good performance often leads to high rewards, which, in turn, lead to high satisfaction and thus they predict that job satisfaction should be related to performance only where rewards are related to performance. Lawler and Porter (1967b) present some data to support their prediction, and it is in agreement with the view that satisfaction is sometimes strongly related to performance but at other times not.

The model in Figure 13-2 suggests that pay dissatisfaction possibly can affect job performance. Pay dissatisfaction leads to a stronger desire for more pay, which, as was stressed in Chapter 6, can lead to a strong motivation to perform. This, of course, will happen only where good performance is seen to lead to higher pay. According to this line of reasoning, it is possible to predict that pay dissatisfaction should lead to better performance when workers feel that pay is based upon performance. To the extent that this tendency operates, it should lead to a negative relationship between pay satisfaction and performance. It is also possible that pay dissatisfaction and a desire for more money may lead to lower productivity. Whyte (1955) has pointed out that workers on piece rates sometimes restrict their production in an effort to induce management to raise the rates. Thus, rather than producing more in order to earn more, they produce less—at least on a short-term basis. Still, it is important to note that they are motivated to produce less by a desire to earn more.

These are not the only tendencies that are likely to influence the relationship between pay satisfaction and performance. As was pointed out in Chapter 12, pay satisfaction is influenced by the amount of money a person receives and by the amount he feels he should receive. Where good performers actually receive more pay than poor performers, there should be a tendency for pay satisfaction to be positively related to performance because of the ability of good performance to lead to higher pay and the ability of higher pay to lead to greater pay satisfaction. In this situation there should be a positive relationship between pay satisfaction and performance.

Overall, it appears that there is one tendency that could lead to a negative correlation between pay satisfaction and performance (pay dissatisfaction→desire for pay) and another that could lead to a positive correlation (performance→pay→pay satisfaction). Given these conflicting tendencies, it is no wonder that there has often been confusion about the relationship between pay satisfaction and job performance. If these two tendencies are of equal strength, then one would expect a zero relationship between pay satisfaction and performance. One would also expect a zero relationship between pay satisfaction and performance where pay is not related to performance, since for either of these tendencies to come into play, pay must be related to performance. Depending upon which of the tendencies is stronger, one would expect a different kind of relationship to exist between pay and performance. If the pay dissatisfaction-causes-performance tendency is stronger, then performance should be negatively related to pay satisfaction, but if the performance-leads-to-pay tendency is stronger, then pay satisfaction should be positively related to performance.

There are some good reasons to believe that the performance-leads-to-pay tendency will be stronger in most situations and that, because of this, pay satisfaction typically will be positively related to performance. Desire for pay is only one of many factors that influence performance, and pay satisfaction is only one of several factors that influence desire for pay. Thus, the causal link from pay satisfaction to performance is inevitably a very weak one and for this reason would rarely be expected to create a strong tendency for pay satisfaction to affect performance. On the other hand, the causal link from performance to pay can be quite strong, as can the link from pay to pay satisfaction. Thus, it is possible that performance can fairly strongly influence pay satisfaction. According to this line of reasoning, it would be expected that where pay is based upon performance, pay satisfaction should be positively related to performance. Where pay is not based upon performance, however, pay satisfaction and performance should not be related. Where pay is negatively related to performance, then pay satisfaction should be negatively related to performance. Finally, it should be noted that pay satisfaction might be negatively related to performance where pay is not related to performance, but where people feel they can obtain more pay by performing well. This situation is unlikely to exist, but if it did, a negative relationship should exist because of the tendency of people who are dissatisfied with their pay to work harder in order to earn more money. The performance-leads-to-pay tendency would not be operating in this case and thus there would not be the offsetting tendency that might lead the higher performers to be more satisfied with their pay.

Two studies have specifically focused on the relationship between pay satisfaction and performance under conditions of pay based upon performance and under conditions of pay not based upon performance. These studies are, of course, just what is needed to test the view that performance will be positively related to pay satisfaction where pay is based upon performance, but not related where pay is not based on performance. In the more interesting of these studies Schneider and Olson (1970) found a correlation of .25 between performance and pay satisfaction in a merit pay hospital, but a 0 correlation between them in a hospital where pay was based upon seniority. Porter and Lawler (1968a) have reported somewhat similar data, showing that, for a group of managers whose pay was not based upon performance, no relationship existed between pay satisfaction and performance. For a group whose pay was performance-based, however, they found a positive relationship. This evidence suggests that the stronger causal tendency is that of performance causing pay satisfaction, rather than pay satisfaction causing performance, since a positive relationship would be expected from the view that performance causes pay satisfaction. It also supports the view that pay satisfaction will be related to performance only when pay is based upon performance. These two points lead to some extremely important implications for practice that will be discussed in Chapter 14.

JOB SATISFACTION

Figure 13-2 shows that pay dissatisfaction tends to decrease the attractiveness of a job and, as a result, tends to lead to high job dissatisfaction. When a person says he is dissatisfied with his pay, he is saying that one aspect of his job (his pay) is not attractive to him or, in other words, not what he feels it should be. Since a person's feeling of job satisfaction is influenced directly by his feeling with respect to the adequacy of the important elements of the job, it follows that a person who is dissatisfied with his pay is likely to be less satisfied with his job than is a person who is satisfied with his pay. Pay satisfaction, however, should not be expected to bear a very close relationship to overall job satisfaction. It is only one of a number of important influences on how satisfied a person will be with his job. In order to predict job satisfaction well, one must know how satisfied a person is in all the areas of the job that are important to him (Schaffer, 1953). Knowing how satisfied a person is with his pay provides one clue about how satisfied he is with his job. In some instances, it may turn out to be a surprisingly good predictor of job satisfaction. One of the reasons is that the degrees of satisfaction which employees express concerning different aspects of their jobs often are correlated moderately well (Vroom, 1964). Thus, when a person says he is dissatisfied with his pay, he is also likely to be dissatisfied with other aspects of his job, and therefore to express high overall job dissatisfaction.

Studies have tried to determine the impact of pay satisfaction on job satisfaction by asking employees what influences their job satisfaction. Typically employees have reported that pay satisfaction influences job satisfaction. In one of the earlier studies of this type, Walker and Guest (1952) found that of 180 workers interviewed, 126 gave "good pay" as an important reason for liking their jobs. In another early study of this type,

Evans and Laseau (1950) found that 41 percent of the employees at G.M. reported that wages were an important determinant of job satisfaction.

More recently a number of studies of this type have been done, almost all of them designed to test Herzberg's two-factor theory of job satisfaction. It is beyond the scope of this book to review all this research, but it is important to note a few of the points which are relevant to pay satisfaction. Based upon their initial study, Herzberg et al. (1959) classified pay as a dissatisfier, that is, as a factor which contributes to or affects only dissatisfaction. According to this view, feelings of pay satisfaction cannot lead to feelings of job satisfaction, but feelings of pay dissatisfaction can lead to feelings of job dissatisfaction. The data from that study, however, supported the view that pay can operate both as a dissatisfier and a satisfier. That is, the data showed that when people are satisfied with their pay they feel good about their job, but when they are dissatisfied with their pay they feel dissatisfied with their job. At least fifty studies have tested Herzberg's theory since 1959, and they have consistently tended to replicate the finding of the original study as far as pay is concerned. Pay is mentioned as a factor that can cause dissatisfaction and as a factor that can cause satisfaction (House & Wigdor, 1967). This would seem to provide strong support for the view that pay satisfaction/ dissatisfaction can and does influence job satisfaction/dissatisfaction. This evidence is particularly important since it provides some support for the view expressed in the model—that it is pay satisfaction that influences job satisfaction rather than the reverse.

A second approach to studying the relationship between job satisfaction and pay satisfaction involves simply correlating the two factors. According to our model, the expectation would be that they should bear a moderate positive relationship to each other. Data from a number of studies are in agreement with this view. Wernimont (1964) has reported a correlation of .19 between pay satisfaction and job satisfaction. Hulin and Smith (1967) have reported correlations of .32 and .30 between pay satisfaction and job satisfaction for male and female office workers. Of particular interest in this study is the finding that feelings of pay satisfaction correlated with subjects' statements about both their feeling of job saisfaction and their feeling of job dissatisfaction. This is important since it supports the view that people's feelings of satisfaction with their pay influence their feelings of both job satisfaction and job dissatisfaction. Thus, it appears that at least for pay it does not make sense to speak of job satisfaction and job dissatisfaction as on two seperate continuums a la Herzberg. Pay satisfaction seems to affect employees' feelings of job satisfaction and job dissatisfaction as if a continuum stretching from satisfied to dissatisfied existed.

Armstrong (1968) has reported correlations of .18 and .37 between pay satisfaction and job satisfaction. Hinrichs (1968) reports that pay satisfaction correlates between .28 and .43 with job satisfaction for five groups of employees. Thus, it seems that pay satisfaction typically correlates around .30 with job satisfaction. This is not a high correlation, but it is in line with the view that pay satisfaction is just one of a number of variables which influence job satisfaction. Overall, a large amount of evidence has been reviewed which supports the view that pay satisfaction is an important influence on job satisfaction. When employees are satisfied with their pay, this contributes to their feeling of job satisfaction, and when they are dissatisfied, this contributes to their feelings of dissatisfaction.

PAY AND JOB SATISFACTION

A number of studies have shown that the amount of pay a person receives for holding his job correlates with his job satisfaction. This, of course, should be expected from the relationship found between pay satisfaction and job satisfaction. Amount of pay influences pay satisfaction, and pay satisfaction influences job satisfaction. It does not follow, however, that amount of pay should be very highly correlated with pay satisfaction. As was pointed out in Chapter 12, amount of pay is only one of a number of influences on pay satisfaction, and as has been stressed, pay satisfaction is only one of the factors which influence job satisfaction.

Typical of the actual relationships found between pay rates and job satisfaction is that reported by Smith and Kendall (1963). Within the plants they studied, they found a mean correlation of .25 between wage rate and job satisfaction. Studies which report positive correlations between satisfaction and income have been done on college graduates (Barnett, Handelsman, Stewart, & Super, 1952; Miller, 1941; Thompson, 1939), on British factory workers (Marriott & Denerley, 1955), and on a national sample of American workers (Centers & Cantril, 1946). Stockford and Kunze (1950) report that workers who begin a new job with wages that are low compared with their previous wages have more negative attitudes toward the employer and are more likely to quit. This finding fits with the view that the impact of pay rate on satisfaction is influenced by both actual pay level and by wage history. In this study, as would be expected, attitudes were more closely related to relative wage rate than to absolute wage rate. When all the evidence is considered together, a rather strong case can be made to support the view that wage rates bear a moderate relationship to job satisfaction.

UNION MEMBERSHIP, STRIKES, AND GRIEVANCES

Joining a union, filing grievances, and going on strike are behaviors which employees can use to obtain more money. The model shows that employees who want more money are particularly prone to engage in these activities. Since pay dissatisfaction causes an increased desire for more money, it follows that pay dissatisfaction should lead to more strikes and grievances. There is quite a bit of evidence to support the view that pay dissatisfaction and the resultant desire for more pay are an important influence on union membership, strikes, and grievance behavior. Stagner (1956) reports data which show that employees see unions as organizations who can help them to obtain higher wages and that employees join unions in order to obtain higher wages. Related to these points is a study by Smith (1962). His data show that employees who are dissatisfied with their jobs feel more positively toward unions than do satisfied employees. Thus, it appears that when employees are dissatisfied with their jobs and want more pay, they feel more positively toward unions and are likely to join them because of the perceived ability of unions to obtain more money for most employees.

A study by James (1951) shows a direct relationship between pay satisfaction and strike behavior. He compared a group of striking workers with a comparable control group of workers who were not striking. The strikers showed much higher levels of pay dissatisfaction than did the controls. Unfortunately, James had no measure of the workers' attitudes before the strike. It would be helpful to know if the level of pay dissatisfaction could predict the occurrence of strikes. Still, the data do provide some support for the view that pay dissatisfaction can lead to strikes, and there is a great deal of evidence that pay dissatisfaction is an important influence on employees' willingness to strike. Basically, the research evidence suggests that dissatisfaction with wages, hours, and fringe benefits is given by unions as the principal cause for 70 to 80 percent of all strikes. The evidence also suggests that strike frequency in a country is closely related to some economic indicators. One relationship shows that as unemployment goes up, strikes tend to be less frequent. This undoubtedly reflects the fact that people are more satisfied with their own job when they see many other people out of work, and it probably reflects the riskiness of a strike in periods of economic downturn. Strike frequency is not perfectly related to economic conditions, however.

It is all too easy to overemphasize the role that economic issues play in causing strikes because such issues are easy to identify and talk about. The evidence is clear that they are just one of a number of causes of strikes. They may be the most important, but this remains to be shown.

All that is clear at this point is that they are important and that they are the most frequently talked about reason for going on strike. One difficulty encountered in doing research on this topic is that it is socially acceptable to talk about striking for more money, but it is not so easy to talk of striking for more interesting work. Thus, about all that can be concluded is that, as shown in the model, strikes are motivated by economic conditions.

Practically the same points that were made in discussing strikes can be made in discussing grievances. Grievances do frequently seem to be filed as a result of pay dissatisfaction, and a large number of them are specifically concerned with economic issues, particularly where wage incentive plans are in effect (Whyte, 1955). But like strikes, grievances are often caused by other kinds of dissatisfaction. They can be an effective way of harassing management and venting employee hostility over other issues. Grievances over economic issues like strikes are a socially acceptable way to express these kinds of dissatisfaction. Because of this situation, we must be careful not to overinterpret the role of pay dissatisfaction in producing grievances.

In summary, the evidence quite clearly shows that, as suggested by the model, pay dissatisfaction can lead employees to join unions, go on strike, and file grievances. In general, the link between these behaviors and pay dissatisfaction seems to be stronger than the link between pay dissatisfaction and such behaviors as absenteeism and performance. Overall, it is clear that pay dissatisfaction can be quite costly to organizations. It erodes people's commitment to their jobs and leads to absenteeism, turnover, and other important but not always fully appreciated causes of low productivity, poor performance, and high costs.

THE EFFECTS OF OVERPAYMENT

It was stressed in Chapter 12 that perceived overpayment produces quite a different reaction in people from perceived underpayment. Overpayment produces feelings of guilt, discomfort, and anxiety which, as equity theory stresses, people try to reduce. There are a number of ways in which this can be done. Figure 13-3 lists four of the most important ways.

Unfortunately, very little research has been done on how people reduce feelings of inequity due to overpayment, although some research has been done on the effects of overpayment on productivity and quality (Chap. 8). There has also been relatively little research on why people choose different modes of inequity reduction.

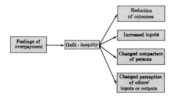

FIGURE 13-3. *Ways to reduce feelings of overpayment.*

Altering Outcomes

The evidence reviewed in Chapter 8 suggested, as shown in Figure 13-3, that people will reduce their outcomes when they are paid on a piece rate by restricting their productivity. There is little research to prove it, but it seems that people may also decrease their outcomes by reducing the preceived value or amount of some of the nonmonetary outcomes of their job. They may, for example, come to feel that a task is boring and uninteresting and thereby reduce the intrinsic outcomes of the job. Changing their cognition of the outcomes is probably the preferred way of reducing feelings of overpayment for most people, at least it is probably preferable to decreasing pay outcomes. The latter is obviously financially expensive, whereas changing cognitions about task interest and value involves relatively little cost.

Altering Inputs

Figure 13-3 suggests that when subjects are overpaid they may increase their inputs in order to reduce their feeling of inequity, although as was stressed in Chapter 8, it is not clear that this actually leads them to work harder. There is evidence that it may lead them to increase their perceptions of their inputs. Thus, in one study (Lawler, Koplin, Young, & Fadem, 1968), it was found that overpaid subjects reported higher qualifications than equitably paid subjects, despite the fact that the former were initially made to feel overpaid by being told that they had low job qualifications. It is hardly surprising that people are more inclined to increase their perception of their inputs than to increase their actual inputs. Clearly, the former is much easier and less costly. People can also increase their perceived inputs by increasing their perception of the difficulty of the job they are doing. Again, changing this perception is much easier than actually working harder. Unfortunately, very little attention has been given to the effects of overpayment on employees' perceptions of their own inputs. Most of the research has tried to measure the behavioral consequences of overpayment. This is too bad, since it is quite possible that in actual work situations employees change their perception of their inputs rather than their behavior when confronted with feelings of over-payment. Thus, the strongest impact of overpayment may be on percep-tions rather than on job behavior directly.

Changing Comparison Other

People may reduce feelings of overpayment by changing their comparison other. Although this subject has received little research attention, Patchen (1961) has established that comparisons are important and that subjects who make certain kinds of comparisons feel inequity while others do not. Patchen also found that very few people chose comparison others who had less favorable input-outcome balances than themselves. It would seem to follow that by changing the comparison other from someone who has a less favorable input-outcome balance to someone who has a balance similar to or better than himself, a person could reduce his feelings of overpayment. This may be a common method of reducing feelings of over-payment, since it is certainly easy to do and, according to equity theory, should be very effecive.

Other's Inputs and Outcomes

Overpayment inequity may be reduced by changing one's perception of the input-outcome balance of the comparison other. Specifically, this might involve upgrading other's outcomes or downgrading his inputs. Lawler (in press) has presented a great deal of evidence to show that subjects often do distort the pay outcomes of others. What is more, other's pay outcomes are usually distorted upward, and the more they are dis-torted upward, the less likely is the person who is distorting them to feel overpaid. This provides at least some evidence that distorting other people's outcomes is a viable way to reduce one's feelings of being over-paid, and it suggsts that people use it to reduce feelings of inequity due to overpayment. It is also possible to downgrade the inputs of others in order to reduce or prevent a feeling of overpayment. Adams (1965) has presented some evidence that this does in fact happen, but other support-ing evidence is very sparse. It would seem to be a relatively frequent approach to reducing feelings of overpayment, since it can be done at a relatively low cost and does not require a serious realignment of one's self-image or perceptual system.

PREFERRED METHODS OF REDUCING FEELINGS OF INEQUITY DUE TO OVERPAYMENT

Adams (1965) has presented some propositions that attempt to predict which inequity reduction approach people will choose. He suggests, as has been stressed here, that certain types of cognitive changes may be the most frequently chosen. As a general rule it seems that people will avoid choosing an inequity reduction approach that:

1. Will result in their losing positively valued outcomes (e.g., money)
2. Will have negatively valued consequences for them (e.g., getting tired from working hard for extra productivity or quality)
3. Will involve a major change in their self-image or concept

Thus, the preferred methods of reducing feelings of inequity due to overpayment will be (roughly in order of preference):

1. Changing comparison other (unless it is long established and related to a person's self-concept)
2. Changing the perception of comparison person's inputs and/or outcomes
3. Raising the perception of own inputs (unless low inputs are central to self-image)
4. Reducing the perceived value of own outcomes

These four relatively preferred approaches involve cognitive changes. Actually altering one's inputs and outcomes clearly would rank very low in such a list. This suggests that more support for equity theory might be found in studies that examine cognitive changes than has been found in the studies that have looked for behavioral changes. Many of the latter studies may have missed important cognitive changes that were going on.

Given the large number of ways of reducing feelings of overpayment and the ease with which many of them can be employed, it is hardly surprising that most researchers have reported that very few employees actually feel overpaid (Lawler, 1965a). Still, the effect of overpayment is of interest, particularly on a theoretical level, since by studying how people reduce feelings of overpayment, one can learn something about how people deal with uncomfortable feelings, such as guilt. Clearly, the whole topic of why people choose different approaches to reducing inequity is open to research.

Overall, the evidence shows that both underpayment and overpayment affect pay satisfaction. The effects of underpayment have been researched more extensively, and they also seem to be more relevant for organizations, since they include such things as absenteeism, turnover, and strikes—which have a direct impact on organizational effectiveness. Overpayment on the other hand seems to be dealt with on a cognitive level. It is possible for employees to deal with underpayment on a cognitive level. They could for example change their comparison other or increase their perception of their inputs but there is little evidence to suggest that they do deal with their feelings of perceived underpayment this way. Feelings of underpay seem to be effectively dealt with only by an increase in pay and probably because of this they are much more stable and long lasting than are feelings of overpayment.

Chapter 14
PAY SATISFACTION: IMPLICATIONS FOR PRACTICE

It hardly seems necessary to say that managers should be concerned about the level of pay satisfaction in their organizations. Chapter 13 showed that pay dissatisfaction can lead to strikes, grievances, absenteeism, and turnover. In short, pay dissatisfaction can lead to a liquidation of the human assets of an organization. It is quite obvious that strikes cost organizations great amounts of money, but it is not always recognized that grievances, absenteeism, and turnover are also very expensive. Most organizations simply do not know how expensive turnover is, for example, and as a result, they underestimate the importance of keeping it low. Many of the costs associated with it are hidden, such as the cost of having an inexperienced worker doing a job. Other costs, such as those related to training, recruitment, and clerical tasks are more obvious, but managers seldom appreciate how closely they are tied to turnover. Some firms that have attempted to assess the costs of turnover figure that even on low-level jobs it can cost as much as $2,000 to replace each employee who quits. At the executive level the cost can be $25,000 or more. Turnover has also been very high in many companies. The Bell System reported a 21 percent turnover rate during 1969, and other companies have reported much higher rates.

Given that pay satisfaction influences a number of crucial factors, what practical steps can an organization take to prevent the negative consequences of pay dissatisfaction? Perhaps the simplest answer is that pay satisfaction should be kept high. This, however, is much easier said than done. Designing a pay program that will lead to a high level of satisfaction for all employees is a difficult and potentially costly undertaking. The Model of the Determinants of Pay Satisfaction can be of some help in designing such a program. It directly suggests some of the things that organizations can do to raise pay satisfaction. Some of these things are rather obvious, but others, like installing cafeteria-style wage plans and eliminating pay secrecy, are not. A number of practical suggestions will be discussed in the pages that follow. At this point, however, it is important to describe what we mean by a "high level of pay satisfaction."

One way to ensure that a high level of pay satisfaction exists in an organization is to make every member of the organization satisfied with his pay. In this situation there would not only be a high average level of pay satisfaction, but also a low variance in the pay satisfaction of different people in the organization. It is also possible to have a high variance in the pay satisfaction of employees and a fairly high level of pay satisfaction. This condition would exist where most people are satisfied with their pay but a small number are very much dissatisfied. A high variance situation seems to be preferable to a low variance situation. The specific reasons for this will be discussed at the end of this chapter in the section, "Who Should Be Satisfied with Their Pay?" The issue is raised at this time only to stress the view that in our discussion of high pay satisfaction, the objective is not to describe how conditions can be created under which everyone will be satisfied, but to emphasize approaches to creating a pay system where, although the average pay satisfaction of employees will be high, there will be considerable variance in how satisfied individual employees are.

RAISING THE PAY OUTCOMES

The Model of the Determinants of Pay Satisfaction rather clearly indicates that raising a person's pay should increase his pay satisfaction because it increases his perception of the value of the rewards he receives. This, of course, serves to reduce the discrepancy between what the person feels his pay should be and what he feels it is, since it raises his perception of what his pay is. One problem with this approach to increasing pay satisfaction is that it can cost a great deal of money. As was pointed out in Chapter 1, a small change in a company's payroll can have a large effect on its profitability. A second possible problem with this approach is that it might lead to a decreased motivation on the part of employees to obtain more money. As has been noted, when given enough money, some people lose interest in it and it ceases to motivate their behavior (Gellerman, 1968). Although this may happen in some circumstances, it is unlikely to result from a systematic attempt on the part of an organization to raise the pay satisfaction level of its employees; it is unlikely that an organization could pay out enough money to create this condition. It is likely to occur only if a person is highly paid for a long time, so that he becomes independently wealthy. Relevant here also is the point made in Chapter 13 that pay satisfaction probably does not influence performance very strongly; therefore, job performance should not be a major consideration when pay satisfaction is discussed. It is possible that pay dissatisfaction can lead to higher performance, but only under special conditions, and at best pay dissatisfaction is only one of a number of indirect influences on performance.

There is one additional problem with simply increasing salaries in order to increase pay satisfaction. Increasing employees' salaries will automatically increase their feelings of satisfaction with respect to external pay comparisons (external equity). That is, their pay will look better when they compare it with the pay of others like themselves in other organizations, and to this extent, they probably will be more satisfied with their pay. But within an organization, pay comparisons are important (internal equity), and giving everyone a raise will not necessarily make everyone more satisfied with them. In fact, it may make some people more dissatisfied. If high performers see their incompetent co-workers getting raises, for example, an organization may find itself paying out more money but creating dissatisfaction among its more effective employees. Intraorganization pay comparisons are crucial to employees, and because of this, pay differences among employees are important even where pay is high. An employee can be satisfied with his external pay comparisons but be dissatisfied with his pay if he sees that others around him who are less competent than he or who do a less demanding job are paid as much as or more than he. Thus, just paying everyone higher wages is not the answer to pay dissatisfaction. The answer lies in paying high salaries and at the same time establishing differences among people that are perceived by them to be equitable. Job evaluation and performance evaluation are the tools that must be used to establish equitable differences, and these will be discussed later.

How worthwhile is it to spend money on increasing the pay satisfaction of employees? Certainly, it is possible to err on the side of spending too much money on pay. But most companies probably do not commit enough of their income to salaries simply because they do not perceive salaries as a way to buy pay satisfaction and as an investment in the human assets of the company. The evidence is quite clear that money spent to raise employees' pay satisfaction is not wasted. It can buy less absenteeism, less turnover, fewer grievances, fewer strikes, and higher job satisfaction. These are commodities which clearly are worth investing in and as such represent good reasons for paying high enough wages so that employees will be satisfied with their pay.

At some point, of course, additional money spent on pay will not be well spent. It will just buy feelings of overpayment; and as the Model of the Consequences of Pay Dissatisfaction shows, such feelings are likely to be short-lived and have no positive outcomes for the organization. Feelings of overpayment can be counted on to produce certain realignments on the part of the person—but that is all. Thus, an organization that is trying to decide how much to invest in employees' pay must seek an amount that is neither too high nor too low if it is to get the highest rate of return on its money. Some ideas on how this amount can be determined will be discussed in the remainder of this book, but unfortunately, little research has been directed toward this subject. Also, the problem is to some extent different for each organization, since its solution depends upon how expensive absenteeism, turnover, and strikes are to an organization. If for some reason these behaviors are not costly at the present time and would not be costly if they occurred, then there is little reason for the organization to spend additional money to increase pay satisfaction. On the other hand, if they are occurring and are costly, serious consideration should be given to investing some of the money that is being spent on turnover, for example, in higher wages so as to reduce the level of turnover.

In addition to looking at the costs of turnover, absenteeism, etc., organizations must collect systematic data on how satisfied employees are with their pay. Such data are very important as a diagnostic tool to determine whether pay dissatisfaction is the cause of absenteeism and turnover. If pay satisfaction is relatively high, then it does not make sense to raise the salaries of employees, even though absenteeism and turnover might be high. If pay satisfaction is high, then these behaviors are probably being caused by other problems, and raising pay rates will not eliminate them. Rather than spending additional money on salaries, an organization might better spend it on redesigning jobs or changing other job aspects that affect turnover. The difficult question is, Where will the additional money yield the greatest return? For some organizations, higher salaries might yield the greatest return, while for others, redesigning jobs might yield the highest return. What is needed is a sophisticated cost benefit analysis that considers such things as the present pay satisfaction level, the characteristics of the jobs in the organization, the local labor market, etc.

A strong argument can be made for continuously monitoring the pay satisfaction of employees. If comparative pay satisfaction data are collected over a period of months or years, then it should be possible to do preventative maintenance as far as pay is concerned. In other words, a drop in the pay satisfaction of employees should be a clue that problems are about to develop. By appropriately adjusting salaries, an organization might be able to prevent these problems from materializing.

Continuous monitoring of pay satisfaction attitudes should also allow organizations to measure the impact of the money they invest in pay raises. To determine how much a raise meant in terms of increased pay satisfaction, an organization would measure the satisfaction of employees soon after they received a pay raise and compare the result with an earlier measure. After doing this a number of times, an organization should be able to develop a model of just how much increase in pay satisfaction a given pay raise can be expected to buy. If at the same time data are collected on levels of absenteeism and turnover, a knowledge of what different levels of pay satisfaction mean in terms of different levels of absenteeism and turnover can be built. Indeed, it should be possible to predict from this kind of model just what kind of change in absenteeism and turnover an organization can expect from investing a given amount of money in wages. If the costs of absenteeism and turnover have been accurately computed, then it should also be possible to determine what the return will be from expending a given amount of money on pay increases. This kind of information would make it possible to determine at just what point putting additional money into wages ceases to be economically profitable. The process of pay administration would no longer be a rule of thumb, fad-ridden, "fly by the seat of the pants" operation, but instead, a decision-making operation that gathers and interprets data and realistically tries to gauge the return that an organization receives on the money it invests in pay. In the absence of such data any decisions about how much should be spent on salaries or about how large an increase should be given must inevitably be based on guesswork and unrelated to the economic realities that they influence.

CAFETERIA-STYLE WAGE PLAN

Actually raising salaries is not the only way to raise employees' perceptions of the amount of pay they receive. One of the important points in the Model of the Determinants of Pay Satisfaction is that it is not the actual amount of pay a person receives, but his perception of that amount, which determines his pay satisfaction. The greater the perceived amount, the greater the pay satisfaction. The perceived amount received and the actual amount received are usually highly related, but not always, particularly when pay comes in more than one form. Today, pay comes in many different kinds of fringe benefits as well as actual cash. Typically, workers underestimate the value of fringe benefits, as well as their cost to the company. In addition, the policy of giving everyone the same benefits means that some people receive fringe benefits that they do not value. Nealey (1963), for example, has shown that married men do not want more time off the job, while unmarried men do, yet the trend is toward giving everyone more time off. Thus, organizations often spend money on fringe benefits and get no return for the expense.

Since employees underestimate the cost of fringe benefits and do not always value the benefits they receive, the money an organization invests in fringe benefits generally does not buy as much in terms of pay satisfaction as it should. With respect to actual cash payments, organizations in general do get credit for the money they pay out. One solution to the fringe benefit problem is to pay employees in cash only or to use the cafeteria-style pay plan that was outlined in Chapter 11. This kind of pay plan was originally discussed by Nealey (1963). It involves telling employees just how much is currently spent on their total pay package and giving them the opportunity to spend this money any way they want. They can choose to take it all in cash or they can choose to take some cash and to use the rest to buy the fringe benefits they actually want. This approach brings home to the employees rather clearly just how much the organization is spending to compensate them, and it assures that the money will be spent only on the fringe benefits the employees want. This will increase an employee's perception of the value of his pay, and this in turn should increase his pay satisfaction. Thus, from a psychological point of view the cafeteria-style plan clearly seems to be superior to the traditional pay and benefit approach.

There are some practical problems with the cafeteria approach, but they are far from insurmountable. One obvious difficulty is that the plan will complicate the bookkeeping aspects of wage and salary administration. With computer assistance this difficulty should be only temporary, however, since individual employee choices can be quantified and fed directly into the computer. In fact, one computer programming company, System Development Corporation, has already developed a computer program to do this. Some managers feel that if employees are given the chance to choose their own pay and benefit package they will be irresponsible and choose only cash; then if illness or other problems come along, the employees will not be protected. This concern can be dealt with on two levels. First, the research evidence indicates that most people will behave responsibly, given the choice. Furthermore, there is real doubt that people taking all cash is a problem that employers should spend their time on. Worrying about the kind of fringe benefit package an employee selects smacks of the kind of corporate paternalism that encourages people to be dependent, passive, and irresponsible (Argyris, 1957).

Probably the most serious practical problem with the cafeteria approach stems from the fact that the cost of many fringe benefits (e.g., insurance plans) is based upon the number of people who subscribe to them. Thus, it might be difficult to price a benefit plan in advance so that an employee could make an intelligent decision about whether or not he wanted to participate in it. This should be a major problem only for small companies. In large companies, a certain minimum number of participants could probably be guaranteed in advance. Smaller companies may have to try to negotiate agreements with insurance companies and others who underwrite aspects of the benefit package, or they may simply have to take some losses when the plan first goes into effect. After some experience with the plan, an organization should be able to judge in advance the number of employees who will select different benefits, and be able to price them accordingly. It also could conduct a survey to get an idea of what people would pick, given a choice. Based on this, reasonably good initial estimates of how many will choose each option could be developed, and the benefits priced accordingly. Survey results could also be used to set up five or six packages that seemed to fit different groups of employees. The employees could then be asked to choose one of these packages. If an organization felt that there were basic benefits its employees "had" to have, they could be included in each of these packages. At the moment very few organizations use cafeteria-style wage plans; it seems likely that such plans will become more common in the future, if, as was suggested in Chapter 11, employees perfer to take jobs with companies that offer such plans.

PAY SECRECY

Most managers argue that pay secrecy at the managerial level prevents managers from making dissatisfying pay comparisons and thereby minimizes pay dissatisfaction (Lawler, 1966c). The Model of the Determinants of Pay Satisfaction emphasizes the influence of pay comparisons, especially the comparison of one's own pay with what one perceives to be the pay of relevant others. There is no evidence to indicate that secrecy eliminates pay comparisons, but there is evidence that when pay secrecy exists, people base their comparisons on inaccurate information, innuendo, and hearsay. From the model, it would seem clear that, if pay secrecy leads employees to estimate the pay of others correctly, then pay satisfaction should be roughly the same with secrecy or without it. The one difference would be that, without secrecy, people who want to confront their boss and ask for a raise can say specifically that "X makes Y amount of money, why don't I?" Thus, if pay information were made public, the typical manager would have to defend his salary decisions more frequently and more adequately. On the other hand, if secrecy leads people to underestimate the pay of relevant others, satisfaction should be higher with secrecy than with openness. Finally, if secrecy leads people to overestimate the pay of others, pay satisfaction should be lower with secrecy. Whether secrecy leads to over, under, or accurate estimations of the comparison other's pay is a researchable topic, and it has been researched fairly extensively. The research shows that secrecy tends to lead people to overestimate the comparison other's pay, and it shows that the greater the overestimation, the greater the dissatisfaction. This finding is congruent with the model, but what is more important, it suggests that pay secrecy may do more to cause pay dissatisfaction than to reduce it.

On the basis of available data, it seems quite possible that, other things equal, an organization might be able to raise the satisfaction level of its employees by making pay rates public. Unfortunately, no research has directly measured the effect on satisfaction of moving from a secret system to a public one. The consequences would probably depend upon how well pay had been administered prior to the change. If it had been poorly administered and a number of unjustifiable pay differences existed, then the change would, at least temporarily, cause quite a few problems. In the long run, however, it would probably be beneficial if it forced the organization to take a critical look at its pay procedures and to straighten out any irregularities that existed. If pay had been well administered, the typical company would seem to have much to gain by making pay public. As was pointed out earlier, accurate pay information can clearly show employees that pay is related to performance, and it can eliminate any pay dissatisfaction that might result from overestimating other's pay.

Data collected by Beer and Gery (1968) suggest what can happen when people gain more information about pay rates. They found that employees who had accurate information about the pay rates in a company were more favorable to the idea of merit pay than were those who had little information. This finding is hardly surprising, since it seems logical that employees will be more willing to accept the risk of a merit system if they have clear evidence that the company can be trusted to distribute pay fairly. With pay secrecy, it is difficult to see how this trust can be built. On the other hand, when pay information is public and pay is well administered, this kind of trust apparently can be established, and workers will be more in favor of a merit pay system.

One question that arises whenever greater openness about pay is discussed is, How much information about pay should be made public? Should everyone's salary be made public, or only pay ranges for the various kinds of jobs? The answer depends upon the individual organization. No rule is valid for all. If the organization has always had strict pay secrecy and is rather autocractically run, then it would be foolish to try to move to complete pay openess overnight. A baby must crawl before it can walk! As a beginning, an organization might release some information on pay ranges and median salaries for various jobs. Schuster and Brady (1969) suggest that employees want to know their salary grades and ranges and the makeup of any raise they receive. Next, organizations might give out information on the size of raises and on who is getting them. Finally, the organization could move to complete openness, but only when it has, as a whole, become more democratic and is characterized by a high level of trust between superiors and subordinates and between peers. This whole process might take as long as ten years to complete. As will be shown in Chapter 16, the pay system must fit the climate of the organization. An authoritarian organization requires a different pay system than does a democratic organization. The latter can easily tolerate openness about pay and the basing of pay upon performance, while it is much less clear that this can be easily tolerated in an authoritarian organization.

TYING PAY TO PERFORMANCE

As we have seen, pay serves to motivate employees when it is closely tied to performance. As we have also seen, the research evidence shows that people are more satisfied with their pay when they feel that it is based upon performance. This suggests that organizations can increase pay satisfaction by increasing the relationship between pay and performance. It is significant that the same condition which motivates employees also leads to higher pay satisfaction. This fact strengthens our argument that pay should be tied closely to performance. Chapter 9 discussed how pay can be tied to performance and the difficulties of doing it. As was pointed out there, it is difficult to tie pay to performance in many situations, but this should not be an excuse for not tying pay to performance in those situations where it is appropriate, particularly when success promises such great rewards.

One additional comment about the expected impact of this condition on pay satisfaction: It may be important whether pay is tied to the employee's perception of his performance or to the superior's perception of the employee's performance. Where these perceptions coincide, this issue is not important, and indeed, under a good performance appraisal system, the two should correspond rather closely. If they do not correspond closely, it seems likely that pay satisfaction will be high when pay is tied to the employee's perception of his performance and low when it is tied to the boss's perception. Employees react in terms of their own perceptions of the situation, and in order for them to be satisfied with their pay, they must feel that it is proportionate to their performance (inputs). If pay is based upon the superior's perception of performance—and it differs from the employees' perceptions—employees will not see their pay as proportionate to their inputs. Hence, they will not be satisfied with their pay.

This does not mean that pay should be based upon employee's self-perceptions of performance rather than upon superior's perceptions. It means that self-perceptions are important and must be considered. The organization should try to determine where the employees' self-perceptions and the superior's perceptions converge and where they diverge, and then try to establish a performance appraisal system that can bring them closer together.

Another point that needs to be made is that just tying pay to performance will not necessarily lead to high pay satisfaction. The amount of pay must approximate the employees' perception of what it should be. An organization may tie pay to performance and still have high pay dissatisfaction if the level of pay in the organization is scaled too low relative to other organizations.

JOB EVALUATION

The Model of the Determinants of Pay Satisfaction emphasizes that employees base their perception of what their pay should be partially on the demands of their job. The more demanding the job, the more pay employees feel they should receive. Thus, if pay satisfaction is to be high, pay rates must vary according to job demands in such a way that each perceived increment in a job demand factor will lead to increased pay. In general, organizations do pay higher wages to the holders of more demanding jobs. But that alone is not enough. The size of the difference in pay for higher- and lower-level jobs is just as important as the absolute amount paid. Organizations usually make salary surveys to decide what the absolute amount of a person's pay should be; these surveys will be discussed later. In this section the emphasis is on job evaluation techniques which are used to establish pay differentials.

One common source of pay dissatisfaction is that job holders feel the demands of their jobs have been undervalued and that, as a result, their pay rate has been set too low. Just as employees may evaluate their performance more highly than their superior does, they may also evaluate their jobs more highly than their company's job evaluation system does. As a way of understanding how this and other problems can arise in job evaluation, let us look at two hypothetical jobs. Suppose that the results of the job evaluation show that job A should receive a higher salary than job B, and thus, people doing A are paid more. Suppose, in addition, that the job A holders feel that their job is roughly equal to job B, and as a result they would be satisfied with the salary that is paid to the job B holders. They are not likely to turn down the extra money, but it is probable that the company is not investing the money wisely by giving it to them. Although they may feel surprised initially, and perhaps guilty, about getting more than they feel is necessary, they will rather quickly revise their perception of themselves and the job so that they come to feel that the new salary is fair. But what about the holders of job B? They, too, probably feel that their job is about equal to A. Once they see that workers on A are being paid more, they surely will raise their perception of what their own job is worth and begin to agitate for higher pay, to match that of job A. This probably would not have happened if job A had not been given the higher rate to start with. It is obvious that this job evaluation did not lead to an overall increase in pay satisfaction. It is hardly necessary to go into all the kinds of problems that can develop when job evaluation systems are used. There is an enormous number of ways in which an actual pay system can deviate from what some set or sets of job holders feel it should look like in order for them to be satisfied with their pay.

There is no easy solution to the problem of establishing pay rates for different jobs. But an important cue as to how this can best be done is apparent if we remember the purpose of any job evaluation program: to produce a high level of pay satisfaction at the lowest possible cost. A good job evaluation program can do this. What are the characteristics of a good job evaluation program? First, and most important, it should involve the people whose jobs are being evaluated, so that their perceptions can be taken into account. After all, it is their perceptions that ultimately will determine the success or failure of the system. Their perceptions are probably the single most important input to the job evaluation program. But, in addition, they must be involved in the decision-making process, and they must understand how jobs are evaluated. In many companies not everyone can take part in the job evaluation, but some employees should be involved so that the others will feel they have been represented and so that those who did participate will be able to explain and defend the job evaluation process to their peers. Under this kind of system, the rates decided upon are likely to be closer to what the workers see as fair, because their views have been consulted. This brings us to the second characteristic of a good job evaluation system. It must be understandable, and the whole process of its use must be creditable. Unless these conditions exist, the results of the system, no matter how valid they are, will not lead to high pay satisfaction.

Most companies have extensive job evaluation schemes for deciding the pay differences that should exist between jobs. Highly technical systems are used, job evaluation committees (made up primarily of management people) are formed, and beautifully logical and precise job evaluations are produced. To management the evaluations look fair and consistent. Often, however, the people whose jobs have been evaluated do not share this view. They do not understand the process, and what is more, their perceptions of the jobs are sometimes different from those held by management. When the employees speak out against the system, management typically defends it, pointing out its technical features and explaining its operation. At this point, explanations are too late. The situation is hardly calculated to produce high pay satisfaction among employees. The simple fact is that the technical features of the plan are not as important as how they are used and who is involved in the decision-making.

The literature on pay administration abounds with discussions of which method of job evaluation is best: the point method, the factor comparison method, the classification method, and so on. My feeling is that it does not make much difference which of the better-known methods is used; what makes a tremendous difference, however, is who uses the method and how. Without employee involvement, the results of the evaluation probably will look good and logical to the members of management, but they will be seen by the workers as a management decision that is arbitrary and at points irrational. On the other hand, if the workers are legitimately involved in the process, the results may not look as neat and logical to management, but the important point is that they will not need to be defended to the employees. The employees who were involved in setting the rates will take on this role.

In summary, the success of a job evaluation plan seems to depend very heavily on how much low-level involvement there is. A job evaluation should produce that pay structure which gives employees high pay satisfaction, and this may not be the same structure which looks neat and logical to management and which is easy to administer. The argument for the involvement of job holders in the evaluation of their jobs is that it will lead to higher pay satisfaction (1) because the resulting decision will be improved by the information contributed by job holders, and (2) because the job holders will be more likely to accept the decisions if they are involved in making them. Organizations seem to avoid employee participation in job evaluation out of a fear that the employees will only be motivated to get the highest rate they can for their own job. This is particularly ironic, since there is some evidence to suggest that job holders are less prone to overpay for jobs than are managers (Lawler & Hackman, 1969).

SALARY SURVEYS

Salary surveys can be an important tool in establishing what wage rate is required in a certain job if a high level of pay satisfaction is to be obtained. The reason for this is apparent in the Model of the Determinants of Pay Satisfaction: The model clearly shows that a person's pay satisfaction is influenced by what the perceived relevant others make.

Thus, if one company is paying janitors X amount and another is paying them $X + Y$, it is inevitable that, if the janitors in the first company know about those in the second, they will be dissatisfied with their pay. The use of salary surveys can prevent this from happening, since they can inform the first company that its pay is low and that pay dissatisfaction is likely to exist or develop among its janitors.

Certainly no one can argue against an organization's using salary surveys as a method of keeping its salaries roughly comparable to what is being paid in other companies and as a way of anticipating pay satisfaction problems and preventing them. Organizations frequently make two mistakes when they use salary surveys. The first was discussed in Chapter 11. There it was pointed out that companies sometimes base their surveys on comparison jobs that are actually irrelevant. The only jobs that are worth surveying are those which the employees know about and compare their pay with. Their pay satisfaction is influenced by what they see others around them making, and since salary surveys should be directed at solving pay dissatisfaction problems, the surveys should focus on the organizations and jobs which the employees actually use for comparison purposes.

The second mistake is that salary surveys are often done without the participation of lower-level employees. Having lower-level employees involved can prevent wrong comparison jobs from being chosen. Lower-level participation in salary surveys can be valuable for other reasons as well. It was emphasized earlier that employees react to their pay in terms of their sometimes inaccurate perceptions of other's pay, not in terms of what other's pay actually is. Organizations try to deal with this problem by releasing the results of salary surveys, hoping that this will correct the misperceptions of employees and convince them that their pay rates are equitable. This is one approach, and it is probably worth the effort. It may not be effective in changing employee perceptions, however, particularly if employees mistrust management. It is likely to be much more effective if the employees themselves actually take part in the salary survey. Then it will be their survey, and they will be more likely to see the results as valid. Just as in job evaluation, when the workers participate in the process, management does not have to defend the adequacy of the survey. The employees who took part in it will do that, and to other workers, their word is perhaps more acceptable than that of management.

WHO SHOULD BE SATISFIED WITH THEIR PAY?

At the beginning of this chapter it was stressed that a high average level of pay satisfaction is desirable. It was also noted, however, that this does not mean that everyone in an organization should have an above average level of satisfaction. It seems likely that an organization should contain some employees who are very much satisfied with their pay, a large group which is above average in its pay satisfaction, and a third group which is highly dissatisfied. This kind of variation in pay satisfaction is desirable in an organization, however, only if careful control is maintained over who is dissatisfied and who is satisfied. Pay satisfaction certainly should not vary randomly. Stated most simply, an organization should make a real effort to see that the best performers are the most satisfied with their pay and that the worst performers are the least satisfied. The reason for this is evident from the data presented in the previous chapters: Dissatisfied employees quit their jobs, are absent more, etc. It is far better to risk losing poor performers through turnover than to risk losing good performers. What is really being argued for here is a strategy of investing in the good performers in order to hold them in the organization while minimizing the investment in the poor performers.

To create this kind of positive relationship between pay satisfaction and performance, it is not necessary to spend more money on salaries. It is necessary to tie large differences in salaries directly to performance so that the good performer will be making substantially more than the poor performer. The good performer must make substantially more because he sees himself as having higher inputs, and it will probably require more pay just to have him as satisfied as the poorer performer. But he should not be just as satisfied as the poor performer, he should be more satisfied, and for this to be so, he must be paid substantially more.

It is interesting to note what this line of argument suggests would happen in an organization that paid everyone roughly the same. Since the good performers have higher inputs, they expect more pay than the poorer performers, and if they are not getting it, they will be more dissatisfied with their pay than the poor performers. Thus, a negative relationship between pay satisfaction and performance will exist, and the people most likely to leave the organization will be the good performers, because their pay dissatisfaction is higher. This is hardly a wise investment of the money used for salaries.

The same amount invested differently could produce far greater returns for an organization. If the bulk of it were given to the good performers, then they would be more satisfied, and the turnover would center among the poorer performers. In the long run this approach might lead to less total turnover. The good performers should show less turnover, and the poor ones would probably have about the same as before. Granted the poor performers will be more dissatisfied, but they are likely to leave only if they can find a better job. This may not be easy for them if in fact they are not very competent. All that is required to accomplish this kind of situation is the adoption of a strategy of investing the organization's financial resources in those employees who really are vital to the success of the organization.

Porter and Lawler (1968b) have stressed that a study of the relationship between pay satisfaction and performance in an organization can provide some very important insights into the effectiveness of its reward system. They argue that a strong positive relationship between satisfaction and performance indicates a reward system that is functioning well and that is rewarding good performance. On the other hand, a zero relationship between satisfaction and performance or a negative one indicates a poorly functioning reward system and should be taken as a signal of potential problems. Specifically, it means that motivation is likely to be low because rewards are not clearly tied to performance. It also means that turnover in the organization is likely to be centered among the better performers. This line of reasoning is congruent with our discussion of pay satisfaction, and it suggests that organizations should constantly monitor the relationship between pay satisfaction and performance.

Part IV
OVERVIEW: PAY IN ORGANIZA- TIONS

The problem is to fit economic incentives and human relations together, to integrate them.

(Whyte, 1955)

Chapter 15
A
THEORETICAL
OVERVIEW

Each section of this book has presented a separate model to explain the relationship between pay and the psychological issue treated in that section. Four separate models have been presented: one to explain the determinants of the value of pay; a second to explain how pay can influence motivation; a third to explain the determinants of pay satisfaction; and a fourth to explain the consequences of pay dissatisfaction. Although these models were presented separately, they are related; and this chapter will be devoted to integrating them and giving a theoretical overview of the psychological issues concerned with pay. It is important that the models be integrated, since many issues have implications not just for one topic but for all the topics discussed. Problems concerned with the importance of pay, for example, are related to the role of pay in influencing motivation, just as those concerned with the determinants of pay satisfaction are relevant to a consideration of the consequences of pay dissatisfaction. Hopefully, by stating clearly how importance, motivation, and satisfaction are related, we shall be able to see how changes in one can affect the others.

THE IMPORTANCE OF PAY AND ITS ROLE
IN INFLUENCING MOTIVATION

Chapter 6 showed that the importance attached to pay determines to a large extent how effective pay will be in motivating behavior. The more important pay is, the more power it has to motivate behavior. Increasing the importance of pay will therefore increase its power to motivate. Figure 15-1 shows the part of the Motivation Model which emphasizes the role of the importance of pay in influencing the ability of pay to motivate and to influence effort. It shows that the valence or the importance of pay combines multiplicatively with the perceived probability that performance will lead to pay to constitute the second component of the motivation equation. The first component is, of course, provided by the subjective probability that effort will lead to performance. Provided that E→P is greater than 0, and provided that P→O is greater than 0 for pay, then the more important pay is to a person the more effort he will put out to perform well.

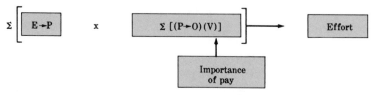

FIGURE 15-1. Determinants of effort.

MOTIVATION AND SATISFACTION

In Chapter 13, it was pointed out that there are some conditions
under which motivation and pay satisfaction may be related. Performance
can, under certain conditions, influence satisfaction rather directly. It can
influence satisfaction when it leads to rewards which influence satisfaction (Fig. 15-2). It is probably important here to separate extrinsic rewards (e.g., pay and promotion) and intrinsic rewards (e.g., feelings of
growth and status) because of the different relationships they have to
performance. Extrinsic rewards are given by someone else, and for this
reason they may not be in close accord with a person's performance. If
they are not, then we might expect a zero or negative relationship between
satisfaction and performance. This statement is based on two findings that
have already been discussed. First, as the amount of pay received increases, so does satisfaction. Second, as people feel they are performing
better, they expect greater amounts of reward (Porter & Lawler, 1968a).
Thus, in a situation where good performers are paid the same as poor
performers, a negative relationship should exist between satisfaction and
performance: The better performers will receive the same rewards as the
poor performers, but will feel they should receive more. In short, for the
good performers, there will be a greater discrepancy between what they
receive and what they feel they should receive.

In a situation where rewards are tied to performance, a positive
relationship between satisfaction and performance should exist: The good
performers will receive more rewards and should be more satisfied. The
one qualification that is necessary here concerns the size of the difference
in the rewards received by the good and poor performers. If the difference
is small, then it is not likely that a substantial positive relationship will
exist, because good performers have higher aspirations than poor performers, and it will take more than a small difference in reward level to
make them more satisfied.

The situation is somewhat different for intrinsic rewards, since they
are given by the person to himself when he performs well. Thus, they are

closely tied to performance, and because of this, satisfaction with them should be more closely tied to performance than is satisfaction with other kinds of rewards. The one qualification that is necessary here centers around the kind of job the person holds. There is some evidence (e.g., Blauner, 1964) that good performance on certain kinds of jobs simply is not intrinsically satisfying. On these jobs no relationship would be expected between intrinsic satisfaction and performance (Lawler & Porter, 1967b). Basically, jobs that allow the holder low control, jobs that are not challenging, and those which provide little feedback would seem to fall into this category.

Figure 15-2 shows that a person's satisfaction with his pay affects the importance that he attaches to pay. As has been seen the more satisfied a person is with his pay, the less important pay is likely to be to him, and the less effective it will be as a source of motivation. Thus, high satisfaction can lead to lower motivation. This is not the only process operating that influences the relationship between satisfaction and motivation, however, and thus it is rare to find a negative relationship between an employee's satisfaction and motivation. Much of the research on animal behavior shows that a negative relationship does exist where subjects are motivated only by such rewards as food and water (Cofer & Appley, 1964). Animal researchers frequently point out that a satisfied need does not motivate behavior.

At this point it should be obvious that the relationship between satisfaction and motivation is very complex. Satisfaction can be both a cause and a consequence of performance. In some situations, a strong negative relationship between the two will exist, while in others a strong positive relationship will exist. There is one process operating which leads to a negative relationship between the two, and that is the tendency of satisfaction to decrease the importance of most rewards. This tendency, however, may be neutralized or even reversed by the ability of performance to influence satisfaction if performance leads to rewards. If there is a strong link between performance and reward, a strong positive relationship can exist because the good performers will feel that they are better rewarded.

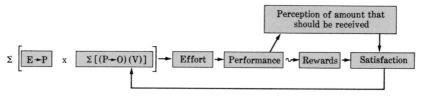

FIGURE 15-2. Relationship of effort to performance and satisfaction.

THE FINAL MODEL: RELATIONSHIPS AMONG MOTIVATION, IMPORTANCE, AND SATISFACTION

Figure 15-3 represents an attempt to combine the models and to illustrate the relationships among motivation, importance, and satisfaction. To keep the model simple, we have omitted some of the influences. Still, it indicates the relationships among the major variables, points out the importance of feedback loops, and shows how the different models are related.

Probably the best way to look at this model is to imagine a new employee going through the sequences shown in it. Upon finding himself in a new job situation our hypothetical employee should make some estimates of both his E→P probability and the various P→O probabilities for that situation. Once he has done this, he will be motivated to perform well to the extent that he feels he can perform well and to the extent that he feels good performance will lead to positively valued outcomes. Assuming that the employee is motivated to perform well, he will perform well if he has the ability, if he has the correct perception of how to do it, and if the situational factors are right. Once he has performed well or poorly he may or may not receive the rewards that he perceived were likely to result from good performance. If he receives them for performing well, this should strengthen his P→O beliefs and thereby increase his motivation when he again finds himself in that situation. If he performs well and does not get the rewards, however, his P→O beliefs will be weakened, and he will be less motivated next time around. His success in performing well presumably will influence his E→P probability the next time he finds himself in a similar situation.

If the person does receive the rewards (regardless of how he performed), his satisfaction will increase, although just how satisfied he will be depends upon what he perceives to be a fair level of reward for him. As

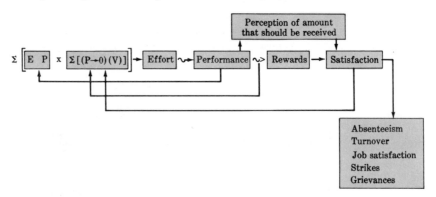

FIGURE 15-3. Motivation-performance-satisfaction cycle.

he becomes more satisfied with the level of the rewards he receives in a certain area, the less important these rewards will be to him and, hence, the less motivational power they will have for him. As satisfaction increases, so does the attraction of the job to the person, and as a result, the less likely he is to be absent or to quit. Once the person has completed his performance and assessed its impact, he will presumably cycle back to the beginning of the model. His motivation to perform will again be determined by his E→P and P→O probabilities, which may have changed as a consequence of his first attempt.

Thus the model presented in Figure 15-3 shows performance, importance, satisfaction, and motivation influencing one another and being influenced by one another as the steps in the model are repeatedly gone through. For example, although performance is shown to be capable of influencing satisfaction when it brings rewards, satisfaction is also shown to influence performance because it has an impact on reward importance, which in turn influences motivation. Thus, although as the model indicates, satisfaction at least initially in any behavioral sequence probably is a dependent outcome variable, it may later influence motivation and performance. Because of this, it is difficult to say that satisfaction is never a determinant of motivation. Similarly, while reward importance is usually a determinant of performance, it is a variable that can be influenced by performance where performance leads to rewards. In one sense, then, it can be both a determinant of motivation and an indirect consequence of it. All this argues that it is not profitable to think in terms of a simple static model of performance that shows one set of variables as determinants of performance and another as consequences of performance. Rather, it seems logical to think of a continuous ongoing process where at some moment one factor is causing another and where at a later moment it is being caused by it. Therefore, the model presented here can best be thought of as a representation of the sequence of events that a person goes through in performing his job, a sequence that is repeated many times.

Since the relationship among satisfaction, motivation, and importance is a dynamic multicausal one, it is possible to picture it in a number of ways, depending upon where in the causal sequence the time slice is taken. Starting toward the end of the sequence, as shown here, one would see that satisfaction causes performance and importance. Many of the seemingly contradictory stands that have been taken by researchers concerned with satisfaction, motivation, and importance may be due to the fact that they have chosen different starting points for their models. They may be saying somewhat similar things, but since they have used different starting points and have failed to stress the dynamic aspects of the relationship, this is not always obvious.

The present model starts with the variables E→P, P→O, and V; it is assumed that these are the initial causal factors or major "start-up" influences when a person encounters a new situation. In this sense they cause the other factors. At a later point in time, however, they may both cause the other factors and be caused by them. Thus, we must be cautious in making statements about whether one factor causes another or is caused by it. All we can say is that initially one variable seems to cause another or that one variable seems to have more causal effect on a second variable than the second variable has on it. It is in this spirit that the model shows the causal relationships it does and picks as its starting point the motivational terms. With this criterion, it makes the most sense to speak of performance as being determined by outcome importance and by E→P and P→O probabilities. Satisfaction, on the other hand, is seen as a factor that is primarily determined by performance, and is only indirectly a cause of performance.

Perhaps the clearest implication of the model is that, in order to understand the relationship between satisfaction and performance, one must look at a number of variables. A similar point can be made for any other pairs of variables that appear in the model. It does not make sense to look at just two of them in isolation. This means that future research must be more complex and must look at more than two variables. Two-variable research simply is not appropriate, given the complexity of the relationships among the variables and given the high degree of interrelationship among them. Multiple-variable research and thinking are admittedly more difficult, but they are also potentially more rewarding because of the increased explanatory power they offer.

Chapter 16
THE ROLE OF PAY IN ORGANIZATIONS

In the last fifty years, scholars have advanced a number of rather completely developed yet different approaches to organization management (see, e.g., Miles, 1965; Scott, 1961). All of these approaches deal to some extent with pay administration. Not surprisingly, they tend to assign pay relatively different roles. The scientific management approach, for example, assigns it the primary role in motivating employees to follow the orders of their superiors, while modern management theory tends to ignore pay almost entirely or to see it as only one of a large number of possible influences on motivation (see e.g., Likert, 1961). Probably the one issue which should be considered by all organization theories is the relationship between pay and performance. Time and time again the issue has come up as a crucial issue in our discussion of pay and organizational effectiveness. No theory of organization can be said to be complete unless it deals with this issue. If the decision is made to try to relate pay to performance, then the issue of how this can be accomplished must also be dealt with. It is a difficult problem and one that is not adequately dealt with by most theorists.

Given our discussion of pay, it is difficult to argue with the view that relating pay to performance can contribute to organizational effectiveness. But it is also clear that under some conditions (e.g., subjective criteria, low trust) it cannot be done effectively. When pay is tied to performance, it can motivate performance. In addition, satisfaction will be related to performance, and as a result, turnover and absenteeism will be lower among high performers. Further, tying pay to performance leads to high pay satisfaction. Finally, it can increase the importance of pay. Figure 16-1 shows that tying pay to performance influences all the major psychological issues that have been discussed in this book. It also shows

FIGURE 16-1. *Effects of relating and not relating pay to performance.*

that an organization can realize a number of tangible benefits from relating the two closely.

THEORIES OF ORGANIZATION AND PAY

Not all theories of organization argue that pay should be tied to performance. Those that do differ widely on how they say this should be done and on how important they feel it is that it be done. Figure 16-2 shows one way of classifying the different approaches to administering pay in an organization. It presents a four-cell table that divides approaches according to whether they tie pay to performance and according to whether pay is administered on a democratic or an authoritarian basis.

In Figure 16-2 the names of different approaches to management and organizations are placed in three of the four cells. Paternalistic management is placed in the cell where authoritarian control is practiced and pay is not related to performance. This approach is called paternalistic because of the dependency realtionship this type of pay administration creates between employer and employee and because, like the parent, the employer gives rewards for things other than performance. Scientific management falls under the approach of autocratically tying pay to performance: Taylor's work emphasizes the primary role of management in setting piece rates and tying pay to performance. There clearly is no room in Taylor's system for employee participation in discussions about how pay should be administered. Using democratic or participative management but not tying pay to performance is called the "human relations" or "socialist management" approach. In one sense, neither of these labels perfectly fits this approach to administering pay. There is a strong current of this kind of thinking in the writing of most writers who are identified with the human relations movement (e.g., Mayo, Roethlisberger), and certainly there is an element of this kind of thinking in the socialist management approach. The socialist approach stresses involving the workers in administrative decisions and relating their pay more to their needs than to their performance.

The name of no management style appears in the cell in which pay is democratically tied to performance. The reason for this is simple: none of the currently identifiable approaches to management have articulated this point of view adequately. The spirit of this approach is partially contained in the writings of many of the modern organization theorists. They are, however, far from unanimous in expressing this orientation toward pay administration. Many of them are more interested in the motivating power of higher-order needs, the importance of self-control, and the inappropriateness of the pyramidal structure.

Writers like Argyris (1964), Haire (1956), and McGregor (1960, 1967) are the exceptions here. They emphasize the importance of tying pay to performance, and they also express a preference for participative management. But even these writers put forward only tentative views of how pay and performance are to be related. Typically, they single out the Scanlon Plan for praise and cite it as an example of what can be done. The Scanlon Plan is an interesting effort in this direction. Clearly, however, there are problems associated with it, and it is not universally applicable.

Most modern organization theorists concentrate their fire on building an organization in which people will be motivated by intrinsic rewards such as a desire for growth and competence. Indeed, as Schein (1965) has stated, they are concerned with motivating "self-actualizing man." There is, of course, some validity to this view, just as there is validity to the view of scientific management. Schein has said that organization theorists

Approach to administering rewards

	Authoritarian	Democratic
Pay not related to performance	Paternalism	Human relations Socialism
Pay related to performance	Scientific management	

FIGURE 16-2. Management style and the relationship between pay and performance.

should think in terms of what he calls "complex" man. As was pointed out in Chapter 1, such a view of man is necessary, particularly if we wish to see the role of pay in its proper perspective—somewhere between the high place given it by scientific management and the low place given it by many of the human relations movement writers. The research evidence reviewed in this book shows that pay is important and that, if related to performance, it can contribute to organizational effectiveness. Still some organizations probably should not try to relate pay to performance, and among those that should, widely different approaches are needed. As we shall see, such things as the climate, technology and structure of an organization strongly influence whether and how pay should be related to performance.

ORGANIZATION CLIMATE AND PAY

The pay system in an organization must, above all, fit the human relations climate of that organization. Although it makes some sense to talk about general principles of pay administration, specific procedures must fit the conditions that exist in a particular organization. Consider for a moment the suggestion that salaries be made public. In the kind of organization that generally adopts a democratic or participative approach to management, this practice should develop naturally. As employees begin to participate more in evaluating themselves and others, they will gradually come to know other people's salaries, as well as the general pay structure of the organization. On the other hand, in an autocratically run organization the policy of openness just will not fit. Salary openness demands trust, open discussion of performance, and justification of salaries. None of these are likely to occur in an authoritarian organization. They are, however, an integral part of a democratic approach to management. Participative performance appraisal is another practice that is necessary if salary is to be clearly tied to performance. It too is likely to fit well in a participative, but not in an authoritarian, style of management. Similarly, widespread employee participation in a job evaluation program should present no problem in an organization that practices participative management day in and day out; but in one that does not, it may be quite impossible.

Piece rate plans with rates set by industrial engineers and other "semiautomated" payment plans were developed within the context of scientific management. Traditionally, such plans have been established as a management control device. Only with the advent of unions were workers given some say in how they were set up and administered. The fact that piece rate plans have typically been run in an authoritarian manner does not, of course, mean that they have to be. They could fit into a democratic approach to management if they were participatively developed and if greater self-control were built into the system. These plans are so strongly identified with more traditional styles of management, however, that it is difficult to convince people that they can be democratically administered. In fact, the traditional association of incentive pay and authoritarian management may account for the slight attention that many modern organization theorists have given to incentive plans.

What kind of pay incentive plan will work in an organization run on traditional lines? The evidence reviewed in this book suggests that the more "objectively" based the plan, the more likely it is to be successful. Plans that tie pay to "hard" criteria, such as quantity of output, profits, or sales, and thus require a minimum level of trust, stand a much better chance of succeeding in the traditional organization than approaches which depend on joint goal setting and soft criteria. Piece rate plans that are administered in a consistent and fair manner and have rates that are set fairly do work sometimes. So do sales bonuses for salesmen and profit-sharing plans in small organizations. But where trust is low, these plans seldom reach their full potential.

The problem for traditional organizations occurs in jobs where there are no hard criteria for measuring performance and where trust and participation are needed if pay is to act as an incentive. Here, the traditionally managed organization has difficulty in getting pay to work as a motivator because the conditions are not right for participative performance appraisal and joint goal setting. In this kind of job situation, a Theory Y organization is in a better position to use pay to motivate performance than is the traditional scientific management approach. In such job situations, this approach, which is built upon the idea of using pay as an incentive, cannot be used because it does not believe in employee participation or the other power-equalization approaches to management. On the other hand, many of the newer approaches to organization theory —approaches which were not designed to rely on pay to motivate—can use it. Many modern organization theorists do not capitalize on this advantage of their approach by actually saying how pay can be used to motivate performance within their system.

In summary, it has been argued that one of the factors which influences the type of pay plan an organization can use is the human relations climate or management style that exists in the organization. For illustrative purposes, organizations characterized by an authoritarian style of management were contrasted with those characterized by a more participative approach. It was stressed that the potential for using pay to motivate performance is greater in the latter than in the former, despite the fact that the authoritarian approach has given greater emphasis to the use of pay to motivate performance.

TECHNOLOGY AND PAY

The human relations climate that exists in an organization is only one of the factors that determine how appropriate different pay plans will be. Certainly, the kind of product that is being produced must be considered, since it influences how an organization is technically organized, and this in turn influences the appropriateness of different pay plans.

Woodward (1965) distinguishes among industrial organizations that engage in mass production, unit production, and process production. Piece rate incentives, probably can be used in unit and mass production plants, but they hardly make sense in a process production firm. Plant-wide bonuses would seem to be well suited to many process production plants but not to most unit and mass production plants. This difference arises because of the difficulty of identifying individual contributions in process production. If we expand our discussion to include nonindustrial professionally staffed service organizations, such as hospitals and schools, this point becomes even more obvious. Neither of these types of organizations could use piece rate plans or organizationwide bonuses. They could, perhaps, use a system based upon participative performance appraisals and joint goal setting if the climate were right.

In short, the type of product an organization produces influences the technology and production method of the organization. Production methods in turn differ in the degree to which individual performance is identifiable and measurable, as well as in the degree to which cooperation among the members of the organization is necessary. Because of this, organizations that differ in the kinds of products they produce need different pay systems, even though they may be similar in other ways. For example, in Chapter 9 it was stressed that group plans lead to cooperation. In process production plants where cooperation is important and individual performance is difficult to measure, a group plan makes sense. In a consulting firm, however, where cooperation probably is not so important and individual performance is measurable, a more individualized plan makes sense, but not a piece rate plan, since individual performance in this situation probably does not lend itself to piece measurement.

ORGANIZATION STRUCTURE AND PAY

In addition to the human relations climate and technological factors, other characteristics affect the kind of pay system that will be appropriate for an organization. Size is a crucial variable. Another is the degree of centralization. Small organizations can do things that large organizations cannot. They can, for example, use incentive and bonus pay plans that are based upon organizationwide performance. In a small organization, most employees will feel that their behavior affects the performance of the total organization. In a large organization this is not likely to be so (except at the very top), and as a result an organization-wide plan is not likely to motivate performance. Pressures toward uniform policy statements and systematic pay and appraisal practices are also more prevalent in large organizations. Thus, it is more difficult to tailor an individual's pay package to his own situation. This is unfortunate, because much can be gained by individualizing fringe benefit packages and setting up individual pay incentive plans. People differ in how frequently they should be evaluated, in how they should be evaluated, and in the kind of pay system (i.e., bonus increase, stock options) that is most likely to motivate them. Using individualized pay programs to capitalize on these differences is difficult in large organizations because they entail tremendous increases in administrative overhead. They can be installed, however, in small organizations. In short, small organizations have a potential advantage over large organizations because they have more options open to them.

The degree of centralization-decentralization is relevant to pay administration because it affects the kind of performance criteria data that are available. In a centralized organization, for example, the performance of a subpart, or a particular plant, is often difficult to measure unless a decentralized responsibility-based accounting system is used. Even if it is possible to measure an individual plant's performance, this is often not a good criterion upon which to base pay, because the plant employees often are not in control of the plant. As a result they do not feel responsible for the plant's performance. If substantial decision-making power is vested in the central office, local plant management can hardly be evaluated on the basis of how the plant performs. In fact, the management may resent being evaluated on this basis. This is not true when decision making is decentralized and accounting data are gathered on subparts of the organization. This point is particularly important in a large organization. It means that pay plans that use large group, plant-wide, or divisionwide performance as a criterion are practical only if the organization is to some extent decentralized. It is only within the context of a decentralized organization that this type of criterion can be meaningful.

Compared with firms with centralized authority, decentralized organizations have more pay administration options. As has already been mentioned, they can more easily use plantwide and subunitwide plans. In addition, they can more easily tolerate different pay practices in different parts of the organization. In fact, decentralization would seem to encourage different parts of an organization to establish different pay practices, while centralization would seem to discourage such tailoring. To the extent that it makes sense to tailor pay plans to fit the organization—which is the thesis on which this chapter is based—decentralization should have the advantage over centralization.

Table 16-1 attempts to summarize the points made so far on the relevance of organization factors to pay plans. The human relations climate of an organization, the type of production it engages in, its size, and its degree of centralization—all affect the kind of pay system that is appropriate for an organization. Each of these factors limits the possible types of merit pay plan that can be successfully used. Only certain kinds of plans are appropriate for large organizations, for example, and only certain kinds are appropriate for mass production organizations. In order to state what kind of plan can be used in a specific organization, one must classify the organization according to each of the four variables listed in Table 16-1. An organization might, for example, practice authoritarian management, engage in mass production, and be large and centralized. The pay plan that is appropriate for this organization is determined by all these factors. In other words, the plan that is chosen for this firm must be one that cannot be ruled out on the basis of any of these four characteristics.

TABLE 16-1. Relevance of four organizational factors to pay plans

Human relations climate	Authoritarian	Need objective hard criteria; pay clearly tied to performance
	Democratic	Can use participative goal setting and softer criteria
Production type	Mass and unit	Can usually develop hard criteria; rewards on individual or small group basis
	Process	Need to encourage cooperation; individual performance not highly visible or measurable
	Professional organizations (i.e., hospital, school, consulting firms)	Individually based plans; soft criteria; high individual involvement in own evaluation
Size	Large	Organizationwide bonuses poor for all but a few top-level managers
	Small	Organizationwide bonuses possible in some situations
Degree of centralization	Centralized	Hard to base performance on subunit (i.e., plant) performance
	Decentralized	Pay can be based on profit center or subunit performance for members of management

Since each of the factors (being of a certain size, having a highly centralized administration, etc.) serves to rule out some kinds of pay plans, it is possible that for some organizations there is no pay plan that can be labeled appropriate. Table 16-2 shows this by listing all the types of organizations that can be identified, using the crude classification system developed here. As indicated, in some (e.g., authoritarian, centralized, large, and professionally staffed service organizations), there is simply no type of merit or performance-based pay system that is appropriate. In these organizations, it is advisable not to try to base pay on performance, and to pay on the basis of attendance and membership. In fact, in many types of organizations there is no really satisfactory merit pay system, but it is possible to design merit pay systems that will be adequate (e.g., most authoritarian organizations).

The most important point that Table 16-2 illustrates is that pay systems exist in the context of organizations and that the characteristics of the organizations must be taken into account when pay systems are developed. No one pay system will fit all organizations; there are too many situational factors that must be considered. Our discussion has emphasized only a few of the most salient. There are others which, if considered, would further complicate the thinking shown in Table 16-2 (e.g., age of company, hiring policies, characteristics of workers). One of the problems with the research on pay is that little of it has tried to identify the relevant situational factors and to elaborate on their treatment. There is a good deal of research showing what basic conditions must exist if pay is to motivate (e.g., it must be important, and it must be related to performance) and what must happen if people are to be satisfied with their pay (e.g., inputs must match outcomes). Missing, however, is "developmental" research (Haire, 1964)—that is, research concerned with (1) how these broad principles can be applied to the situations existing in particular organizations and (2) what the specific situational factors are that determine how the principles can be converted into practice. As was pointed out in Chapter 1, however, investigators are showing a growing tendency to do research on the psychology of pay. It is hoped that the trend will continue and that this kind of research problem will be attacked.

PAY AS A CHANGE AGENT

The discussion so far has emphasized the important relationship between organization climate and pay administration. We have said that the kind of climate that exists very much limits the kind of pay practices that an organization can use. Further, we have assumed that pay practices

TABLE 16-2. Appropriate merit pay plans for various types of organizations

Authoritarian	Mass and unit	Large	Cent.	Individual basis; objective criteria
			Decent.	For workers—individual; for managers—group plan possible on profit center basis; for all objective criteria
		Small	Cent.	Individual basis; objective criteria
			Decent.	For workers—individual; for managers—group plan possible on profit center basis; for all objective criteria
	Process	Large	Cent.	None very appropriate; companywide bonus possible for managers
			Decent.	Group plan based upon objective subunit performance criteria
		Small	Cent.	Organizationwide bonus plan
			Decent.	Group plan based upon objective subunit performance measures
	Professional service	Large	Cent.	None appropriate
			Decent.	None appropriate
		Small	Cent.	None appropriate
			Decent.	None appropriate
Democratic	Mass and unit	Large	Cent.	Individual plans based on objective criteria as well as soft criteria, such as participatively set goals
			Decent.	Same as centralized, but for managers use data from their subpart of organization
		Small	Cent.	Some consideration to performance of total organization; individual plans based on objective criteria as well as soft criteria, such as participatively set goals
			Decent.	Same as centralized except subpart performance can be used as criteria in both individual and group plans
	Process	Large	Cent.	Organizationwide plan based on objective and subjective criteria; individual appraisal based on soft criteria
			Decent.	Group plan based on plant performance; objective and subjective criteria
		Small	Cent.	Organizationwide plan based on company performance
			Decent.	Group plans based on subunit performance
	Professional	Large	Cent.	Design individual plans; high input from employees; joint goal setting and evaluation
			Decent.	Same as centralized but some consideration to performance of subparts
		Small	Cent.	Some consideration to performance of total organization; design individual plans; high input from employees; joint goal setting and evaluation
			Decent.	Same as centralized, except that data for subpart of organization may be relevant

must be adjusted to fit the climate. This assumption is open to question. Is it not possible that the pay system can change the climate? There is some evidence that this has happened in companies that have tried the Scanlon Plan and the Lincoln Electric Plan. The installation of these plans seemed to help the organizations move toward a more democratic style of management. In effect, the pay plans seemed to be agents of change.

It is not difficult to see how pay administration policies can affect organization climate. Pay is important to people, and decisions about pay are carefully watched by everyone in an organization. Pay is a common language shared by all, and because of this it is a medium through which an organization can communicate with all its employees. Thus, pay practices can influence the whole climate of the organization. Pay administration is one place where management philosophy can be clearly and immediately converted into action. It is a concrete manifestation of leadership and management style. Because of this, changes in pay policy can be a direct indication to employees of a change in management thinking or management style. Actually delivering on promised pay raises or merit increases, for example, can be concrete evidence that management means what it says. Such acts can increase the credibility of management and potentially lead to greater trust between management and workers. Actually involving workers in pay decisions is a clear way to indicate that management is moving toward a more democratic climate. Similarly, giving employees a share of company profits is a clear way to indicate that the organization wants to establish a climate in which employee-employer relations are characterized by trust, cooperation, and, indeed, respect.

Little research has been done on the use of pay as a change agent in organizations. With the exception of the Scanlon Plan and a few others, pay plans simply have not been thought of as a way of changing organizations. This is unfortunate because potentially pay administration represents a powerful tool for effecting change. Interest in organization change at this time emphasizes interpersonal issues rather than structural changes. The typical change program seems to begin with management training, using T-groups, grid sessions, role playing, etc. This may be the best approach in many organizations, but in others, changes in organization policy or procedures may be better. At present, we know very little about which approach is more effective. In particular, we know little about when to choose a specific approach.

Even when an organization decides that the pay system is not a good place to start a change effort, it is important that the pay system not be forgotten or overlooked. In the long run, an anachronistic or inappropriate pay system can be a powerful retarding force. For example, where an attempt is being made to change toward a more participative style of management, keeping the traditional pay plan can slow progress considerably. Unfortunately, many attempts at organizational change have concentrated only on revising leadership styles or increasing interpersonal competence. For maximum effectiveness these changes should be accompanied by changes in the pay system; changes in the pay system can reinforce the other changes and make it clear that they are not just another management gimmick. Money speaks, and administered in a traditional way, it can say that an avowed move toward participative management is not sincere; administered in new ways, it can say that a real change is taking place. It is hoped that, as more is learned about the psychological aspects of pay administration, more people interested in organizational change will see pay system changes as an important element in any change effort.

SUMMARY

The major theme of this chapter has been that a pay plan must fit the characteristics of an organization if it is to be effective; it must be individualized in terms of organization size, management style, etc. There are two ways organizations and pay systems can be matched. First, the task can be viewed as a problem of choosing the correct pay plan for an organization, taking into account the characteristics of the organization as it is presently administered. But as the last part of the chapter emphasized, there is a second way. Instead of fitting the plan to the organization, management can change the organization to fit the plan. The pay plan can be viewed as a stimulant or lever to effect change in the organization. A pay plan can be used to initiate movement toward a more participative management style. This can be done but we are just beginning to understand the process. The key would seem to be in choosing a pay plan that will start the organization moving and reinforce any movement that is made.

REFERENCES

Adams, J. S. Toward an understanding of inequity. *Journal of Abnormal and Social Psychology*, 1963, **67**, 422–436. (a)

Adams, J. S. Wage inequities, productivity and work quality. *Industrial Relations*, 1963, **3** (1), 9–16. (b)

Adams, J. S. "Injustice in social exchange." In L. Berkowitz (Ed.), *Advances in experimental social psychology*. Vol. 2, New York: Academic, 1965, 267–299.

Adams, J. S. *A study of the exempt salary program*. Crotonville, N.Y.: General Electric Behavioral Research Service, 1966.

Adams, J. S. Effects of overpayment: Two comments on Lawler's paper. *Journal of Personality and Social Psychology*, 1968, **10**, 315–316.

Adams, J. S. & Jacobsen, P. R. Effects of wage inequities on work quality. *Journal of Abnormal and Social Psychology*, 1964, **69**, 19–25.

Adams, J. S. & Rosenbaum, W. B. The relationship of worker productivity to cognitive dissonance about wage inequities. *Journal of Applied Psychology*, 1962, **46**, 161–164.

Alderfer, C. P. *Differential importance of human needs as a function of satisfaction obtained in the organization*. Unpublished doctoral dissertation, Yale University, 1966.

Alderfer, C. P. An empirical test of a new theory of human needs. *Organizational Behavior and Human Performance*, 1969, **4**, 142–175.

Allport, G. W. *Personality: A psychological interpretation*. New York: Holt, 1937.

Allport, G. W., Vernon, P. E. & Lindzey, G. *Study of values*. (Rev. ed.) Boston: Houghton Mifflin, 1951.

Anderson, B. & Shelly, R. K. Reactions to inequity II: A replication of the Adams' experiment and a theoretical reformulation. Mimeographed paper, Michigan State University, undated.

Anderson, E. E. The externalization of drive: I. Theoretical considerations. *Psychological Review*, 1941, **48**, 204–224. (a)

Anderson, E. E. The externalization of drive: III. Maze learning by nonrewarded and by satiated rats. *Journal of Genetic Psychology*, 1941, **59**, 397–426. (b)

Andrews, I. R. (Ed.). *Managerial Compensation*, Ann Arbor, Mich: Foundation for Research on Human Behavior, 1965.

Andrews, I. R. Wage inequity and job performance: An experimental study. *Journal of Applied Psychology*, 1967, **51**, 39–45.

Andrews, I. R. & Henry, M. M. Management attitudes toward pay. *Industrial Relations*, 1963, **3**, 29–39.

Andrews, I. R. & Valenzi, E. R. Overpay inequity or self-image as a worker: A critical examination of an experimental induction procedure, *Organizational Behavior and Human Performance*, 1970, **5**, 266–276.

Argyris, C. *Personality and organization.* New York: Harper, 1957.

Argyris, C. *Integrating the individual and the organization.* New York: John Wiley, 1964.

Armstrong, T. B. *Occupational level as an indicator of "satisfiers" and "dissatisfiers": A test of the Herzberg et al. theory.* Paper presented at I.B.M. Personnel Research Conference, August 1968.

Arrowood, A. J. *Some effects on productivity of justified and unjustified levels of reward under public and private conditions.* Unpublished doctoral dissertation, University of Minnesota, 1961.

Ash, P. The S. R. A. employee inventory—A statistical analysis. *Personnel Psychology*, 1954, **7**, 337–364.

Atkinson, J. W. Towards experimental analysis of human motivation in terms of motives, expectancies, and incentives. In J. W. Atkinson, (Ed.). *Motives in fantasy, action, and society.* Princeton, N.J.: Van Nostrand, 1958, 288–305.

Atkinson, J. W. *An introduction to motivation.* Princeton, N.J.: Van Nostrand, 1964.

Atkinson, J. W. & Reitman, W. R. Performance as a function of motive strength and expectancy of goal attainment. *Journal of Abnormal and Social Psychology*, 1956, **53**, 361–366.

Ayllon, T. Untitled paper presented at McKinsey Foundation conference on manager motivation and money, Tarrytown, New York, 1967.

Ayllon, T. & Azrin, N. H. The measurement and reinforcement of behavior of psychotics. *Journal of the Experimental Analysis of Behavior*, 1965, **8**, 357–383.

Babchuk, N. & Goode, W. J. Work incentives in a self-determined group. *American Sociological Review*, 1951, **16**, 679–687.

Baehr, M. E. A factorial study of the S. R. A. employee inventory. *Personnel Psychology*, 1954, **7**, 319–336.

Balderston, C. C. *Group incentives.* Philadelphia: University of Pennsylvania Press, 1930.

Barnett, G. J., Handelsman, I., Stewart, L. H., & Super, D. E. The occupational level scale as a measure of drive. *Psychological Monographs*, 1952, **66**, No. 10 (Whole No. 342).

Bass, B. M. *Organizational Psychology.* Boston: Allyn and Bacon, 1965.

Bass, B. M. Ability, values, and concepts of equitable salary increases in exercise compensation. *Journal of Applied Psychology*, 1968, **52**, 299–303.

Bass, B. M., Hurder, W. P., & Ellis, N. *Assessing human performance under stress*. Unpublished technical report, Contract AF 33(616)134. Baton Rouge: Louisiana State University, 1954.

Bavasi, B. Money makes the player go. *Sports Illustrated*, 1967, **26** (21), 44–55.

Beer, M. *Leadership, employee needs, and motivation*. Columbus: Ohio State University, Bureau of Business Research, 1966.

Beer, M., & Gery, G. J. Individual and organizational correlates of pay system preferences: Implications for planned change of a pay system and for the effects of pay systems on motivation and satisfaction. Mimeographed paper, Corning, N.Y., undated.

Beer, M., & Gery, G. J. *Pay systems preferences and their correlates*. Paper presented at A.P.A. convention, San Francisco, August 1968.

Behrend, H. Absence and labour turnover in a changing economic climate. *Occupational Psychology*, 1953, **27**, 69–79.

Bendig, H. W., & Stillman, E. L. Dimensions of job incentives among college students. *Journal of Applied Psychology*, 1958, **42**, 367–371.

Berdie, R. F. Can factors in vocational choice be weighted? *Occupations*, 1943, **22**, 43–46.

Bhatt, L. J. Incentives and the working class. *Psychological Studies Mysore*, 1962, **7** (2), 51–61.

Bindra, D. *Motivation: A systematic reinterpretation*. New York: Ronald, 1959.

Birch, H. G. The role of motivational factors in insightful problem solving. *Journal of Comparative Psychology*, 1945, **38**, 295–317.

Blauner, R. *Alienation and freedom*. Chicago: University of Chicago Press, 1964.

Blodgett, H. C. The effect of the introduction of reward upon the maze performance of rats. *University of California Publications in Psychology*, 1929, **4**, 113–134.

Blood, M. R., & Hulin, C. L. Alienation, environmental characteristics, and worker responses. *Journal of Applied Psychology*, 1967, **51**, 284–290.

Blough, R. M. Price and the public interest. *U.S. Steel Quarterly*, 1958, **12** (4), 7.

Blum, M. L., & Russ, J. J. A study of employee attitudes toward various incentives. *Personnel Psychology*, 1942, **19**, 438–444.

Bose, S. K. *Man and his work*. Presidential Address to the section on Psychology and Educational Science, 38th Indian Science Congress, Bangalore, 1951.

Brayfield, A. H., & Crockett, W. H. Employee attitudes and employee performance. *Psychological Bulletin*, 1955, **52**, 396–424.

Brenner, M. H., and Lockwood, H. C. Salary as a predictor of salary: A 20-year study. *Journal of Applied Psychology*, 1965, **49**, 295–298.

Brissenden, P. F., & Frankel, E. *Labor turnover in industry*. New York: Macmillan, 1922.

Brown, J. A. C. *The social psychology of industry*. Baltimore: Penguin, 1954.

Brown, J. S. Problems presented by the concept of acquired drive. In J. S. Brown, et al., *Current theory and research in motivation: A symposium*. Lincoln: University of Nebraska Press, 1953. Pp. 1–21.

Brown, J. S. *The motivation of behavior*. New York: McGraw-Hill, 1961.

Brown, W. *Piecework abandoned*. London: Heinemann, 1962.

Burnett, F. *An experimental investigation into repetitive work*. Industrial Fatigue Research Board Report No. 30. London: H. M. Stationery Office, 1925.

Calvin, J. S., Bicknell, A., & Sperling, D. S. Establishment of a conditioned drive based on the hunger drive. *Journal of Comparative and Physiological Psychology*, 1953, **46**, 173–175.

Campbell, D. T., & Stanley, J. C. Experimental and quasi-experimental designs for research on teaching. In N. L. Gage (Ed.), *Handbook of research on teaching*. Chicago: Rand McNally, 1963, 171–246.

Campbell, H. Group incentives. *Occupational Psychology*, 1952, **26**, 15–21.

Campbell, J. P., Dunnette, M. D., Lawler, E. E., & Weick, K. E. *Managerial behavior, performances and effectiveness*. New York: McGraw-Hill, 1970.

Cantril, H. Identification with social and economic class. *Journal of Abnormal and Social Psychology*, 1943, **38**, 74–80.

Cantril, H., & Allport, G. W. Recent applications of the study of values. *Journal of Abnormal and Social Psychology*, 1933, **28**, 259–273.

Carey, A. The Hawthorne studies: A radical criticism. *American Sociological Review*, 1967, **33**, 403–416.

Carlson, R. E., Dawis, R. V., England, G. W., & Lofquist, L. H. *The measurement of employment satisfaction*. Minnesota Studies in Vocational Rehabilitation. XIII. Bulletin 35, p. 49. Minneapolis: University of Minnesota, Industrial Relations Center, 1962.

Centers, R. Motivational aspects of occupational stratification. *Journal of Social Psychology*, 1948, **28**, 187–217.

Centers, R., & Bugental, D. E. Intrinsic and extrinsic job motivation among different segments of the working population. *Journal of Applied Psychology*, 1966, **50**, 193–197.

Centers, R., & Cantril, H. Income satisfaction and income aspiration. *Journal of Abnormal and Social Psychology*, 1946, **41**, 64–69.

Chalupsky, A. B. Incentive practices as viewed by scientists and managers of pharmaceutical laboratories. *Personnel Psychology,* 1964, **17**, 385–401.

Chant, S. N. F. Measuring the factors that make a job interesting. *Personnel Journal,* 1932, **11**, 1–4.

Charnofsky, H. Mister major league, *Sports Illustrated,* 1968, **29** (3) 14–16.

Clarke, A. V., & Grant, D. L. Application of a factorial method in selecting questions for an employee attitude survey. *Personnel Psychology,* 1961, **14**, 131–139.

Cofer, C. N. *Motivating effects of money: Theoretical approaches.* Paper presented at McKinsey Foundation conference on manager motivation and money, Tarrytown, N.Y., 1967.

Cofer, C. N., & Appley, M. H. *Motivation: Theory and research.* New York: Wiley, 1964.

Collins, B. E. *An experimental study of satisfaction, productivity, turnover, and comparison levels.* Unpublished doctoral dissertation, Northwestern University, 1963.

Collins, O., Dalton, M., & Roy, D. Restriction of output and social cleavage in industry. *Applied Anthropology,* 1946, **5** (3), 1–14.

Conrad, R., & Jaffe, H. *Occupational choice and values in a mass society.* Paper read at American Sociological Association meetings, New York, August, 1960.

Cowles, J. T. Food tokens as incentives for learning by chimpanzees. *Comparative Psychology Monographs,* 1937, **14**, No. 5, Whole No. 71.

Cravens, R. W. and Renner, K. E. Conditioned appetitive drive states: Empirical evidence and theoretical status. *Psychological Bulletin,* 1970, **73**, 212–220.

Crespi, L. P. Quantitative variation of incentive and performance in the white rat. *American Journal of Psychology,* 1942, **55**, 467–517.

Crespi, L. P. Amount of reinforcement and level of performance. *Psychological Review,* 1944, **51**, 341–357.

Dabas, Z. S. The dimensions of morale: An item factorization of the S.R.A. employee inventory. *Personnel Psychology,* 1958, **11**, 217–234.

Dalton, M. The industrial "rate-buster": A characterization. *Applied Anthropology,* 1948, **7**, 5–18.

Dashiell, J. F. *Fundamentals of objective psychology.* Boston: Houghton Mifflin, 1928.

Davis, N. M. Attitudes to work among building operatives. *Occupational Psychology,* 1948, **22**, 56–62.

Despain, D. Let workers write the pay checks. *Nations Business,* 1945, **33** (July), 23.

Dickinson, C. Ratings of job factors by those choosing various occupational groups. *Journal of Counseling Psychology,* 1954, **1,** 188–189.

Dickinson, Z. C. *Compensating industrial effort.* New York: Ronald, 1937.

Dill, W. R. *GSIA alumni: Their progress and their goals.* Unpublished manuscript. Pittsburgh: Carnegie Institute of Technology, 1962.

Dunnette, M. D. (Ed.). The role of financial compensation in managerial motivation. *Organizational Behavior and Human Performance,* 1967, **2,** 175–216.

Dunnette, M. D., & Bass, B. M. Behavioral scientists and personnel management. *Industrial Relations,* 1963, **2** (3), 115–130.

Dunnette, M. D., Campbell, J. P., & Hakel, M. D. Factors contributing to job satisfaction and job dissatisfaction in six occupational groups. *Organizational Behavior and Human Performance,* 1967, **2,** 143–174.

Dyson, B. H. *Whether direct individual incentive systems based on time-study, however accurately computed, tend over a period to limitation of output.* Paper read at Spring Conference, British Institute of Management, London, 1956.

Edwards, W. The theory of decision making. *Psychological Bulletin,* 1954, **51,** 380–417.

Englander, M. E. A psychological analysis of vocational choice: Teaching. *Journal of Counseling Psychology,* 1960, **7,** 257–264.

Evans, E. E. & Laseau, LaV. N. My job contest. *Personnel Psychology.* Monograph No. 1, 1950.

Evans, M. G. *The effects of supervisory behavior upon worker perception of their path-goal relationships.* Unpublished doctoral dissertation. Yale University, 1968.

Evans, M. G. Conceptual and operational problems in the measurement of various aspects of job satisfaction. *Journal of Applied Psychology,* 1969, **53,** 93–101.

Evans, M. G., & Molinari, L. Equity, piece-rate overpayment, and job security: Some effects on performance. *Journal of Applied Psychology,* 1970, **54,** 105–114.

Factory. What the factory worker really thinks about his job, unemployment, and industry's profit. *Factory Management and Maintenance,* 1947, **105** (12), 86–92.

Ferster, C. B. & DeMyer, M. K. A method for the experimental analysis of the behavior of autistic children. *American Journal of Orthopsychiatry,* 1962, **32,** 89–98.

Festinger, L. A theory of social comparison processes. *Human Relations,* 1954, **7,** 117–140.

Festinger, L. *A Theory of cognitive dissonance.* Evanston, Illinois: Row, Peterson, 1957.

Festinger, L. *Some changes in attitudes and values following promotion in General Electric*. Crotonville, N.Y.: General Electric Behavioral Research Service, 1964.

Fleishman, E. A., Harris, E. F., & Burtt, H. E. *Leadership and supervision in industry*. Columbus: Ohio State University, Bureau of Educational Research, 1955.

Foreman Facts. Do you know your workers' wants? 1946, **9**, (21), 1–4.

Fortune Survey. *Fortune*, 1947, **35**, 10.

Fosdick, S. J. Speech reported in *Handbook on Pensions* (Studies in Personnel Policy No. 103). New York: National Industrial Conference Board, 1950.

French, E. G. Effects of interaction of achievement, motivation and intelligence on problem-solving success. *American Psychologist*, 1957, **12**, 399–400. (Abstract)

Friedman, A., & Goodman, P. S. Wage inequity, self-qualifications, and productivity. *Organizational Behavior and Human Performance*, 1967, **2**, 406–417.

Galbraith, J. R. *Motivational determinants of job performance*. Unpublished doctoral dissertation. Indiana University, 1966.

Galbraith, J. R. & Cummings, L. L. An empirical investigation of the motivational determinants of task performance: Interactive effects between instrumentality-valence and motivation-ability. *Organizational Behavior and Human Performance*, 1967, **2**, 237–257.

Ganguli, H. C. An inquiry into incentives for workers in an engineering factory. *Indian Journal of Social Work*, 1954, **15**, 30–40.

Gellerman, S. W. *Management by motivation*. New York: American Management Association, 1968.

Georgopoulos, B. S., Mahoney, G. M., & Jones, N. W. A path-goal approach to productivity. *Journal of Applied Psychology*, 1957, **41**, 345–353.

Ghiselli, E. E. The forced-choice technique in self-description. *Personnel Psychology*, 1954, **7**, 201–208.

Ghiselli, E. E. & Brown, C. W. *Personnel and industrial psychology*. (2d ed.) New York: McGraw-Hill, 1955.

Giles, B. A. and Barrett, G. V. The utility of merit increases. *Experimental Publication System*, 1970, No. 4, Ms. 148A.

Gilmer, B. V. H. Psychological aspects of women in industry. *Personnel Psychology*, 1957, **10**, 439–452.

Glennon, J. R., Owens, W. A., Smith, W. J., & Albright, L. E. New dimensions in measuring morale. *Harvard Business Review*, 1960, **38**, 106–107.

Goodman, P. S. An empirical examination of Elliott Jaques' concept of time span. *Human Relations*, 1967, **20**, 155–170.

Gordon, B. F., & Lowin, A. *Qualifications, co-worker characteristics and productivity—An extension and critique of Adams' inequity theory.* Technical Report, December 15, 1965, Bell Telephone Laboratories.

Gordon, M. E. An evaluation of Jaques' studies of pay in the light of current compensation research. *Personnel Psychology,* 1969, **22**, 369–389.

Graen, G. Instrumentality theory of work motivation: Some experimental results and suggested modifications. *Journal of Applied Psychology Monograph,* 1969, **53** (2), 1–25.

Graham, D. & Sluckin, W. Different kinds of reward as industrial incentives. *Research Review,* 1954, **5**, 54–56.

Gruenfeld, L. W. A study of the motivation of industrial supervisors. *Personnel Psychology,* 1962, **15**, 303–314.

Gruenfeld, L. W. & Weissenberg, P. Supervisory characteristics and attitudes toward performance appraisals. *Personnel Psychology,* 1966, **19**, 143–152.

Hackman, J. R., & Porter, L. W. Expectancy theory predictions of work effectiveness. *Organizational Behavior and Human Peformance,* 1968, **3**, 417–426.

Haire, M. *Psychology in management.* New York: McGraw-Hill, 1956.

Haire, M. The social sciences and management practices. *California Management Review,* 1964, **6** (4), 3–10.

Haire, M. *Questionnaire on pay.* Unpublished paper. Cambridge, Mass.: M.I.T.

Haire, M., Ghiselli, E. E., & Gordon, M. E. A psychological study of pay. *Journal of Applied Psychology Monograph,* 1967, **51** (4), (Whole No. 636).

Haire, M., Ghiselli, E. E., & Porter, L. W. Psychological research on pay: An overview. *Industrial Relations,* 1963, **3** (1), 3–8.

Haire, M., Ghiselli, E. E., & Porter, L. W. *Managerial thinking: An international study.* New York: Wiley, 1966.

Hall, D. T., & Nougaim, K. E. An examination of Maslow's need hierarchy in an organizational setting. *Organizational Behavior and Human Performance,* 1968, **3**, 12–35.

Hardin, E., Reif, H. G., & Heneman, H. G. Stability of job preferences of department store employees. *Journal of Applied Psychology,* 1951, **35**, 256–259.

Harlow, H. F. Mice, monkeys, men and motives. *Psychological Review,* 1953, **60**, 23–32.

Harrison, R. Cumulative communality cluster analysis of workers' job attitudes. *Journal of Applied Psychology,* 1961, **45**, 123–125.

Heller, F. A., & Porter, L. W. Perceptions of managerial needs and skills in two national samples. *Occupational Psychology,* 1966, **40**, 1–13.

Hersey, R. B. Psychology of workers. *Personnel Journal,* 1936, **14**, 291–296.

Herzberg, F. *Work and the nature of man.* Cleveland: World Publishing, 1966.

Herzberg, F., Mausner, B., Peterson, R. O., & Capwell, D. F. *Job attitudes: Review of research and opinion.* Pittsburgh: Psychological Service of Pittsburgh, 1957.

Herzberg, F., Mausner, B., & Snyderman, B. *The motivation to work.* (2d ed.) New York: Wiley, 1959.

Heslin, R., & Blake, B. Performance as a function of payment, commitment, and task interest. *Psychonomic Science,* 1969, **15**, 323–324.

Hickson, D. J. Motives of workpeople who restrict their output. *Occupational Psychology,* 1961, **35**, 110–121.

Hinrichs, J. R. A replicated study of job satisfaction dimensions. *Personnel Psychology,* 1968, **21**, 479–503.

Hinrichs, J. R. Correlates of employee evaluations of pay increases. *Journal of Applied Psychology,* 1969, **53**, 481–489.

Ho, C. J. Health and labor turnover in a department store. *Personnel Journal,* 1930, **9**, 216–221.

Holland, J. G., & Skinner, B. F. *The analysis of behavior.* New York: McGraw-Hill, 1961.

Homans, G. C. *Social behavior: Its elementary forms.* New York: Harcourt, Brace and World, 1961.

Hoppock, R. *Job satisfaction.* New York: Harper, 1935.

Horney, K. *The neurotic personality of our time.* New York: Norton, 1937.

Horney, K. *New ways in psychoanalysis.* New York: Norton, 1939.

Horney, K. *Our inner conflicts.* New York: Norton, 1945.

Horney, K. *Neurosis and human growth.* New York: Norton, 1950.

House, R. J., & Wigdor, L. A. Herzberg's dual-factor theory of job satisfaction and motivation: A review of the evidence and a criticism. *Personnel Psychology,* 1967, **20**, 369–390.

Hulin, C. L. Job satisfaction and turnover in a female clerical population. *Journal of Applied Psychology,* 1966, **50**, 280–285.

Hulin, C. L. Effects of changes in job-satisfaction levels on employee turnover. *Journal of Applied Psychology,* 1968, **52**, 122–126.

Hulin, C. L., & Blood, M. R. Job enlargement, individual differences, and worker responses. *Psychological Bulletin,* 1968, **69**, 41–55.

Hulin, C. L., & Smith, P. C. Sex differences in job satisfaction. *Journal of Applied Psychology*, 1964, **48**, 88–92.

Hulin, C. L., & Smith, P. C. A linear model of job satisfaction. *Journal of Applied Psychology*, 1965, **49**, 209–216.

Hulin, C. L., & Smith, P. A. An empirical investigation of two implications of the two-factor theory of job satisfaction. *Journal of Applied Psychology*, 1967, **51**, 396–402.

Hull, C. L. *Principles of behavior.* New York: Appleton-Century, 1943.

Hull, C. L. *Essentials of behavior.* New Haven, Conn.: Yale, 1951.

Hull, C. L. *A behavior system.* New Haven, Conn.: Yale, 1952.

James, J. An experimental study of tensions in work behavior. *University of California Publications in Culture and Society*, 1951, **2** (4), 203–242.

Jaques, E. *Equitable payment.* New York: Wiley, 1961.

Jones, L. V., & Jeffrey, T. E. A quantitative analysis of expressed preferences for compensation plans. *Journal of Applied Psychology*, 1964, **48**, 201–210.

Jones, M. R. (Ed.) *Nebraska symposium on motivation.* Lincoln: University of Nebraska Press, 1955.

Jurgensen, C. E. Selected factors which influence job preferences. *Journal of Applied Psychology*, 1947, **31**, 553–563.

Jurgensen, C. E. What job applicants look for in a company. *Personnel Psychology*, 1948, **1**, 433–445.

Kahn, R. L. Human relations on the shop floor. In E. M. Hugh-Jones (Ed.), *Human relations and modern management.* Amsterdam: North-Holland, 1958.

Kahn, R. L. Productivity and job satisfaction. *Personnel Psychology*, 1960, **13**, 275–286.

Kaponya, P. G. Salaries for all workers. *Harvard Business Review*, 1962, **40** (3), 49–57.

Katz, D. An overview of the human relations program. In H. Guetzkow (Ed.), *Groups, leadership and men.* Pittsburgh: Carnegie Press, 1951.

Katzell, R. A. Personal values, job satisfaction, and job behavior. In H. Borow (Ed.), *Man in a world of work.* Boston: Houghton Mifflin, 1964, pp. 341–363.

Kaufman, H. *Task performance, expected performance, and responses to failure as functions of imbalance in the self-concept.* Unpublished doctoral dissertation, University of Pennsylvania, 1962.

Kelleher, R. T., & Gollub, L. R. A review of positive conditioned reinforcement. *Journal of the Experimental Analysis of Behavior*, 1962, **5**, 543–597.

Kerr, W. A., Koppelmeir, G., & Sullivan, J. J. Absenteeism, turnover and morale in a metals fabrication factory. *Occupational Psychology*, 1951, **25**, 50–55.

Keys, A., Brožek, J., Henschel, A., Mickelsen, O., & Taylor, H. *The biology of human starvation*. Minneapolis: University of Minnesota Press, 1950. 2 vols.

Klein, S. M. & Maher, J. R. Education level and satisfaction with pay. *Personnel Psychology*, 1966, **19**, 195–208.

Korman, A. K. Self-esteem variable in vocational choice. *Journal of Applied Psychology*, 1966, **50**, 479–486.

Koufax, S. The Sandy Koufax story: My salary fights. *Look*, 1966, **30** (12), 90–102.

Kuhlen, R. G. Needs, perceived need satisfaction opportunities, and satisfaction with occupation. *Journal of Applied Psychology*, 1963, **47**, 56–64.

Kuriloff, A. H. *Reality in management*. New York: McGraw-Hill, 1966.

Lahiri, D. N. & Choudhuri, P. K. Perceived importance of job factors by technical and nontechnical employees. *Personnel Psychology*, 1966, **19**, 287–296.

Langer, W. C. *Psychology and human living*. New York: Appleton-Century-Crofts, 1937.

Lawler, E. E. *Managers' job performance and their attitudes toward their pay*. Unpublished doctoral dissertation, Univ. of Calif., Berkeley, 1964.

Lawler, E. E. Managers' perceptions of their subordinates' pay and of their superiors' pay. *Personnel Psychology*, 1965, **18**, 413–422 (a).

Lawler, E. E. Secondary reinforcement value of stimuli associated with shock reduction. *Quarterly Journal of Experimental Psychology*, 1965, **17**, 57–62. (b)

Lawler, E. E. Ability as a moderator of the relationship between job attitudes and job performance. *Personnel Psychology*, 1966, **19**, 153–164. (a)

Lawler, E. E. Managers' attitudes toward how their pay is and should be determined. *Journal of Applied Psychology*, 1966, **50**, 273–279. (b)

Lawler, E. E. The mythology of management compensation. *California Management Review*, 1966, **9**, 11–22. (c)

Lawler, E. E. Review of "Managerial Compensation." *Personnel Psychology*, 1966, **19**, 237–239. (d)

Lawler, E. E. Attitude surveys and job performance. *Personnel Administration*, 1967, **30** (5), 3–5, 22–24. (a)

Lawler, E. E. The multitrait-multirater approach to measuring managerial job performance. *Journal of Applied Psychology*, 1967, **51**, 369–381. (b)

Lawler, E. E. Secrecy about management compensation: Are there hidden costs? *Organizational Behavior and Human Peformance*, 1967, **2**, 182–189. (c)

Lawler, E. E. A correlational-causal analysis of the relationship between expectancy attitudes and job performance. *Journal of Applied Psychology*, 1968, **52**, 462–468. (a)

Lawler, E. E. Effects of hourly overpayment on productivity and work quality. *Journal of Personality and Social Psychology*, 1968, **10**, 306–314. (b)

Lawler, E. E. Equity theory as a predictor of productivity and work quality. *Psychological Bulletin*, 1968, **70**, 596–610. (c)

Lawler, E. E. The pay check as an (expensive) communication device. *Innovation*, 1969, **1** (3), 48–56.

Lawler, E. E. Secrecy and the need to know. In R. House, M. Dunnette, & H. Tosi (Eds.) *Readings in Managerial Motivation and Compensation*, in press.

Lawler, E. E. & Hackman, J. R. The impact of employee participation in the development of pay incentive plans: A field experiment. *Journal of Applied Psychology*, 1969, **53**, 467–471.

Lawler, E. E., Koplin, C. A., Young, T. F., & Fadem, J. A. Inequity reduction over time in an induced overpayment situation. *Organizational Behavior and Human Performance*, 1968, **3**, 253–268.

Lawler, E. E. & O'Gara, P. W. Effects of inequity produced by underpayment on work output, work quality and attitudes toward the work. *Journal of Applied Psychology*, 1967, **51**, 403–410.

Lawler, E. E. & Porter, L. W. Perceptions regarding management compensation. *Industrial Relations*, 1963, **3**, 41–49.

Lawler, E. E. & Porter, L. W. Predicting managers' pay and their satisfaction with their pay. *Personnel Psychology*, 1966, **19**, 363–373.

Lawler, E. E. & Porter, L. W. Antecedent attitudes of effective managerial performance. *Organizational Behavior and Human Performance*, 1967, **2**, 122–142. (a)

Lawler, E. E. & Porter, L. W. The effect of performance on job satisfaction. *Industrial Relations*, 1967, **7**, 20–28. (b)

Lefcourt, H. M. Internal versus external control of reinforcement: A review. *Psychological Bulletin*, 1966, **65**, 206–220.

Lewin, K. *The conceptual representation and the measurement of psychological forces*. Durham, N.C.: Duke University Press, 1938.

Lewis, M. Psychological effect of effort. *Psychological Bulletin*, 1965, **64**, 183–190.

LIAMA, *College student attitudes toward a life insurance career*. Hartford, Conn. Research Report, 1967—2, File 415, 1967.

Likert, R. *New patterns of management*. New York: McGraw-Hill, 1961.

Lincoln, J. F. *Incentive management.* Cleveland: Lincoln Electric Company, 1951.

Lindhal, L. G. What makes a good job. *Personnel,* 1949, **25,** 263–266.

Locke, E. A. The interaction of ability and motivation in performance. *Perceptual and Motor Skills,* 1965, **21,** 719–725.

Locke, E. A. *What is job satisfaction?* Paper presented at A.P.A. convention, September 1968.

Locke, E. A. What is job satisfaction? *Organizational Behavior and Human Performance,* 1969, **4,** 309–336.

Locke, E. A. & Bryan, J. F. *Goals and intentions as determinants of performance level, task choice and attitudes.* Washington, D.C.: American Institute for Research, 1967.

Locke, E. A., Smith, P. C., Kendall, L. M., Hulin, C. L., & Miller, A. M. Convergent and discriminant validity for areas and methods of rating job satisfaction. *Journal of Applied Psychology,* 1964, **48,** 313–319.

Lolordo, V. M. Positive conditioned reinforcement from aversive situations. *Psychological Bulletin,* 1969, **72,** 193–203.

Lytle, C. W. *Wage incentive methods: Their selection, installation, and operation.* New York: Ronald, 1942.

McArthur, C., & Stevens, L. B. The validation of expressed interests as compared with inventoried interests: A fourteen-year follow-up. *Journal of Applied Psychology,* 1955, **39,** 184–189.

McClelland, D. C. *The achieving society.* Princeton, N.J.: Van Nostrand, 1961.

MacGregor, J. The honor system. *The Wall Street Journal,* 1970, **175,** No. 100.

McGregor, D. *The human side of enterprise.* New York: McGraw-Hill, 1960.

McGregor, D. *The professional manager.* New York: McGraw-Hill, 1967.

McKersie, R. B. Wage payment methods of the future. *British Journal of Industrial Relations,* 1963, **1,** 191–212.

Mahoney, T. Compensation preferences of managers. *Industrial Relations,* 1964, **3,** 135–144.

Maier, N. R. F. *Psychology in industry.* (2d ed.) Boston: Houghton-Mifflin, 1955.

Marriott, R. Size of working group and output. *Occupational Psychology,* 1949, **23,** 47–57.

Marriott, R. *Incentive payment systems: A review of research and opinion.* London: Staples, 1957.

Marriott, R. & Denerley, R. A. A method of interviewing used in studies of workers' attitudes: II. Validity of the method and discussion of the results. *Occupational Psychology*, 1955, **29**, 69–81.

Maslow, A. H. A theory of human motivation. *Psychological Review*, 1943, **50**, 370–396.

Maslow, A. H. *Motivation and personality*. New York: Harper, 1954.

Mathewson, S. B. *Restriction of output among unorganized workers*. New York: Viking, 1931.

Mayo, E. *The human problems of an industrial civilization*. Cambridge, Mass.: Harvard Business School, Division of Research, 1946.

Metzner, H., & Mann, F. Employee attitudes and absences. *Personnel Psychology*, 1953, **6**, 467–485.

Meyer, H. H., Kay, E., & French, J. R. P. Split roles in performance appraisal. *Harvard Business Review*, 1965, **43** (1), 123–129.

Miles, R. E. Human relations or human resources, *Harvard Business Review*, 1965, **43** (4), 148–163.

Miles, R. E. The affluent organization. *Harvard Business Review*, 1966, **44** (3), 106–114.

Miller, D. C. Economic factors in the morale of college trained adults. *American Journal of Sociology*, 1941, **47**, 139–156.

Miller, N. E. Studies of fear as an acquirable drive: I. Fear as motivation and fear-reduction as reinforcement in the learning of new responses. *Journal of Experimental Psychology*, 1948, **38**, 89–101.

Miller, N. E. Learnable drives and rewards. In S. S. Stevens (Ed.), *Handbook of Experimental Psychology*. New York: Wiley, 1951. Pp. 435–427.

Moore, L. M. *Effects of wage inequities on work attitudes and performance*. Unpublished master's thesis, Wayne State University, 1968.

Morse, N. C. *Satisfactions in the white-collar job*. Ann Arbor: University of Michigan, Institute for Social Research, Survey Research Center, 1953.

Myers, M. S. Who are your motivated workers? *Harvard Business Review*, 1964, **42** (1), 73–88.

Nealey, S. Pay and benefit preferences. *Industrial Relations*, 1963, **3**, 17–28.

NICB *Some problems in wage incentive administration*. National Industrial Conference Board, No. 19, 1940.

NICB *Personnel activities in American business*, New York: National Industrial Conference Board, No. 86, 1946.

NICB *Factors affecting employee morale*. New York: National Industrial Conference Board, No. 85, 1947.

NICB *The Kaiser-Steel union sharing plan,* Studies in Personnel Policy, National Industrial Conference Board, No. 187, 1963.

Opinion Research Corporation. *Wage Incentives.* Princeton, N.J.: 1946.

Opinion Research Corporation. *"Productivity" from the worker's standpoint.* Princeton, N.J.: 1949.

Opinion Research Corporation. *Employee cooperation on productivity.* Princeton, N.J.: 1951.

Opshal, R. L., & Dunnette, M. D. The role of financial compensation in industrial motivation. *Psychological Bulletin,* 1966, **66**, 94–118.

Organization for Economic Cooperation and Development. *Wages and labor mobility.* Paris: 1965.

Osgood, C. E. *Method and theory in experimental psychology.* New York: Oxford University Press, 1953.

Parkes, E. H. *Establishment of a conditioned drive based on hunger.* Unpublished master's thesis, University of Maryland, 1958.

Patchen, M. *The choice of wage comparisons.* Englewood Cliffs, N.J.: Prentice-Hall, 1961.

Peak, H. Attitude and motivation. In M. R. Jones (Ed.), *Nebraska symposium on motivation.* Lincoln: University of Nebraska Press, 1955. Pp. 149–188.

Penner, D. D. *A study of the causes and consequences of salary satisfaction.* Crotonville, N.Y.: General Electric Behavioral Research Service (mimeo), 1966.

Poduska, J. *A study of the nature and stability of value patterns found among Sears retail executives.* Psychological Services Section, National Personnel Department, Sears, Roebuck & Co., Chicago, Ill.

Porter, L. W. A study of perceived need satisfactions in bottom and middle management jobs. *Journal of Applied Psychology,* 1961, **45**, 1–10.

Porter, L. W. Job attitudes in management: II. Perceived importance of needs as a function of job level. *Journal of Applied Psychology,* 1963, **47**, 141–148.

Porter, L. W. *Organizational patterns of managerial job attitudes.* New York: American Foundation for Management Research, 1964.

Porter, L. W., & Lawler, E. E. Properties of organization structure in relation to job attitudes and job behavior. *Psychological Bulletin,* 1965, **64**, 23–51.

Porter, L. W., & Lawler, E. E. *Managerial attitudes and performance.* Homewood, Ill.: Irwin-Dorsey, 1968. (a)

Porter, L. W., & Lawler, E. E. What job attitudes tell us about motivation. *Harvard Business Review,* 1968, **46** (1), 118–126. (b)

Puckett, E. S. Productivity achievements—a measure of success. In F. G. Lesieur (Ed.), *The Scanlon Plan*. Cambridge, Mass.: M.I.T., 1958, Pp. 109–117.

Rapaport, D. The structure of psychoanalytic theory: A systematizing attempt. In S. Koch (Ed.), *Psychology: A study of a science*. Vol. 3. New York: McGraw-Hill, 1959. Pp. 55–183.

Rapaport, D. On the psychoanalytic theory of motivation. In M. R. Jones (Ed.), *Nebraska symposium on motivation, 1960*. Lincoln: University of Nebraska Press, 1960. Pp. 173–247.

Reitinger, H. *Sound wage incentives*. New York: Emerson Engineers, 1941.

R.I.A. *Sales compensation practices, an RIA survey*. New York: Research Institute of America, File No. 32, 1965.

Rim, Y. Dimensions of job incentives and personality. *ACTA Psychologica*, 1961, **18**, 332–336.

Roach, D. E. Dimensions of employee morale. *Personnel Psychology*, 1958, **11**, 419–431.

Rodney, T. C. Can money motivate better job performance? *Personnel Administration*, 1967, **30** (2), 23–29.

Roethlisberger, F. J., & Dickson, W. J. *Management and the worker*. Cambridge, Mass.: Harvard, 1939.

Ronan, W. W. Individual and situational variables relating to job satisfaction. *Journal of Applied Psychology Monograph*, 1970, **54**, No. 1, Part 2, 1–31. (a)

Ronan, W. W. Relative importance of job characteristics. *Journal of Applied Psychology*, 1970, **54**, 192–200. (b)

Rosen, H. & Weaver, C. G. Motivation in management: A study of four management levels. *Journal of Applied Psychology*, 1960, **44**, 386–392.

Rosenberg, M. *Occupations and values*. Glencoe, Ill.: Free Press, 1957.

Ross, I. C., & Zander, A. F. Need satisfaction and employee turnover. *Personnel Psychology*, 1957, **10**, 327–338.

Rotter, J. B. *Social learning and clinical psychology*. Englewood Cliffs, N.J.: Prentice-Hall, 1954.

Rotter, J. B. The role of the psychological situation in determining the direction of human behavior. In M. R. Jones (ed.), *Nebraska Symposium on Motivation, 1955*. Lincoln: University of Nebraska Press. Pp. 245–268.

Rotter, J. B. Generalized expectancies for internal versus external control of reinforcement. *Psychological Monographs*, 1966, **80** (1), 1–28.

Roy, D. Quota restriction and gold bricking in a machine shop. *American Journal of Sociology*, 1952, **57**, 427–442.

Sayles, L. R. *Behavior of industrial work groups: Prediction and control.* New York: Wiley, 1958.

Scarborough, B. B. & Goodson, F. E. Properties of stimuli associated with strong and weak hunger drive in the rat. *Journal of Genetic Psychology*, 1957, **91**, 257–261.

Schaffer, R. H. Job satisfaction as related to need satisfaction in work. *Psychological Monographs*, 1953, **67** (14), Whole No. 364.

Scheflen, K. C., Lawler, E. E., & Hackman, J. R. The long-term impact of employee participation in the development of pay incentive plans: A field experiment revisited. *Experimental Publication System*, 1970, No. 4, Ms. 154A.

Schein, E. H. *Organizational Psychology.* Englewood Cliffs, N.J.: Prentice-Hall, 1965.

Schneider, B. & Olson, L. K. Effort as a correlate of an organizational reward system and individual values. *Personnel Psychology*, 1970, **23**, 313–326.

Schreiber, R. J., Smith, R. G., & Harrell, T. W. A factor analysis of employee attitudes. *Journal of Applied Psychology*, 1952, **36**, 247–250.

Schuh, A. J. The predictability of employee tenure: A review of the literature. *Personnel Psychology*, 1967, **20**, 133–152.

Schultz, G. P. Variations in environment and the Scanlon Plan. In F. G. Lesieur (Ed.), *The Scanlon Plan.* Cambridge, Mass.: MIT, 1958, Pp. 100–108.

Schuster, J. R. Another look at compensation preferences. *Industrial Management Review*, 1969, **10**, 1–18.

Schuster, J. R. & Brady, T. P. Applying employee attitudes to a decision-making process. *Personnel Journal*, 1969, **48**, 201–204.

Schwartz, M., Jenusaitis, E. & Stark, H. Motivational factors among supervisors in the utility industry. *Personnel Psychology*, 1963, **16**, 45–53.

Schwartz, M., Jenusaitis, E. & Stark, H. A comparison of the perception of job-related needs in two industry groups. *Personnel Psychology*, 1966, **19**, 185–194.

Scott, W. G. Organization theory: An overview and an appraisal. *Journal of the Academy of Management*, 1961, **4** (1), 7–26.

Siegel, P. S. Drive shift: A conceptual and experimental analysis. *Journal of Comparative and Physiological Psychology*, 1943, **35**, 139–148.

Siegel, P. S., & MacDonnell M. F. A repetition of the Calvin-Bicknell-Sperling study of conditioned drive. *Journal of Comparative and Physiological Psychology*, 1954, **47**, 250–252.

Simon, H. A. *Administrative Behavior.* (2d ed.). New York: Macmillan, 1957.

Singh, P. M. & Wherry, R. J. Ranking of job factors by factory workers in India. *Personnel Psychology*, 1963, **16**, 29–33.

Skinner, B. F. *Science and human behavior*. New York: Macmillan, 1953.

Smith, F. J. & Kerr, W. A. Turnover factors as assessed by the exit interview. *Journal of Applied Psychology*, 1953, **37**, 352–355.

Smith, K. H. *Psychological inquiry into attitudes of industrial draftsmen toward unionism*. Unpublished doctoral dissertation, Wayne State University, 1962.

Smith, P. C. & Kendall, L. M. *Cornell Studies of job satisfaction: VI. Implications for the future*. Unpublished manuscript, Cornell University, 1963.

Solomon, R. L., Kamin, L. J., & Wynne, L. C. Traumatic avoidance learning: The outcomes of several extinction procedures with dogs. *Journal of Abnormal and Social Psychology*, 1953, **48**, 291–302.

Spence, K. W. *Behavior theory and conditioning*. New Haven, Conn.: Yale, 1956.

Spitzer, M. E. *Goal-attainment, job satisfaction and behavior*. (Doctoral dissertation, New York University) Ann Arbor, Mich.: University Microfilms, 1964, No. 64-10, 048.

Stagner, R. Psychological aspects of industrial conflicts: II. Motivation. *Personnel Psychology*, 1950, **3**, 1–16.

Stagner, R. *Psychology of industrial conflict*. New York: Wiley, 1956.

Stagner, R., & Rosen, H. *Psychology of union-management relations*. Belmont, Calif.: Wadsworth, 1965.

Stockford, L. O., & Kunze, K. R. Psychology and the pay check. *Personnel*, 1950, **27**, 129–143.

Stone, C. H. The personality factor in vocational guidance. *Journal of Abnormal and Social Psychology*, 1933, **28**, 274–275.

Stromsen, K. E., & Dreese, M. Attitudes of NIPA interns toward a career in the federal service. *Public Administration Review*. 1950, **10**, 254–261.

Strong, E. K., Jr. *Vocational interests of men and women*. Stanford, Calif.: Stanford University Press, 1943.

Stuhr, A. W. The reward system and general morale. *Social Science Research Reports: IV. Surveys and Inventories*. Standard Oil of New Jersey, 1962.

Svetlik, B. Prien, E., & Barrett, G. Relationships between job difficulty, employee's attitudes toward his job, and supervisory ratings of the employee effectiveness. *Journal of Applied Psychology*, 1964, **48**, 320–324.

Taylor, F. W. *The principles of scientific management*. New York: Harper, 1911.

Taylor, J. Toad or butterfly? A constructive critique of executive compensation practices. *Industrial and Labor Relations Review*, 1968, **21**, 491–508.

Thompson, W. A. Eleven years after graduation. *Occupations,* 1939, **17**, 709–714.

Thorndike, E. L. *Animal intelligence: Experimental studies.* New York: Macmillan, 1911.

Tiffin, J., & Lawshe, C. H. War labor board decision trends. *Personnel,* 1945, **22**, 78–83.

Tolman, E. C. Purpose and cognition: The determiners of animal learning. *Psychological Review,* 1925, **32**, 285–297.

Tolman, E. C. *Purposive behavior in animals and men.* New York: Appleton-Century, 1932.

Tolman, E. C., & Honzik, C. H. Introduction and removal of reward and maze performance in rats. *University of California Publications in Psychology,* 1930, **4**, 257–275.

Troxell, J. P. Elements in job satisfaction. *Personnel,* 1954, **31**, 199–205.

Valenzi, E. R., & Andrews, I. R. Effect of underpay and overpay inequity when tested with a new induction procedure. *Proceedings, APA Convention,* 1969. Pp. 593–594.

Van Zelst, R. H., & Kerr, W. A. Workers' attitudes toward merit rating. *Personnel Psychology,* 1953, **6**, 159–172.

Vernon, P. E., & Allport, G. W. A test for personal value. *Journal of Abnormal and Social Psychology,* 1931, **26**, 231–248.

Viteles, M. S. *Motivation and morale in industry.* New York: Norton, 1953.

Vroom, V. H. *Work and motivation.* New York: Wiley, 1964.

Vroom, V. H. *Motivation in management.* New York: American Foundation for Management Research, 1965.

Vroom, V. H. Organizational choice: A study of pre- and postdecision processes. *Organizational Behavior and Human Performance,* 1966, **1**, 212–225.

Walker, C. R., & Guest, R. H. *The man on the assembly line.* Cambridge, Mass.: Harvard, 1952.

Wanous, J. Instrumentality perceptions and objective data. Unpublished paper. Yale University, Department of Administrative Sciences, 1969.

Watson, G. Work satisfaction. In G. W. Hartmann & T. Newcomb (Eds.), *Industrial Conflict.* New York: Wiley, 1939. Pp. 114–124.

Weick, K. E. Reduction of cognitive dissonance through task enhancement and effort expenditure. *Journal of Abnormal and Social Psychology,* 1964, **68**, 533–539.

Weick, K. E. The concept of equity in the perception of pay. *Administrative Science Quarterly,* 1966. **2**, 414–439.

Weick, K. E. Preferences among forms of inequity. *Organizational Behavior and Human Performance*, 1968, **3**, 400–416.

Weitz, J., & Nucklos, R. C. The validity of direct and indirect questions in measuring job satisfaction. *Personnel Psychology*, 1953, **6**, 487–494.

Wernimont, P. F. *Intrinsic and extrinsic factors in job satisfaction.* Unpublished doctoral dissertation, University of Minnesota, 1964.

Wherry, R. J. An orthogonal re-rotation of the Baehr and Ash studies of the SRA employee inventory. *Personnel Psychology*, 1954, **7**, 365–380.

Wherry, R. J. Industrial morale (a symposium). 4. Factor analysis of morale data: Reliability and validity. *Personnel Psychology*, 1958, **11**, 78–89.

White, R. W. Motivation reconsidered: The concept of competence. *Psychological Review*, 1959, **66**, 297–333.

Whitsett, D., & Winslow, E. K. Analysis of studies critical of the motivation-hygiene theory. *Personnel Psychology*, 1967, **20**, 391–415.

Whyte, W. F. *Human relations in the restaurant industry.* New York: McGraw-Hill, 1948.

Whyte, W. F. (Ed.) *Money and motivation: An analysis of incentives in industry.* New York: Harper, 1955.

Wickert, F. R. Turnover, and employees' feelings of ego-involvement in the day-to-day operations of a company. *Personnel Psychology*, 1951, **4**, 185–197.

Wiener, Y. Performance orientation and overcompensation. *Organizational Behavior and Human Performance.* 1970, **5**, 191–208.

Wike, E. L., & Barrientos, G. Secondary reinforcement and multiple drive reduction. *Journal of Comparative and Physiological Psychology*, 1958, **51**, 640–643.

Wilkins, L. T. Incentives and the young worker. *Occupational Psychology*, 1949, **23**, 235–247.

Wilkins, L. T. Incentives and the young male worker in England. *International Journal of Opinion and Attitude Research*, 1950–51, **4**, 540–561.

Winslow, E. K., & Whitsett, D. Dual-factor theory: A reply to House and Wigdor. *Personnel Psychology*, 1968, **21**, 55–58.

Wolf, A. V. *Thirst: Physiology of the urge to drink and problems of water lack.* Springfield, Ill.: Charles C Thomas, 1958.

Wolfe, J. B. Effectiveness of token-rewards for chimpanzees. *Comparative Psychology Monographs*, 1936, **12**, 15.

Wood, I. & Lawler, E. E. The effect of piece rate overpayment on productivity. *Journal of Applied Psychology*, 1970, **54**, 234–238.

Woodward, J. *Industrial organization: Theory and practice.* London: Oxford University Press, 1965.

Woodworth, R. S. & Schlosberg, H. *Experimental psychology* (Rev. Ed.). New York: Holt, 1954.

Worthy, J. C. Organizational structure and employee morale. *American Sociological Review,* 1950, **15,** 169–179.

Woytinsky, W. S. *Three aspects of labor dynamics.* Washington, D.C., Social Science Research Council, 1942.

Wyatt, S. *Incentives in repetitive work: A practical experiment in a factory.* (Industrial Health Research Board Report No. 69) London: H. M. Stationery Office, 1934.

Wyatt, S. & Langdon, J. N. *Fatigue and boredom in repetitive work.* (Industrial Health Research Board Report No. 77), London: H. M. Stationery Office, 1937. Pp. 43–46.

Yoder, D. *Personnel management and industrial relations.* Englewood Cliffs, N.J.: Prentice-Hall, 1956.

Zeaman, D. Response latency as a function of the amount of reinforcement. *Journal of Experimental Psychology,* 1949, **39,** 466–483.

Zedeck, S. & Smith, P. C. A psychophysical determination of equitable payment: A methodological Study. *Journal of Applied Psychology,* 1968, **52,** 343–347.

NAME INDEX

SUBJECT INDEX

ST. JOHN FISHER COLLEGE LIBRARY
HD4909 .L27
Lawler, Edward E. cn   010101 000
Pay and organizational effecti

0 1219 0040046 0

DATE DUE

DEC 0 7 1993	

DEMCO, INC. 38-2931